The
FIRES OF
AUTUMN

Fire survivors and ruins, probably Washington School, Cloquet, about October 14, 1918 (photograph by Hugh McKenzie)

The
FIRES OF
AUTUMN

The Cloquet–Moose Lake
Disaster of 1918

Francis M. Carroll and Franklin R. Raiter

MINNESOTA HISTORICAL SOCIETY PRESS
ST. PAUL

THIS BOOK was supported in part by a grant from the Minnesota Historical Society Public Affairs Center, which is funded by the Northwest Area Foundation.

♾ The paper used in this publication meets the minimum requirements of the American National Standard for Information Sciences — Permanence for Printed Library Materials, ANSI Z39.48–1984.

Minnesota Historical Society Press
St. Paul 55101

International Standard Book Number 0–87351–257–X (cloth)
0–87351–258 – 8 (paper)
Manufactured in the United States of America
10 9 8 7 6 5 4 3 2

Library of Congress Cataloging-in-Publication Data

Carroll, Francis M.
   The fires of autumn : the Cloquet–Moose Lake disaster of 1918 / by Francis M. Carroll and Franklin R. Raiter.
      p. cm.
   Includes bibliographical references and index.
   ISBN 0–87351–257–X (acid-free paper) — ISBN 0–87351–258–8 (paperback : acid-free paper)
   1. Forest fires — Minnesota — History — 20th century. 2. Fires — Minnesota — History — 20th century. I. Raiter, Franklin R. (Franklin Roy), 1939– . II. Title. III. Title: Cloquet-Moose Lake disaster of 1918.
SD421.32.M6C37 1990
363.37'9 — dc20   90–40688
                                                                 CIP

To
Murray Carroll
and
Amy Raiter

Contents

Maps

Preface

It is understandable no reader can possibly visualize the horror of that night, since no writer can possibly find words to describe our experiences.
Steve Tomczak

We were both born more than twenty years after the great autumn fires that ravaged the Cloquet–Moose Lake area of northeastern Minnesota on October 12, 1918. Even so, we grew up in Cloquet with stories of how the fire entered the city, how the escape was made, how the night was spent, who survived and who did not. As children we knew the landmarks and the signs of the fires, we knew the buildings that remained, the curve in the road where the car almost went into the ditch, the treasured lumps of metal melted by the heat of the flames. We accepted the phrases "before the fire" and "after the fire" as ways to describe the past. The fires shaped the historic past in local folklore. They were so traumatic and so destructive and involved so many people that they pushed much of the rest of the past from the minds of local people. They were the most important event in the history of the region. Yet, oddly enough, there is no full-scale study of the fires.

There have been writings about them, to be sure. Overwhelmingly, these are accounts by survivors. After we started this project, Ray E. Hemingson's *Death by Fire: The Story of the Great Northeastern Minnesota Forest Fire* came out in 1983; it contributes significantly to the literature of survivors' stories. Edwin E. Manni published in 1978 a large collection of accounts in his *Kettle River, Automba, Kalevala, and Surrounding Area: History, Stories: Also 1918 Forest Fire*. In 1970 Arnold R. Alanen published *The 1918 Fire in Eastern Aitkin County: Personal Accounts of Survivors*. The Women's Friday Club of Cloquet sponsored a contest in 1936 for essays about the fires, some of which appeared in the city's *Pine Knot*. Indeed, the local newspapers have for years, on the anniversary of the fires, published commemorative editions containing stories of survivors. While these accounts make fascinating reading, they are not history so much as they are the raw material from which history is written.[1]

On another level are the good, short studies of the fires in *Burning an Empire: The Story of American Forest Fires* by Stewart H. Holbrook (1943) and *Timber and Men: The Weyerhaeuser Story* by Ralph W. Hidy, Frank Ernest Hill, and Allan Nevins (1963). These brief discussions, together with the survivors' accounts, seemed to point the way to what could be done in a full-scale study.[2]

In 1980, after years of talking about the need for a book that told the whole story of the great adventure and tragedy of the fires, we decided to write it ourselves. We wanted to explain how the fires started, where they burned, how people survived, how the region recovered, why the court battles were so prolonged, how the United States Congress got involved. It is a vast story. Steve Tomczak's warning stayed with us. How could we find words to recapture the terror, the pain, and the labor of the experience?[3]

Nevertheless, it has been a wonderful adventure to write this history, for we think it is an epic with courage, determination, and vision, with heroes and villains. Furthermore, much of it has never before been told. We wanted to go beyond the horrifying experiences of the survivors — although they are a central part — and to tell as much as we could of the whole story. They have been remembered mainly in northern Minnesota, but the autumn fires of 1918 were more than a local event. They shook the state, and their consequences finally gripped the attention of Congress and the White House.

Following every event affecting thousands of people, there are many versions of what happened. Every survivor and every survivor's family has a separate account. We do not want this book in any way to diminish anyone's experience or account. No historian and no single book could completely encompass this momentous event. We have tried to tell the story as fully as we could, but we admit that much has been left out. Where documents and written accounts, personal contacts and interviews were silent we have not been able to extend our narrative.

The books by Hemingson, Manni, and Alanen are a valuable start toward publishing survivors' accounts. The Carlton County Historical Society, the Northeast Minnesota Historical Center at the University of Minnesota-Duluth, and the Minnesota Historical Society have made serious efforts to collect accounts in both written documents and oral history interviews. We urge readers with a further interest in the fires to consult these books and societies, as well as the other sources that we cite. Indeed, we hope to stimulate others to record their recollections or those of their families, or to write their own histories. Particularly needed are the experiences of survivors in the outlying areas such as Bain, Willow River, and Bruno. Even the experiences of people in such central places as Carlton or Esko have been largely unrecorded. We will be pleased and flattered if our effort brings forth more accounts and works.

A word about sources. We have checked everything in print related to the fires and tried to utilize every relevant manuscript or archival collection. But accounts of the fires presented a special problem of their own. The written materials are uneven in geographic coverage, and they alone would not have enabled us to write as broad a narrative as we wished. Interviewing survivors was difficult because we both now live away from northern Minnesota. Furthermore, by the 1980s people who had experienced the fires were getting on in years; indeed most of them had been young children in 1918.

Our solution to this problem came in the course of research on the court cases following the fires. Six key cases, which represented most of the major fire areas, went to the Minnesota Supreme Court: *Anderson v. Minneapolis, St. Paul & Sault Ste. Marie Railway Company; Borsheim v. Great Northern Railway Company; Carr v. Davis; Hall v. Davis (Peterson v. Hines); McCool v. Davis;* and *Ringquist v. Duluth, Missabe & Northern Railway Company.* These cases produced hundreds of pages of testimonies printed in volumes called records that are part of the brief (set of documents) for each case. They are available in the collections of major law libraries in Minnesota. In addition, the Minnesota State Archives at the Minnesota Historical Society holds the Supreme Court case files, which often include the record volumes, for most of the cases.

In these testimonies are eyewitness accounts of the fires—how they started, how they burned, how people survived—accounts given in court under questioning by skilled lawyers and subject to cross-examination and refutation. This seemed to us the best possible material with which to reconstruct the facts and the drama of the fires. We think that the use of this material gives the book a considerable degree of accuracy and a significant methodological innovation: testimony as a form of oral history that is acquired and collected under exacting circumstances, contemporaneously with the event being investigated.

We have followed available sources in identifying people and spelling their names. Discrepancies were resolved by using the spelling apparently preferred by the person or most commonly used by others. As we read the testimonies, it became evident that some of the court reporters had difficulty with Finnish names in particular. We also noticed that several of the witnesses probably spoke a language other than English as their first tongue and so occasionally talked in a seemingly unclear manner as they tried to describe the terror of the fires while testifying under great emotional pressure in court.

For purposes of identification, whenever possible we give the first name of a married woman in addition to that of her husband — as for Pearl E. Drew, who was also Mrs. Herbert J. Drew. Reflecting social usage of the time, however, some sources have only a husband's first name, as for Mrs. John Iwasko. We include both unmarried and married surnames for some of the women who were children at the time of the fires and adults when they later recounted their experiences.

A version of Chapter Six was published as " 'At the Time of Our Misfortune': Relief Efforts following the 1918 Cloquet Fire" in the Fall 1983 issue of *Minnesota History* and a version of Chapters Seven, Eight, and Nine was published as "The People Versus the Government: The 1918 Cloquet Fire and the Struggle for Compensation" in the January 1985 issue of the *Journal of Forest History*. We thank these journals for permission to reprint parts of the articles, and we give special thanks to Mary D. Cannon, editor of *Minnesota History*, and Ronald J. Fahl and Alice E. Ingerson, former and present editors, respectively, of the *Journal of Forest History*, for their help with the texts and their expertise in dealing with illustrations.

FRANCIS M. CARROLL
Winnipeg, Manitoba

FRANKLIN R. RAITER
Washington, D.C.

Acknowledgments

Many people and institutions deserve to be thanked for their assistance, and we do so with great pleasure. For a grant that enabled us to carry out part of the research, we gratefully acknowledge the support of the Minnesota Historical Society's Public Affairs Center. We express our gratitude as well to Lawrence R. Yetka, associate justice of the Minnesota Supreme Court, for permission to use the papers of his father, Frank Yetka, and for his suggestions and encouragement; the Weyerhaeuser Family Associates Inc. for permission to use the Weyerhaeuser Family Papers and the F. Weyerhaeuser and Company Records; the late Mary Olesen Gerin for permission to quote her mother, Anna Dickie Olesen, and for the interview she graciously gave us; Nancy Hursh Bagley for permission to use the letters of her grandmother, Anne B. Cook Woodworth; Elizabeth Coy Walter for permission to use the letters of her father, Sherman L. Coy; and the late Lester J. Blomberg for permission to use material from an interview and for his inspiration to undertake this project.

Of absolutely unfailing help and encouragement were Barbara Sommer, former director of the Carlton County Historical Society; Lawrence J. Sommer, director of the Montana Historical Society and former executive director of the St. Louis County Historical Society; Ellen Quinn, present director of the Carlton County Historical Society; Patricia Maus, administrator, Northeast Minnesota Historical Center, University of Minnesota-Duluth; Jean A. Brookins, assistant director for publications and research, Ann Regan, managing editor, Deborah Swanson, assistant editor, Alan Ominsky, production supervisor (who also prepared five of the maps), Kathleen Mahoney, word processing secretary, and Sarah P. Rubinstein, editor, all of the Minnesota Historical Society Press; Carol Kennedy, copy editor; and Pete Steen, executive director, Forest History Society.

Library and archives staff members assisted us in locating material, photocopying documents, reproducing photographs and maps, and making suggestions for doing research by long distance and preparing mansucript drafts. We thank Michele Des Rosier, law librarian, St. Louis County Law Library; Dallas R. Lindgren, reference archivist, Ruth Ellen Bauer, reading room supervisor, Steven E. Nielsen, reference assistant, Alissa Rosenberg, librarian, Alice Grygo, librarian, Bonnie Palmquist, archival cataloger, P. A. Hutchens, chief photographer, and Pamela M. Owens, photo lab assistant, all of the Minnesota Historical Society; Dale C. Mayer, archivist, Herbert Hoover Presidential Library; Frances M. Seeber, senior supervisory archivist, Franklin D. Roosevelt Presidential Library; William F. Sherman, Judicial, Fiscal and Social Branch, Civil Archives Division, National Archives and Records Service; and Mary Beth Johnson, former librarian, Forest History Society.

Many people have also given us their advice, lent us material and photographs, photocopied documents in their possession, recalled and searched out information, and in diverse ways helped us along. Our grateful thanks go to Charles E. Twining, research associate of the Forest History Society, currently with the Weyerhaeuser Company Archives; Arnold R. Alanen, School of Natural Resources, University of Wisconsin; Daniel W. Anderson, Educational Center, Fond du Lac Indian Reservation; Donald A. Haines, North Central Forest Experiment Station; Frank D. Irving, School of Forestry, University of Minnesota; Bill Beck, Lakeside Writers' Group, Duluth; Beverly Hermes, librarian and archivist, Olmsted County Historical Society; the members of the Moose Lake Historical Society; Becki Peterson, archivist, and Mary Bennett, photo archivist, both of the State Historical Society of Iowa; C. Patrick Labadie, director, Canal Park Marine Musuem, Duluth; Ramona Thompson, Fond du Lac Indian Reservation; LaVerne L. Olson of Bloomington, Bessie Olson Blomgren of Cloquet, and Helen Mae Olson Maslowski of Cloquet, son, sister, and daughter, respectively, of Olaf (Oliver) Olson; Marjorie Bull of Falcon Heights, daughter-in-law of William Bull; Phyllis M. Johnson of Kettle River, daughter-in-law of Aina Jokimaki Johnson; Marjorie Adams and W. Gordon Adams, Duluth; and the staff of the Minnesota State Law Library.

Special thanks are also due to C. Thomas Shay, Walter R. Henson, and Jack M. Bumsted of the University of Manitoba for their advice and suggestions concerning the technical literature about forest fires and disasters. As part of his continuing study of Minnesota photographers from 1850 to 1930, Alan R. Woolworth, research fellow at the Minnesota Historical Society, wrote the appendix, which discusses the most prominent photographers — Hugh McKenzie, Olaf (Oliver) Olson, Earl L. Irish, Fred Levie, and William Bull — whose works illustrate this book.

Finally, to our families, who because of this book have also grown up with the great autumn fires of 1918, our many thanks.

PART ONE

Introduction

Burned trees and house ruins in woods, St. Louis County, October 1918 (McKenzie)

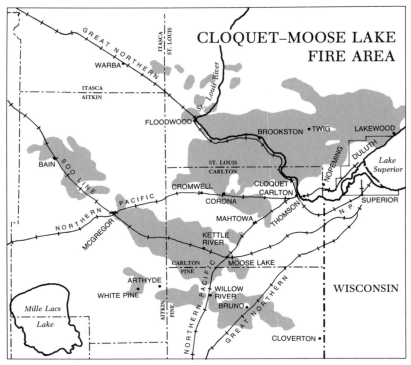

Area of northeastern Minnesota stricken by Cloquet–Moose Lake fires, October 1918

CHAPTER ONE

Fires in the Woods

It was the greatest calamity ever to occur in northern Minnesota. Indeed, the forest fires of October 1918 were the worst disasters ever to befall the state, both in lives lost and in property destroyed. No train crash, shipwreck, or mining accident, no hotel fire, tornado, or flood created so much havoc, misery, or destruction as did these fires. The ordeal affected thousands, and the experience stamped a whole generation. The face of the countryside was changed utterly and the way of life in the region sharply altered. In short, northeastern Minnesota was never the same after October 12, 1918. The great Cloquet–Moose Lake fires were the watershed; for decades afterward people spoke of the past as either "before the fire" or "after the fire."

The people of the nation, preoccupied with reports from the western battlefields of World War I, learned of the calamity by their own senses rather than from the newspapers. Charred papers and stationery from the Northern Lumber Company, destroyed by the flames at Cloquet, were blown as far as Black River Falls, Wisconsin, 190 miles away. Ash and cinders fell in Wisconsin, Michigan, and Illinois. Clouds of acrid bluish smoke, pungent with the smells of the burning forest, obscured the sun throughout the midwestern and eastern states during the next several days. Even the fleet well out to sea in the North Atlantic observed the signs of smoke and haze. Nevertheless, the dimensions of the tragedy never gripped the country.[1]

Years later, when the courts found the United States Railroad Administration, the federal agency that ran the railway companies during the war, to be responsible for the fires, the government refused to accept the responsibility. The result was both a court and a legislative battle that was not fully resolved until 1935 — seventeen years after the fire.

For people living after World War II, the words *holocaust*, *conflagration*, and *local devastation* have rather specific connotations and do not always serve well to describe events outside the war context. Similarly, the term *fire storm* generally refers to the results of a particular kind of tactical bombing, although it was first used in 1871 to describe a forest fire. Thus, when these words are used today to describe a forest fire, they seem trite and exaggerated. But this was no simple forest fire. The statistics, in their starkness, tell the story: 1,500 square miles destroyed by fire over a region encompassing 8,400 square miles; 453 people killed outright, 85 badly burned, 106 killed by influenza and pneumonia; 11,382 families displaced; and 52,371 people injured, disrupted, or affected to some degree. These figures, taken from the *Final Report* of the Minnesota Forest Fires Relief Commission, are probably conservative; they are well below the inflated newspaper estimates.[2]

Property loss was equally staggering. The relief commission estimated the property destroyed to be worth more than $30 million. Between $65 million and $73 million was claimed in the court cases alone, although the final court judgments came down to a total of $29,743,416.25. At least 4,089 houses were destroyed, 6,366 barns, 41 school buildings (including the brand-new "fireproof" high school building in Cloquet), 4,295 farm animals, and the incredible number of 54,083 chickens. In the aftermath, a Chicago insurance inspection firm compiled a list of the towns and villages affected by the fires, together with an assessment of the amount of damage, shown in Table 1.

Many other towns and settlements, such as Bain, Split Rock, Harney, Sturgeon Lake, Bruno, and Willow River, were not mentioned in this assessment. Definitions of *town* allow for different computations, but between thirty-two and thirty-eight towns or villages were wholly or partially destroyed by the fire. The destruction to the wildlife and the environment of the region can only be surmised.[3]

Forest fires were by no means uncommon in woodland areas in the early twentieth century. On the contrary, they were a fact of life,

TABLE 1.	
Towns and villages burned	*Estimated percent burned*
Arnold	100
Automba	100
Brookston	100
Cloquet	100
Kalevala	100
Kettle River	100
Lawler	100
Lester Park	100
Moose Lake	100
Woodland	100
Duluth (in and near)	heavy losses
Adolph	50
Exeter Farms	50
Five Corners	50
Hermantown	50
Munger	50
Thomson	50
Pike Lake	25
Twig	25
Warba	25
Nopeming	10
Brevator	5
Clifton	5
Floodwood	5
McGregor	5
Proctor	5
Rice Lake	5

about which few people at the time made any complaint. As Tena MacMillan Smith, a Cloquet resident who survived the fires, remembered fifty years later, "We had those every year, we had those [fire] scares every year, so we didn't pay too much attention."[4]

For generations the burning of forests had been the acceptable way of clearing land for agricultural purposes, as Stephen J. Pyne explained in his book, *Fire in America: A Cultural History of Wildland and Rural Fire*. In the early twentieth century the burning of scrub and some second-growth forest was still a common practice, albeit one increasingly discouraged by the forestry profession. Farmers also burned their fields after harvesting their crops. Campers, hunters, and anglers were responsible for carelessly allowing campfires to get out of control. Many fires were caused by lightning during electrical storms.

Timber companies were required to dispose of the slash left behind by logging, lest it contribute to a general fire hazard. The method of eliminating the slash was to burn it in controlled circumstances, although occasionally the fires would get away from those tending them and grow into the very disaster that the burning was supposed to prevent. The unburned slash left in the forest presented a genuine hazard, and if weather conditions postponed the controlled burnings, the cutover lands could present a very real fire danger. Indeed, the major fires in the United States between 1871 and 1918 all took place on cutover land.[5]

By far the largest identifiable cause of forest fires was the railroads. Most railroad fires came from sparks and embers blown from the smokestacks of locomotives. In order to develop full power, coal-burning locomotives used a forced draft in the fire box. This draft sometimes sucked small bits of burning coal the length of the engine and out the smokestack, particularly on steep grades when the engine was laboring with some difficulty. The solution was to place a "spark arrester" in the smokestack or smokebox of the locomotive. These arresters were wire-mesh screens or perforated metal sheets with holes of approximately one-quarter of an inch, through which the smoke would pass. Dangerously large pieces of burning coal would be stopped by the screen and broken into relatively harmless small particles. Unfortunately, the screens also tended to reduce the draft, and irate trainmen sometimes took them out or broke large holes in them. Furthermore, the extreme heat and pressure to which the screens were subjected were likely to warp or break them. Thus, frequent inspection and maintenance were necessary. Live coals also fell from the ashpans of the fireboxes, and section crews burned grass, rubbish, and old ties along the right-of-way.

Legislation existed in most states requiring every locomotive to be equipped with spark arresters and safe fireboxes. In Minnesota the law required the railroad companies to send patrols along the tracks during the fire season and to send section crews out to fight the reported fires. These precautions were not always sufficient, and the manpower demands of the war in 1918 further aggravated the problems of inspection, maintenance, patrols, and crews. Thus, while railroad company officials often spoke enthusiastically about fire prevention and cooperation with foresters, the fact remained that railroads were responsible for a large number of fires along their rights-of-way.[6]

This situation was widely understood, if not actually accepted. Henry Solon Graves, the chief forester of the United States, wrote in 1911, "Railroads in many cases are the most prolific source of fires," and he noted that in some areas more than 50 percent of the fires could be traced to locomotives. The federal district forester in Denver told the regional supervisor of the Railroad Administration in Chicago in June 1918, "More fires are started by railroad locomotives in the National Forests of this District than from any other causes." Of all the fires reported in Minnesota in 1920, wrote State Forester William T. Cox of the Minnesota Forest Service, 515 out of 936, some 55 percent, were of railroad origins.[7]

Thus, forest fires were widespread and commonplace in woodland areas, and nowhere more so than in northern Minnesota. Recent research has shown that for thousands of years fires of varying intensities had periodically burned through the northern forests and that these fires were an important element in the regeneration of the forests.[8] In the nineteenth century, however, logging operations increased the debris on the forest floor, which caused fires to burn more intensely. At the same time agricultural settlement increased the human population in the cutover lands, thereby expanding the potential for tragic results from the fires. In these circumstances, then, occasional disasters took place — for example, the Hinckley fire of 1894 and the Baudette-Spooner fire of 1910, in which many lives were lost and vast tracts of land burned.[9] Both Stephen Pyne in *Fire in America* and Stewart H. Holbrook in *Burning an Empire* focused on the pattern of fires in the cutover land of the Great Lakes states, and Holbrook noted one red pine in Carlton County that bore the scars of fires in 1819, 1842, 1864, 1874, 1885, and 1894. The Cloquet area had seen a dangerous fire in the University of Minnesota's Cloquet Experimental Forest, just west of town, in 1917.[10]

Forest fires were difficult to fight or control. The heavy machinery and sophisticated equipment that facilitate today's fire-fighting techniques had not then been developed. The world of the bulldozer, not to mention the smoke jumper, was years in the future. Indeed, not all of the district rangers in Minnesota even had automobiles to use in the inspection and patrol of their districts. When Percy P. Vibert, the Cloquet district ranger, was appointed in 1911, his equipment was "a shovel, an axe, a grub hoe, and a packsack." In practical terms, these were the basic tools, supplemented by wet gunnysacks. Fighting fire then consisted of volunteers hacking out firebreaks with hand tools and relying on specially constructed or natural obstacles, such as roads or rivers, to contain the fire. When a serious fire threatened to get out of control, the backfire — a fire set in front of the large fire in order to deprive it of fuel — provided a dangerous but powerful weapon with which to fight. But success in fighting any fire depended to a large extent on help from nature through a shift in the wind, which would drive the fire back on itself, or a few days of rain, which would soak down the woods. Thus, fire protection was always chancy at best. The roads or rivers might not stop the fire, the backfires might not be effective, and more importantly, the weather might not cooperate.[11]

Studies of fires show that weather, and particularly humidity, may have been the most important factor contributing to a major blowup. Periodically a sharp fall in the humidity coincided with a particularly dry summer. When this happened, a major fire was almost inevitable. Donald A. Haines and Rodney W. Sando explained the sequence of conditions in a dramatic metaphor:

> The series of events leading to these great fires might be compared to the steps involved in firing a weapon. A large amount of fuel was usually available before the fire; this would be analogous to a rifle shell. A unique series of climatic events prevailed during much of the fire season — *the shell is loaded into the rifle chamber.* Smaller fires were burning in the forests and bogs — *the hammer is pulled back.* A favorable synoptic weather pattern developed over the region — *the trigger is pulled and the bullet is on its way.*

The climatic events are generally rainfall and temperature, and possibly also evaporation and sunshine. The great autumn fires in the up-

*Trees damaged by the winds and fires of October 1918 about a year later,
Carlton County (McKenzie)*

per Midwest, charted in Haines and Sando's study, all took place during very dry summers with generally high temperatures, high rates of
evaporation, and extended periods of sunshine.[12]

The Cloquet–Moose Lake fires differed slightly in that the rainfall
had been abnormally short for several seasons — it had been dry since
1916 — and the temperatures just before the fires were not particularly
high. The synoptic weather pattern that was the triggering event,
however, included these preconditions of low rainfall and high temperatures, together with a sharply falling relative humidity and rising
winds. Haines and Sando drew on the records and conclusions of Herbert W. Richardson, who ran the United States Weather Bureau station in Duluth during the time of the fires and who wrote articles and
testified as an expert witness on the relationship of the weather to the
fires. Richardson's observation was that the humidity in the fire area
on October 12 was lower than had ever been recorded in Duluth. At
noon the relative humidity had fallen to 31 percent; but just two hours
later it had reached 21 percent, 19 percent below the normal level.
Winds, which had been negligible in the morning and early after-

noon, began to reach 30 to 40 miles per hour by 3:00 P.M. By about 6:00 P.M., the winds in Duluth were at speeds of about 65 miles per hour and were probably "blowing at a rate of 80 to 90 miles adjoining the fire fronts from two to six miles or more distant from [Duluth]." In these circumstances any fires, whether bog fires that had smoldered all summer or railroad fires that had started earlier in the week, could be expected to blow up into a major catastrophe.[13]

Stephen Pyne wrote about the "uncanny similarity" of the Lake States fires. They shared a dry summer and autumn, cutover and drained land, railroad and clearing fires that burned for some time, and communities that were unconscious of any danger. At a critical moment the fires blew up, the railroads rescued the communities, and the fires destroyed the towns and countryside. For those beyond reach of the railroads, usually farmers, the closest obvious shelters were streams and swamps — or more disastrously, root cellars or wells, which often brought death by asphyxiation. The descriptions were similar also: a red sun was followed by clouds of smoke and growing darkness, winds reached hurricane force, withering heat caused houses and objects to burst into flame as if spontaneously, firebrands and ashes fell from the sky in advance of the fire, and then "balls of fire" descended from the sky, the "fire balloons" exploded, an ear-splitting roar developed, and at last came sheets of flame — all terms used more recently to describe the great Yellowstone National Park fires of 1988. Pyne described the Peshtigo fire of 1871 in Wisconsin and the Hinckley fire of 1894 in Minnesota, but it is evident that the pattern that he noted resembled to an "uncanny" degree that of the Cloquet–Moose Lake fires of 1918.[14]

What is the reason for this similarity? How could these cataclysmic events be regularly repeated? The answer is found in what is now understood about the dynamics of a forest fire. Richardson's article and testimony, as well as the comments of many observers, show that there was a growing knowledge of what happened in large forest fires, but it was not until after World War II that scientists began to study them. This interest sprang as much from a concern to predict the progress of large fires caused by conventional or atomic bombs as from a desire to explain forest fires. Nevertheless, the results have provided a new technical understanding of what went on in historical catastrophes like the Cloquet–Moose Lake fires.[15]

A "large" fire is more than simply a "small" fire on a bigger scale. The difference is not so much in the size of the area burning as in the character of the fire. In a "small" fire, the flames are typically at the fire edge, and the flames, heat, and smoke drift straight up into the sky. When that fire blows up into a "large" fire, a process that may take as little as fifteen minutes or as much as several hours, the flames consume fuel over a wider area than just the fire edge. More heat is generated by the wider burning area; the surrounding atmosphere is directly affected both by the creation of a convection column of rising flames, heat, and smoke and by the draft of fresh air into the large burning area to provide oxygen.[16]

The "large" fire begins to make its own weather by drawing in fresh air at its base and expelling heat and smoke into the atmosphere. If there are surrounding winds of any velocity, they too have their effect. The convection column of flames, heat, and smoke will likely be bent by the wind to lean over neighboring territory, with the result that heat radiating down at an angle from the column will still further reduce the humidity and raise the temperature of fresh fuel in the path of the oncoming fire. Furthermore, as the chimney effect of the convection column becomes more violent, burning particles, embers, and flaming pine cones — "firebrands" — are drawn up into the air from the fire itself and blown some distance ahead of the fire. Some of these firebrands start "spot fires," which begin to burn independently of the main fire and quickly add their own heat to the original convection column. This "coalescence" of several convection columns increases the draft and the intensity of the affected fires, drawing them together in a "surge." Under these conditions, when the flames have grown to between eight and twelve feet high, several dramatic and terrifying things can happen. In a pine forest the fire explodes into the tops of the trees, creating a "crown fire," the intensity of which greatly increases the volume of firebrands thrown into the air. The smoke becomes black, indicating that the fire is burning so violently that the wood is no longer being burned efficiently. The eerie phenomena of "firewhirls," "tornadic whirls," and "horizontal roll vortices" (or horizontal tornadoes) may occur, producing what witnesses describe as sheets of flame roiling overhead, balls of fire descending from the sky, or surges of flame shooting out horizontally from clouds of smoke. Fires of these dimensions are, Stephen Pyne

Burning trees, Moose Lake, October 1918

declared, "uncontrollable by any means under human manipulation," and only significant changes in the weather or the available fuels will slow them down.[17]

Recent scientific studies of forest fires shed light on the possible dimensions of historic disasters like the Cloquet–Moose Lake fires. The Mack Lake fire in Michigan started on the morning of May 5, 1980, and within two hours it had reached an intensity that caused spot fires to ignite at some distance in dense jack pines on a hillside. The main fire and the spot fires then blew up, and in the next ten hours burned twenty-five thousand acres, destroyed a town with forty-four buildings, and killed one fire fighter. It is estimated that the energy released by this fire was 3.5 trillion British thermal units (Btu), something equivalent to one hundred average thunderstorms or ten Hiroshima-size atomic bombs. Fire-line intensity averaged 9,300 Btu per foot/per second, with peak intensities calculated to reach energy levels of 31,000 Btu per foot/per second. Stephen Pyne asserted in *Introduction to Wildland Fire: Fire Management in the United States* that this is the highest energy release estimated for any fire that has been scientifically studied. It is impossible to calculate measurements for the Cloquet–Moose Lake fires retroactively, but even crude comparisons with the Mack Lake fire or the Sundance fire of 1967 in Idaho help to explain how the 1918 fire spread so quickly and consumed so much territory in so short a time.[18]

Only 2 to 3 percent of all forest fires reach the level of a "large" fire. While the preconditions of rainfall, temperature, and general circumstances of the forest are important, the dynamic ingredient is the sharp drop in humidity — an unusual and unpredictable atmospheric condition. Moreover, the relatively short time necessary in these conditions for a "small" fire to blow up into a "large" fire is an important consideration given the level of communications available in 1918. All of this at least partially explains why there was such a sense of complacency about all of the fires burning in the region in the days before Saturday, October 12. Indeed, it might suggest why there was no effective alarm spread throughout the countryside during the afternoon of the twelfth. These fires were regarded as troublesome nuisances to be worked at steadily. No one expected the runaway fires that would range completely out of control, destroying acres of forest and farmland, burning dozens of towns and villages, killing hundreds, and creating untold misery.

The territory destroyed by the flames on October 12, 1918, was enormous — 250,000 acres. There were really five or six major fires and numerous smaller ones (Richardson claimed there were between fifty and seventy-five fires altogether), all distinct from each other, and the total area affected by all of these fires was much larger than the actual acreage burned. The largest of the fires, generally called the Cloquet fire, extended from west of Brookston (near Mirbat, Paupores, and Milepost 62 along the Great Northern Railway tracks) all the way to Lakeside at the eastern edge of Duluth on the shores of Lake Superior, a distance of forty miles. From north to south this fire burned from near Alborn (in the vicinity of the Duluth, Missabe and Northern Railway tracks) to a line somewhat beyond Cloquet, twenty miles south. Fire also ranged on the extreme western edge of this fire, from Prairie Lake southeast through Corona and Mahtowa, or perhaps twenty-five miles.[19]

The second largest, and equally famous, fire was the Moose Lake–Kettle River fire. It burned from just north of McGregor and Tamarack southeast to Sturgeon Lake and a few miles beyond Moose Lake. This fire covered thirty-one miles at its longest and fourteen miles at its widest. Essentially, the Moose Lake–Kettle River fire was

Railroad tracks distorted by fire heat, Moose Lake, about October 15, 1918

bounded by the Northern Pacific Railway tracks on both the north and the south, with the Minneapolis, St. Paul and Sault Ste. Marie Railway ("Soo Line") tracks running diagonally between them from Moose Lake to McGregor.

Farther north along the Soo Line tracks was another major fire with the town of Bain at its center. South of Moose Lake were three sizable fires: one was centered at White Pine, one was at Arthyde, and one extended from Willow River southeast to Bruno and on into the vicinity of Cloverton, a distance of twenty-two miles. Numerous smaller fires were burning simultaneously west and north of these main fires. The distance from the Bain fire in the extreme west to the eastern outskirts of Duluth is at least seventy-five miles, and the north-south extremities of these fires would be about fifty-five miles. Thus, large sections of Carlton, Pine, and southern St. Louis counties burned, with serious damage in Aitkin, Itasca, Cass, Crow Wing, and Wadena counties also. In truth, this disaster might more accurately be known as the "northeastern Minnesota fires," but the incredible loss of life at Moose Lake and Kettle River and the destruction of the prosperous lumber town of Cloquet have understandably identified those specific place names with the general regional disaster.

The region itself was varied in geography and economy. The western borders of the fire area were dominated by the bogs and swamps that form the watershed of rivers and streams flowing into the Mississippi, the St. Louis, and the St. Croix river valleys. Some of these marshlands had been drained to make more pasture for farmers. The bogs and swamps became particularly vulnerable to fire, and in fact once a fire took hold in the peat or turf it was almost impossible to extinguish. Some bog fires smoldered for months, even through the winter, and they became dangerous in the climatic conditions that preceded the fires of 1918. To the east of the bogs, the land — often sandy or gravelly soil — became more rolling and glacial, essentially cutover pine lands, mainly used for farming but interspersed with stands of second-growth forest. (Indeed, the small towns of Lawler, Automba, and Kettle River had five sawmills between them.) The accumulated slash of the cutover land and the tangled brush of the second-growth forests were a tinderbox, especially in a dry year like 1918. In southern Carlton County and in Pine County the countryside was characterized by cutover lands and second-growth forest on red clay soil, deeply cut by streams and rivers. The lakes that dotted the landscape may have been instrumental in creating "green areas" that escaped the fire and may have helped slow the big blaze in the Moose Lake area. The eastern edge of the fire was the escarpment of rock that formed the ridge above the city of Duluth. This outcropping of rock extended from Duluth right into the St. Louis River valley as far west as Cloquet, or technically Knife Falls.[20]

This kind of country could not be described as "rich farm land," such as might be found in southern or far western Minnesota, but it nevertheless provided a livelihood for a large number of families. That 6,366 barns were destroyed by the fires gives some indication of how intensively the region was farmed. Under the inspired leadership of H.C. Hanson of Barnum, dairy farming and poultry and egg production in central and eastern Carlton County, from Moose Lake to Esko, and in southern St. Louis County, north and west of Duluth, had risen to prominence in state agricultural circles. Vegetables, notably potatoes and cabbages, were grown throughout the area, and in the southern region, some barley and other cereal crops. Turkeys and beef cattle were raised in southern parts of Carlton County. Horses were kept in some number on almost every farm. They were still the primary source of farm power and transportation, and they could be leased to the lumber companies for use in the logging camps in the winter. Hay and oats could be grown locally, making the farms remarkably self-sufficient; these crops could also be sold in town for cash.[21]

The small towns and villages throughout the area were farm-service centers with markets, railroad shipping facilities, farmers' cooperatives, supply stores, feed stores, and banks. Larger towns, such as Floodwood, Brookston, Cloquet, and Moose Lake, had creameries, grain elevators, and perhaps two railroads, as well as the basic farm supplies. Moose Lake was one of the oldest settlements in the region, dating back to the 1850s. It grew up in the shadow of the old "Military Road" (as the federally funded Point Douglas–St. Louis River Road was called locally) and then became a sawmill town on the Moose Horn River. By 1918 Moose Lake was both a thriving farm center of more than five hundred people and also a major railroad junction for the Northern Pacific and the Soo Line. Sawmills and the Soo Line railroad were important features of Kettle River, Automba, and Lawler; but like the smaller settlements of Split Rock, Kalevala, and Salo, these towns were even more significant as centers for the surrounding farming communities. Duluth, of course, was the metropolitan center for all of northeastern Minnesota, to a much greater extent than is the case today. Accessible as much by train as by road, Duluth was the focus of much of the commercial, political, and cultural life of the northern part of the state. Although the city was a major market for farm produce and also a supply and distribution center for the region, the heart of Duluth's economic life consisted of the mining, lumber, railroad, and steamship industries.[22]

Cloquet also was a major farm center, but like Duluth its primary economic focus was industrial. The thriving lumber town of between eight thousand and nine thousand people prided itself on being the "White Pine Capital of the World." The smell of fresh-cut pine and the sound of sawmills were remembered by Walter O'Meara in *We Made It through the Winter: A Memoir of Northern Minnesota Boyhood*, his recollections of Cloquet before the fire.[23] Three mills were immediately prominent: the Cloquet Lumber Company, the Northern Lumber Company, and the Johnson-Wentworth Lumber Company. These companies were owned by a number of individuals and families in the lumber trade, of which the Weyerhaeusers were the most prominent. By 1918, though they had substantial holdings in other parts of the state, Cloquet was the center of Weyerhaeuser operations in Minnesota.[24]

The oldest company was the Cloquet, which had its origins in 1879. Frederick Weyerhaeuser, an early backer, became president of the company when George S. Shaw, one of the founders, died in 1897. In 1918 it was managed by Henry C. ("Harry") Hornby. The Cloquet had two sawmills, a planing mill, large drying yards, power plants, shops, barns, and offices, as well as a subsidiary logging railroad, the Duluth and Northeastern. The Cloquet Lumber Company had a production capacity of about one hundred million board feet of lumber per year and a large volume of products such as lath and shingles. The Northern Lumber Company was formed in 1896 when Frederick Weyerhaeuser, George Shaw, and others bought out the mills of Charles N. Nelson, who had started operations in the town in 1880. In 1918 the Northern was managed by Rudolph M. Weyerhaeuser, one of Frederick's sons. It had two large sawmills, a planer, vast drying yards (which stretched up the St. Louis River beyond the town), power plants, shops, stables, and offices. It too owned a small logging railroad, the Mesabe Southern Railway. The Northern was able to produce about a hundred million board feet of lumber annually. The Johnson-Wentworth Lumber Company had been built in 1894 by Samuel S. Johnson, who sold out to a combination of the Cloquet and Northern companies in 1902. This mill, managed by Joseph R. Wilson, was the largest single sawmill in the country, with three saws, and was able to produce about seventy million board feet a year.

Cloquet also had several other significant forest industries that made it more than just a sawmill town. Perhaps the most important was the Northwest Paper Company, formed in 1898 by the lumber interests to utilize trees that were unsuitable for cutting into high-grade lumber. Originally intended to make mechanically ground newsprint, the mill was upgraded in 1915 to manufacture higher quality papers. Similar objectives marked the establishment of the Cloquet

Carlton County Vidette.

VOLUME NO. XXXI.   THE CARLTON COUNTY VIDETTE, CARLTON, CARLTON COUNTY, MINNESOTA.   FRIDAY, OCTOBER 18, 1918.   NUMBER 46.

AWFULLEST FIRE HORROR IN STATE'S HISTORY!
Probably 900 Lives Gone! Property Loss Also Terrible!

City of Cloquet Wiped Out By a Seething Holocaust With a Loss of Probably Twenty Million Dollars!

Moose Lake and Kettle River, 24 Other Towns Wiped Out With Hundreds Of Lives Lost!

Beggering description was the awful catastrophe which visited this section, the hurricane of flame and burning leaves and smoke which swept at a 60 or 70 mile

INSURANCE NOTICE!

Adjusters for Hartford Fire Insurance Company are on the ground. Claimants please address or communicate with Agent C. P. Osburn, either at Cloquet or Sellwood Building, Duluth.

SPECIAL NOTICE TO FARMERS

The Carlton county authorities urge every farmer not to sell their stock. Unprincipled buyers have been going through the county buying up all stock obtainable at prices much under their value, explaining to the owners that with no feed in the country they will be at least anyway. The authorities are hurrying hay and supplies here as rapidly as can be done, and expect in a few days to have enough feed here to save all stock. Every farmer should

LODGES HASTEN TO RELIEVE THEIR MEMBERS

OCTOBER DRAFT CALL IS CANCELLED NOW

SAVE M'GREGOR AFTER BIG FIGHT

On Thursday Afternoon Town Was Circled By Flames.

The Carlton County Vidette *of Carlton and the* Pine Knot *of Cloquet together produced this first postfire issue at the* Vidette *office, which escaped burning.*

Tie and Post Company in 1900. This firm cut and sold the spruce, cedar, and tamarack trees that the lumber companies could not use. In 1905 the lumber companies formed the St. Louis River Mercantile Company to supply the logging camps and to operate an elaborate boom facility at Cloquet to sort out logs coming down the river, directing them to the appropriate mill or landing. The Rathborne, Hair and Ridgeway Company, with origins in 1904, manufactured wooden boxes to be used by firms across the country for packaging and shipping. In 1905 the Berst-Forster-Dixfield Company began producing such items as clothespins, toothpicks, tongue blades, and eventually wooden matches.[25]

In addition to the forest-related industries, Cloquet in 1918 had a thriving commercial life: five hotels; two banks; at least fifteen public houses; eleven stores dealing in dry goods, hardware, or general merchandise; and many specialty shops. Cloquet also had two telephone companies, a weekly newspaper (the *Pine Knot*), a cooperative creamery association, two retail cooperatives, doctors and lawyers, and schools, a fire department, and a hospital. The city had access to three railroads, the most important being the Great Northern and the Northern Pacific.[26]

All of this industry and commerce made Cloquet a major center for the region and gave it a sense of permanence. That the city and much of the country could disappear overnight was something that no one could imagine.

PART TWO

The Fires of Autumn

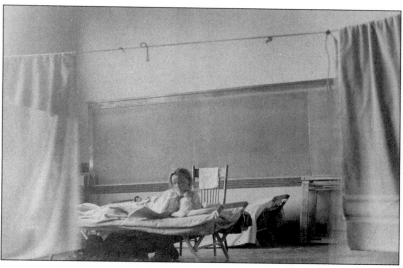

*Young fire refugee on makeshift bed in schoolhouse, Moose Lake, October 1918
(photograph by Earl L. Irish)*

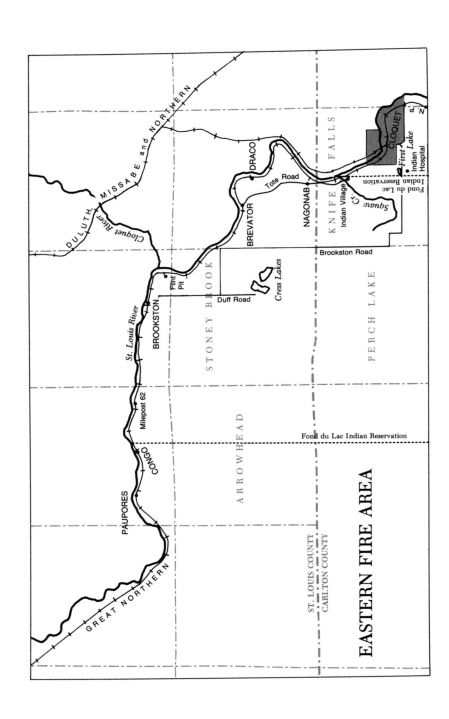

EASTERN FIRE AREA

CHAPTER TWO

Milepost 62 and the Fires in Brookston and Fond du Lac

*I tried to put it out but I ain't
got anything in my hand, you know.*
Steve Koskela

Come, for God's sake, and get out of here.
M. K. Whittemore

The St. Louis River is relatively placid above Cloquet, its smooth water only occasionally broken by shallow rapids and rocks in midstream. The steep banks, between 70 and 150 feet high, covered by birches, maples, and aspens, give the St. Louis a picturesque tranquillity that is particularly beautiful in the autumn. For a millennium Indian people made this river a main artery to the western Great Lakes. For more than two hundred years explorers, fur traders, and missionaries used the St. Louis River as the northern gateway to the Mississippi and as the highway to the Rainy River, Lake of the Woods, and the Canadian West. For lumbermen, the St. Louis watershed was one of the richest pinelands in the upper Midwest. Every spring the river carried logs down to the great mills at Cloquet and Scanlon. And when the Duluth and Winnipeg Railroad pushed west from Cloquet in the late 1880s, it went up the St. Louis River valley along the narrow floodplain on the south bank of the river, until at Floodwood it struck out almost straight for the northwest. The railroad, acquired by James J. Hill in 1896 for his Great Northern, made this stretch of the St. Louis a vital transportation corridor once again, with iron ore from the famous Mahoning mine moving down to the docks at Superior, Wisconsin. Ore trains, logging trains, passenger trains, and

The Indian Village and Holy Family Church on the Fond du Lac reservation appeared in the distance of this view of Cloquet with the tip of Dunlap Island on the right, about 1914 (detail of panorama by Olaf Olson). Logs in St. Louis River booms waited for processing in saw and planing mills while hundreds of piles of sawn lumber dried before being shipped out by railroad.

mixed freights labored up and down the double track along this part of the St. Louis valley, picking up cars, dropping off passengers, taking on water at now-forgotten stations and sidings — Nagonab, Draco, and Brevator between Cloquet and Brookston, Congo, Paupores, and Mirbat between Brookston and Floodwood. Among these small railroad junctions on the south bank of the St. Louis River the great Cloquet–Moose Lake fires started.

Almost all of the south bank of the St. Louis River, from just east of Paupores to Cloquet itself, is the northern border of the Fond du

Lac Indian Reservation. This reservation was created through the Treaty of La Pointe in 1854, in which the Lake Superior Ojibway (or Chippewa) in the region ceded to the United States government most of the present-day "Arrowhead Country" in exchange for reservations at Fond du Lac, Grand Portage, and Nett Lake (Bois Fort) and for cash annuities and various government services. The Fond du Lac Ojibway bands had traditionally enjoyed seasonal migrations up and down the lower St. Louis River valley. The new reservation of about 100,000 acres included their sugar bush camps and the wintering, ricing, and hunting grounds, and under government policy they were encouraged to settle down there. While this was not a perfect arrangement, the Fond du Lac reservation served the three local Ojibway bands better than some reservations in other parts of the United States served the Indians for whom they were intended.[1]

The Fond du Lac Ojibway prospered in numbers at least; in 1918 the population of the reservation was just more than a thousand, almost three times larger than the band had been in 1843. In 1887, however, Congress had passed the Dawes Allotment Act, allowing land on reservations to be allotted to individual Indians. Often these allotments were sold to white settlers or, especially at Fond du Lac, to lumbermen. In either case, a portion of reservation land passed out of the hands of the native people themselves. This was particularly true of Fond du Lac's northern border along the St. Louis River, where the railroad had been built, the timber cut, and the land settled by Finnish immigrants. The first places burned by the great fires, long before they reached Cloquet or Duluth, were the immigrant farmsteads and the Ojibway allotments on the Fond du Lac reservation.[2]

Fires were burning north and west of Cloquet throughout the autumn of 1918. Brush fires, clearing fires, and railroad fires were smoldering all along the Great Northern line from Brevator, just upriver from Cloquet, to Floodwood. All of these fires contributed to both the atmospheric conditions and the staggering intensity of the great fires of October 12. Of the several fires identified, however, one stood out in public opinion as being of such magnitude as to be clearly the source of the disaster. The great fire that destroyed Cloquet and Brookston was the railroad fire along the Great Northern tracks at Milepost 62, four miles west of Brookston on the south bank of the St. Louis River and fifteen miles northwest of Cloquet. Milepost 62 may be almost forgotten today, but its name haunted a whole generation.[3]

On Thursday, October 10, at about 4:30 in the afternoon, a passenger train from Duluth to Hibbing, known locally as the "Wooden Shoe" after the conductor's wooden leg, stopped at Milepost 62 and a siding called O'Brien's Spur. For years private contractors had used the siding, about two thousand feet long, as a loading station for various wood products. It contained large amounts (perhaps ten thousand cords) of pulpwood, cordwood, railroad ties, fence posts, and telephone poles in piles on both sides of the track. Furthermore, the ground was strewn with bark and chips, making the siding a tinderbox in the autumn conditions.[4]

Steve Koskela, who owned a farm a half mile away, was working with John Sundstrom, a neighbor, culling ties at the siding for use in Koskela's barn. "Big Steve" and Sundstrom watched the train stop at the siding, and after it left they saw a small column of smoke rise at the western end of the siding. They rushed over, to find a fire about twenty feet across burning through the tall, dry grass near the piles of wood. Having no tools with them, they attempted to put out the fire by trampling it with their boots. "I tried to put it out," Koskela said, "but I ain't got anything in my hand, you know. . . . I used to tramp it down with my feet, and I couldn't put it out." The grass was too dry, and the fire quickly spread under one of the several piles of cordwood at the siding.

Koskela went to get pails and shovels from home and, together with several other neighbors, began working to dismantle the rows of cordwood in order to make a firebreak. By 6:00 P.M. a Great Northern section foreman came down the track; when his crew arrived an hour and a half later the wind had stirred up the fire. A small railroad speeder came out from Brookston about 8:00 P.M., bringing Charles DeWitt, a Great Northern employee and the Brookston village president, who also had some logs at the landing; J. M. ("Matt") Miettunen, a store owner; Ray Paukka, his bookkeeper; and several others. They joined the section crew in working late into the night fighting the fire but were unable to put it out. The following day, Friday, October 11, the wind moderated; the fire, while still not out, seemed less dangerous. When Koskela went back to the siding early in the morning three crews were there, but they soon left to do work in Brookston and did not return. Even so, the smoke was sufficiently threatening that Anton LaFave, who had a small farm down the tracks near Milepost 61, decided to collect his tools from a small shed he had at the east end of O'Brien's Spur, lest they burn up. Koskela worked on the fire again later that day, although being alone he was unable to confine it to the siding.[5]

On Saturday morning, October 12, Koskela went into Brookston to do some shopping, getting a lift on a railroad speeder with the section crew. The fire was quiet. Returning at 11:30 on the Wooden Shoe, he found the siding now in flames, with lots of black smoke being driven by a strong northwest wind. The environmental conditions favorable to generating the blowup of a major fire — what Haines and Sando described years later — had been met. Several years of dry weather had created the favorable climatic conditions — *"the shell is loaded into the rifle chamber."* Small fires were burning throughout the region — *"the hammer is pulled back."* The passage of a cold front the previous day brought with it dry northwest winds and a record-breaking fall in humidity, such as to create a favorable synoptic weather pattern over the region — *"the trigger is pulled and the bullet is on its way."*[6]

Koskela saw clearly that with the enormous amount of dried wood at the siding, the heat generated by the flames would soon drive the fire out of control. He returned to his farm knowing that it was directly in line with the fire and that he would have to protect his property. "I guess we have to make ready fighting that fire now," Koskela told his family, and sent his sons to pump water and fill pails. He wetted down his buildings, set his animals free, and got his money from the house. By 1:40 P.M. the fire reached the farm from across the pasture. Koskela was able to save his house and family, but lost numerous outbuildings, some of his stock, and his timber. The worst of the fire passed in less than an hour, during which time it also overran Koskela's neighbors. The first refugees of the fire were members of Henry Knutti's household. The Knuttis, who lived about a half a mile east of Koskela, kept boarders, mostly trainmen. After the fire burned them out, they all made their way to Koskela's house for assistance. It was the beginning of a long and tragic day.[7]

At the Iwasko farm, southeast of Milepost 62 and about two miles away from Brookston, the sky was getting dark while Koskela and his neighbors were in the fire. John Iwasko and his wife were alone; one son was in the United States Army and the second son had left that morning for Duluth to report for the draft. The couple began moving their valuable possessions to the root cellar about noon. As burning leaves and ash fell around his house and the sun turned red from the smoke, Mr. Iwasko began fighting small spot fires. When the full force of the blaze reached him, between 2:00 and 3:00 P.M., he told his wife to go to the root cellar while he went to get his team of horses out of the burning barn. The fire was on them in an instant: "Awful quick, like a shot; it was awful big fire, and I jumped for that team right in the barn, that team in the barn, and grabbed the team and run away, and the wind blow the roof right up. . . . I came up from my place this way, you know, and I hit right here the bridge; right here is a big hill, and that wind that raise me away up on that hill there, and after throw me down, and after I slide to the creek, you know."[8]

From the creek Mr. Iwasko could see the flames destroy his horses, still in their harnesses. His wife, meanwhile, found herself trapped in the root cellar, with the door on fire and the room filling with smoke, an experience many others were to suffer elsewhere that day. Wrapping herself in a blanket, Mrs. Iwasko attempted to run from the root cellar one hundred feet to the creek. The wind blew away the blanket and the fire blinded her eyes and burned her face, hands, and legs, but she made it to the creek. Mr. Iwasko himself left the creek about 6:00 P.M. to examine his farm, which was completely destroyed. He found his injured wife when he returned to the creek for a pail of water. He then led and carried her into Brookston for help. But Brookston was gone. "Well," John Iwasko said later, "I never see anything[,] only everything red, you know; I never see that depot, you know?"

The Great Northern had no patrols along this region, and the section crews that had fought the Milepost 62 fire on Thursday were pulled off to work elsewhere on Friday and Saturday. Theodore Kunelius, a fourteen-year-old section hand on the Great Northern, worked out of Congo. Within the past two days he had fought fire at both Milepost 64 and Milepost 62. On Saturday morning Kunelius was sent into Brookston to assist in straightening track. By lunch time, however, he was sent up the tracks with a crew on a speeder to investigate the smoke coming into town. About two miles west of Brookston, shortly after 1:30, they ran into fire burning along both sides of the tracks. The fact that even the railroad ties were on fire made them worry whether the gasoline tank for the engine might explode. Nevertheless, they carried on through the fire to Milepost 62, where the wood piled at the siding was burning with great intensity. The foreman concluded that the passenger train, which was due in from Floodwood and farther north, could not safely pass by, and sent the speeder on to stop the train. The crew found fire burning on the south side of the track all the way to Congo and between Paupores and Mirbat.[9]

Meanwhile, in Brookston, then a town of about five hundred people, Charles DeWitt, the village president, who had worked all night for the railroad, was wakened by his wife at 2:00 P.M. because things were looking ominous. The air was smoky, the sun was red, and the wind was rising. During the next two hours the smoke and wind increased in intensity, coming right down the tracks from the west. Fire first swept by the town just to the south. As DeWitt said, "Well, it seemed — it just seemed like a long roll of smoke going right up and leaning over, just traveling across the country at probably about, oh, six or eight, maybe ten miles an hour."[10]

In the great heat, houses along the streets in the town began to burst into flames even before the fire actually emerged from the woods to the west. There was a freight train in Brookston, ordered to serve as a relief train by George S. Stewart of Superior, the general superintendent of the Great Northern's Lake District. Many of the townspeople made their way to the rail yard and climbed on board. DeWitt recorded that at 4:10 P.M., with the town burning, the relief train pulled out of Brookston with about two hundred people. Remarkably, much of the Great Northern property in Brookston was saved by a section foreman who stayed in the town, working the pumps along the river and hosing down the buildings in the railroad yard.[11]

The relief train escaped from Brookston, but it was not yet out of danger. About a mile down the tracks, where both the river and the tracks turned south, the train encountered fierce flames at Flint pit. The fire that had swept past Brookston had burned east to the St. Louis River, and a great swirl of flame momentarily engulfed the refugees in the open gondola cars of the relief train, scorching many, including DeWitt and his wife and three small children, before they could cover themselves.[12]

Fred Mader, a boom-crew cook who lived five miles down the tracks from Brookston, saw the heavy clouds of smoke and was told by section crews that the fire was coming. First he thought he would try to fight the fire at his cabin, but as the smoke became thicker and the wind became stronger he changed his mind and attempted to bury some of his belongings for safekeeping. (Many people attempted to protect their valuables in this way, but were unable to relocate the "buried treasure" once all points of reference had been obliterated by the fires.) He then walked out onto the track in time to see flames on the hill to the northwest above the crest of the riverbank. Mader started down the track for Brevator, "running wild" as he put it, and was overtaken by the relief train coming through the smoke, blowing its whistle every half minute. The train stopped for about fifteen minutes at Brevator, where Mader and numerous others got on. The relief train then went another ten miles, reaching Cloquet at about 5:00 P.M. The scorched cars and blackened, injured, and hysterical refugees presented a frightening spectacle to many people in town. Water and aid were brought to the train from the nearby hotels, while the refugees warned their comforters that Cloquet could not be saved. The relief train then went on to Carlton and to safety in Superior.[13]

As the fire swept past Brookston, it trapped people attempting to flee by automobile. Matt Miettunen ran a store in Brookston; on Saturdays Earl Miettunen, a sixteen-year-old high-school student, helped his father and Ray Paukka, the bookkeeper and assistant, at the store. Matt Miettunen and Paukka had been out to help at the fire on Friday at Milepost 62, so they knew the dangerous potential of all that burning wood. When Brookston filled with smoke around 3:00 P.M., they decided to leave. Young Earl drove the Overland 80 south toward Cloquet along the Duff road. Five or ten minutes out of Brookston, a great cloud of smoke, sparks, and surface fire blew across the road. The automobile struck a tree blown onto the road and crashed into the ditch. Matt Miettunen, his wife, and Paukka were thrown out into the burning bush. Matt was badly cut and burned from crashing through the windshield and landing in the fire. Earl looked for his mother among the blankets thrown from the automobile and then ran searching for her in the burning woods, but she was never seen alive again. Forced away by the smoke and flames, Earl and Paukka helped Matt up and back onto the road. All three then fled east through the woods, across the tracks near Flint pit, down the bank, and into the St. Louis River.[14]

They made their way out onto a logjam some distance from shore, about a quarter of a mile below where the Cloquet River enters the St. Louis. A few minutes later the surface fire burned right down to the water's edge. That was followed shortly by dense smoke and the great roar of the main fire, which showered sparks and firebrands down on them. "Now she is coming. Better we look for a place where we can duck," Matt Miettunen shouted, as they plunged into the water among the now-burning logs. "I see some chunks of fire flying right over us across the river right up in the air." The flames then spanned the river, igniting the trees on the opposite side. Shortly afterwards the men heard the Brookston relief train, itself passing through the flames at that point. The Miettunens and Paukka stayed in the river until after dark, attempting periodically to warm themselves by moving as close as possible to the burning logs. Later in the night they made their way to shore, where they huddled behind a large rock to keep out of the wind, unable to walk very far in either direction because of the fires still burning. At some point early the next morning, when they heard a train whistle in Brookston, they walked along the now-passable track back toward the town for aid and were taken by the train to the north end of Cloquet.[15]

While these escapes were being effected, the Milepost 62 fire was also traveling even more rapidly inland from the river in a southeasterly direction across the Fond du Lac reservation. Ojibway people south of Brookston had no railroad to deliver them to safety. One such person was Grace Sheehy, who lived on a farm on the Duff road, about three miles due south of Brookston. She was looking after her five children, who were between the ages of twelve years and eleven months, while her husband, Paul, worked in the shipyards in Duluth. In the early afternoon, noticing the smoke and wind, she walked up the road to consult with her neighbors, the Christensens. They were packing up and told her to go home and get her children. The wind was so strong, however, that it was blowing down trees, so that when she got home she did not think she could make it back with all of the children. Sheehy decided to try to save the farm herself. She put the two babies in bed so that they would not interrupt her, donned old shoes, got a shovel, and started to make a firebreak.

At about 3:30 P.M. the neighbors sent Mike Beargrease to help bring her back. Beargrease picked up the little boy, Sheehy wrapped up the baby in a mosquito bar, and they and the older children started north up the Duff road for the Christensens' place. Unfortunately, by that time the flames had crossed the road, so they turned around and walked a mile south toward Cress Lakes (also called Twin Lakes). When they reached a hill near one of the lakes at about 5:00 P.M. they could see fire burning heavily to the north and west of them. They found a boat on the edge of the western lake, and Beargrease paddled them out onto the water. With a great roaring noise, the fire swept past the east side of Cress Lakes. From the boat they could see fire all around them, particularly north and east toward Cloquet, but the fire at the lake did not burn all of the shoreline. They could see other people on land, so about 8:00 P.M. Beargrease brought the boat in to shore. "We couldn't pull the boat up on the shore so we jumped out in the water and I handed him the children and we started to walk around there," Sheehy said later. Beargrease walked over to John and Charlie Cress's farm, assuring Sheehy, "If the fire happen to come there we will go down to the water." By about 9:00 P.M. they all went to the Cress farm, where they and several other people spent the night. Sheehy and her children stayed there until Monday, when they went into Cloquet and found her husband.[16]

News of the fire burning through the Fond du Lac reservation west of town filtered into Cloquet by the late afternoon. "Why, I learned that there was a bunch of homesteader children that were up on the Brookston road that had to be gotten out of there or they would be liable to get burned," said Dr. M. K. Whittemore, a Cloquet dentist. Sometime after 7:00 P.M. Whittemore drove out past the Indian Hospital and then north about a mile and a half on the Brookston road until he was stopped by fire. There he turned onto the Bassett farm, about five and a half miles southeast of Cress Lakes. No one seemed to be around, but upon entering the house Whittemore found a distraught Mrs. Bassett and her four small children. Her husband, Ben,

was "out in the fire," she said in tears. "I think he was burned up."
Just then Mr. Bassett ran in through the smoke. "Come, for God's
sake," Whittemore said, "and get out of here." Mr. Bassett, however,
insisted on saving his horses. Just then they could hear the whistles
blow in Cloquet, and Whittemore remembered, "at that it seemed to
me that there was a tongue of fire that swept around and it broke loose
then terribly, and I whirled and ran into the house and grabbed two
of the children, and the oldest one followed right close behind, and
the mother grabbed the baby, and I threw them into the car, and we
got out of there and started south."[17]

After they had gone about a mile and a half in the automobile they
came to the corner of the Cedar Lake road. Mrs. Bassett said, "Oh,
God, can you go up to a certain place and get my other two children?"
Whittemore turned west on the Cedar Lake road and let Mrs. Bassett
off to pick up her children while he drove on a bit farther. When he
was engulfed in smoke he could hear the voices of people in the woods:
"When I got up there I could hear hollering and screaming, but I saw
that there was no use — well, the fact of the matter, I got scared; I
didn't dare to go in there; I was afraid I could not get out." He turned
back, picked up Mrs. Bassett and her children, and headed once again
for Cloquet.

About two miles northeast of Bassetts' was Joseph Petite's farm.
Petite had spent the whole day picking rutabagas, carrots, and beets,
but by late afternoon, about 4:00 P.M., he began to get worried about
the smoke in the northwest. At about 7:00 P.M. the smoke was very
close, so he and his wife decided to leave. They made their way by
the old road into the Indian Village (the largest of the Ojibway settlements on the Fond du Lac reservation) and past the Holy Family
Catholic church. "We was going to stay in the Indian Village," Petite
recounted, "when we see these sparks falling, so we keep on going to
Cloquet." They continued along the road south, and then down the
riverbank to the Northern Lumber Company yards. At that point the
fire was right behind them: "You could hear it crackling and sparks
coming over us. Of course, I could get away all right but the woman
[sic] couldn't and I don't want to leave them there. They couldn't run
fast." Some of the firebrands were as "big as balls," and he could see
"the fire flying all over us." Although it was not yet burning, Petite
saw no one left in the village when he passed by.[18]

Holy Family Church congregation members with their priest, Father Simon Lampe, at right in foreground, 1908

Southeast of Petite's farm lived Frank Houle with his wife and one child. During the day Houle had been busy pulling tree stumps, oblivious to any approaching danger. By about 5:30 P.M. his wife was sufficiently alarmed by the smoke to leave with their child for the Indian Village. In about an hour's time, Houle himself became concerned, loaded up their furniture on the farm wagon, turned loose his livestock, and by about 7:15 headed for the Indian Village. Just as he pulled away his house burst into flames and sparks and firebrands fell all around. As Houle remembered later, there were "big chunks of fire falling all over, and on the horses and all along the road." Houle found his wife at the church in the village with a large group of women and children. By this time houses in the village had started to burn, so Houle unloaded his furniture, leaving it to be consumed by the oncoming fire, and took the women and children in his wagon down the hill from the village into the Northern Lumber Company yards. Houle's wife and the other passengers got out of the wagon at the Great Northern water tower, and he took the wagon through the lumberyards to the bridges over Dunlap Island to the north side of the river. There he left his rig and recrossed the river by the log boom to

Posey's Island, met his wife, and took her back to the north side of the river.[19]

William Wiselan lived on an eighty-acre farm south of Brevator, just more than a mile from the Great Northern tracks below Draco. He returned to his farm at 2:00 P.M. after spending much of the day cutting trees for the Cloquet Tie and Post Company. From his property he could see quite a distance to the west, and by late afternoon he thought that "it looked as if the whole country was burning up" and that the fire was moving on a front of three to four miles wide. He sent his wife and two children off to Cloquet at about 5:30, walking along the old tote road (or Indian portage) that twisted south from Brevator to the Indian Village — about nine miles. The family got a ride with a neighbor who had a team of horses. Wiselan followed about a half an hour later and caught up with the team. Throughout most of the trip the fire kept just to the west of them, but when they crossed Squaw Creek the fire "kept crossing the road behind them." They too came down the road through the Indian Village, but about a mile and half beyond, the fire "crossed the road ahead of us." Sparks and embers were flying everywhere when Wiselan turned down into the upper yards of the Northern Lumber Company. He saw then that the fire was entering the company property.[20]

The fire burned through much of the northern half of the Fond du Lac reservation, striking the farms and homes of Ojibways and settlers alike. Completely destroyed were the Indian Village and the Holy Family Church, located on the high bluff overlooking the St. Louis River just upriver from Cloquet. George W. Cross, the Fond du Lac agency superintendent, telegraphed his superiors at the United States Office of Indian Affairs (OIA) for help the following day:

> Fond du Lac Reservation devastated by forest fire. City of Cloquet and adjacent towns destroyed. Office records and furniture burned. Many Indians homeless. Loss of life not known. Wire Five Thousand Dollars care First National Bank Duluth Immediate relief.[21]

Cross later reported to the OIA that some fifty-seven Ojibway homes and many more outbuildings were burned. Although sources vary, between 245 and 269 Ojibway suffered sufficient losses to file damage claims in the aftermath of the fires. A great deal of livestock was killed and much of the hay and feed crop was also lost, with the result that

Telegram from Cross to the United States
Office of Indian Affairs

George W. Cross, about 1915

the surviving animals had to be looked after at the Indian Farm (part of the reservation). Cross lamented that many historically valuable Ojibway craft items, such as arrowheads, bows, tomahawks, and beadwork, had been destroyed. Of more commercial importance was the loss of a large supply of decorated blankets that, along with beadwork, were sold for souvenirs and produced a good income for the Ojibway at the reservation.[22]

Fortunately, and perhaps remarkably, no Ojibway were killed in the fire. Both Cross and State Forester William Cox noted that the Ojibway were much more adept at coping with the hazards of woodland living, even dealing with forest fires, than were many of the European immigrants. In this regard, the *Pine Knot* concluded that "their keen wits saved them from perishing." In practical terms this meant getting on the relief trains, finding shelter in one of the local lakes, or crossing onto one of the islands in the St. Louis River that did not burn.[23]

As the afternoon wore on, people who lived near Cloquet began to get anxious. Peter M. Nelson owned a small farm about a mile and a half south of the Indian Village, overlooking the Northern Lumber Company (close to the present-day Cloquet Country Club). Nelson came home from Duluth by train about 5:00 P.M., and because of the smoke walked over to the Indian Village road to see what was going on. Seeing nothing but smoke, he went back home to milk his cows and do the chores. During supper the wind increased to such a force that it shook the house. He thought he would fill some tubs with water in case he should need to put out any fire. He was filling the first pail from a neighbor's well at about 8:00 P.M. when "all at once I see a big blaze right over the tree top of the balsam grove, northwest of me. As soon as I saw this I heard a terrible roaring through the woods. The wind was getting awful strong in the pine trees, and pine trees going up by the roots, and some was breaking off. I went in the house and told the woman we had better get out of there quick, so I grabbed the youngest child in my arms, and we started on the run to get away from there."

They headed south, hoping to get to First Lake, about a half a mile away, but ran through some heavy fire before they got there. On the road they met Harry Ruff and his daughter, who had driven their Ford automobile into the ditch. Nelson, despite having burned his hands in the fire, attempted to help Ruff get the Ford out of the ditch, but the canvas top caught fire while they were pushing. They abandoned the automobile and made for an open potato field nearby. While the fire was now burning in front of them to the south, they heard the whistle at the Northern Lumber Company. They spent much of the night in the field while the fire burned past them, after which they walked to Charlie Main's house near the Indian Hospital. The hospital, the Indian Farm, and several other houses did not burn, protected perhaps by the open area surrounding First Lake, although the fire burned on both the east and west of this area.[24]

In Cloquet Archie Campbell, the street commissioner and waterworks superintendent, was called from his supper at about 6:00 P.M. to look after a substantial brush fire at the Spring Lake pumping station, southwest of town. There he found a fire of about twenty acres that was seriously threatening many of the local wood-frame houses but was of little danger to the pumping station itself, which was built of brick and had a supply of garden hose. Indeed, as the buildings in the vicinity began to catch fire, people fled to the pumping station to spend the night. When Campbell returned to town at about 9:00 P.M. to get more garden hose, the great fire had already entered Cloquet.[25]

Alicia Panger remembered years later her family's frightening experience in the late afternoon as the fire approached Spring Lake. Her father, Fred, had first planned to fight fire on the reservation. He then returned home to take his wife and their eight children to Duluth, but when the fire overtook them they fled to the brick pumping station. Everything seemed to go wrong: the horse would not go in the right direction, the wind was so strong they could not hear each other speak, the axle broke on the wagon, and "a flaming two-by-four flew over our heads and set a field afire." But they made it to the station, where "three families and parts of two others, including 12 children, were jammed into the cement aisles between the whirring engines pumping as though they knew they were saving lives." They prayed and fingered their rosary beads and watched through the windows as the red sky gradually turned black.[26]

The fire that had started at Milepost 62 on October 10 had been stirred up on Saturday at about 11:00 A.M. by a freshening breeze. By noon, when Steve Koskela returned from Brookston, the fires in the huge wood piles along O'Brien's Spur were burning with such an intensity that Koskela recognized the danger immediately. He went home to make preparations, and by 1:30 P.M. the fire was up the hill and into his farm. Six and a half hours later it had traveled fifteen miles to the city limits of Cloquet, at a speed of 2.3 miles per hour, slightly faster than the Mack Lake fire of 1980 in Michigan. It caught the city by surprise. The wind had been rising all afternoon, and the haze and smoke had been getting thicker; at about 6:00 P.M., only an hour after the Brookston relief train arrived in Cloquet, a white ash began to fall on the city. Indeed, it seems to have been these two events, the Brookston train and the falling ash, that alerted the population to real danger. Several survivors' accounts tell of men intending at about this time, from 7:00 to 8:00 P.M., to join volunteer fire-fighting brigades, only to be overtaken by the arrival of the fire in the city before they were ever organized and deployed. As Commissioner Campbell put it, "I didn't know of any fires that was in any ways dangerous, any ways close."[27]

CHAPTER THREE

The Miracle of Cloquet

This town ain't gonna burn.
Johnny Bull

This whole town is going and it is going fast.
Orlo B. Elfes

People in Cloquet were not in ignorance of the fires that were burning northwest of town along the Great Northern tracks. But autumn fires in the Great Lakes states were commonly accepted as part of the annual cycle of the seasons. Moreover, knowledge of a specific fire burning at Milepost 62, some fifteen miles away, would not have been a cause for alarm. Indeed, as has been shown, the railroad section crews were called off the fire on Friday and Saturday to work on more pressing railroad jobs. In Cloquet, Saturday, October 12, dawned with no premonition of anything unusual, much less an impending disaster. The temperature was warm, the early morning sky was clear and sunny; it seemed to be a beautiful autumn day.

Cloquet was laid out largely on the south side of the St. Louis River, which entered the city from the northwest (then called the North End), turned and flowed more or less due east for the length of the settlement, and then turned again southeast below the city. The mills were all built along the south bank of the river, with the exception of the Cloquet Tie and Post Company, which then had facilities just opposite Dunlap Island. South of the mills were the railroad tracks and yards, the commercial sections, and, beginning just about where the hills rose, the residential areas. The Northern Lumber Company had large facilities at the northwest corner of the city. The two mills, planer, allied buildings, and huge lumberyard ran from opposite Dunlap Island up the curve of the south bank of the river al-

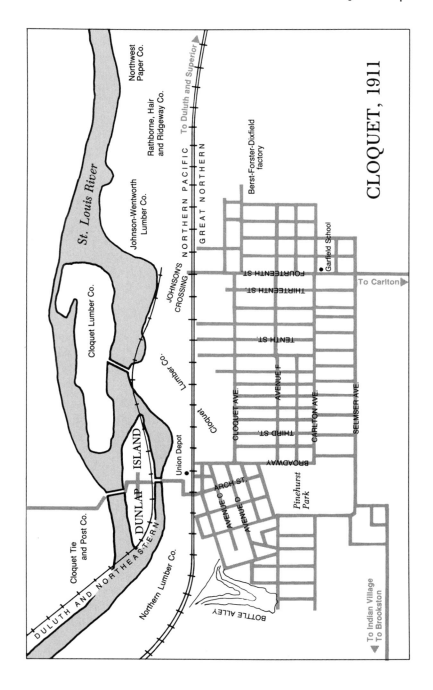

CLOQUET, 1911

Cloquet, about 1914–17, with Cloquet Lumber Company planer (left), Johnson-Wentworth sawmill and burner (center), and Northwest Paper Company (upper right) between the river and Cloquet Avenue (detail of panorama by Olson)

most to the Indian Village. To the east, just beyond Dunlap Island, was the Cloquet Lumber Company. The Cloquet yards began on the island and extended across the river into what is now Veterans Park. Still farther downriver was the Johnson-Wentworth Lumber Company, and beyond it the paper company and the match mill in their present locations. The fire's path through the city was very much shaped by the layout of the city, the river, and the surrounding hills, as well as by the strong northwest wind driving it.

Throughout the afternoon, there had been a growing anxiety in Cloquet about the fire situation and the weather. As the wind and smoke blowing across the city increased, there was an understandable cause for concern. Clothes hanging on lines were whipped like signal flags, and people's eyes and noses were irritated by the smoke and dust in the air. Pearl E. Drew remembered being assured by the district forest ranger that the city was quite safe as long as the wind stayed in the same direction. At about 2:00 P.M. Ranger Percy Vibert drove out west of Cloquet on the Moorhead road to investigate conditions around Corona. He found the area there and near Perch Lake to be threatened by fire, but he perceived no danger to Cloquet. William H. Kenety, the superintendent of the Cloquet Experimental Forest, also drove west to Big Lake to look for fires, but the columns of smoke that he saw were well to the west.[1]

So people went about their normal tasks. Elise Cook Wenzel's husband and sons filled the woodshed with the kindling delivered that day, and her sister's children went to a movie; Alicia Panger went to a picnic in Pinehurst Park; Mrs. A. F. Peterson baked bread and cakes for Sunday; Guy Smith, Tena's husband, worked on war bonds at the First National Bank; Pearl Drew wrote a letter to her husband, Herbert J., who was fighting in France with the American Expeditionary Forces in the Meuse-Argonne campaign. Even so, people were wary. They canceled weekend holiday plans, bought supplies, buried valuables, packed clothes. The news of the burning of Brookston and rumors of fire on the reservation, the falling ash in the city, the red glow in the western sky as the daylight faded, together with the increasing wind, caused growing alarm. "About six o'clock that evening," remembered Evelyn Swanson Elshoss, "popular opinion had doomed the city."[2]

Rudolph Weyerhaeuser and Sherman L. Coy, the manager and secretary respectively of the Northern Lumber Company, returned to Cloquet from a business trip on Saturday afternoon. Coy and Weyerhaeuser were met at the depot in Carlton by Coy's family and driven home by about 7:00 P.M. They all had an anxious supper together (young Edward D. Coy was so upset that he could not eat and wanted to leave town right away), but understood that the fire was a half mile away. After supper they decided to find out the news from town, but, Coy remembered, "I happened to look back after we had gone a block [toward town] and saw a huge sheet of flame over the hill back of his [Weyerhaeuser's] house a short distance away. I turned to go back immediately and he followed. We went over the hill by our garden and into the ravine yard. The fire was then only a few feet from the lumber piles. I turned in the alarm from the box right there and then ran to the pump house for full pressure, and had the engineer blow the siren and keep it up."[3]

The mill sirens and whistles that Coy started were heard throughout the city and the surrounding countryside, as far away as the Bassett farm on the Brookston road, the Indian Village, and Spring Lake.

In Cloquet the alarms told people unmistakably what they had been reluctant to believe possible: the fire was in the city.

The city fire department responded immediately and attempted to get out to the lumber piles, but got stuck in the ditch. Some lumber company horses were used to pull the truck free, but it could not get to the flames. Meanwhile, Weyerhaeuser and Coy found the yard foreman, the watchman, and Joseph Wilson at the mill; in Weyerhaeuser's words, "We went out, five men, to combat the flames." With great exertion they got out two hose carts with some 250 feet of hose and shot a stream of water at the now-burning piles of lumber. But the wind was blowing fiercely and sending sparks from the burning lumber all over the rest of the lumberyard. This was exhausting work for five men, and they could see that the fire was quickly getting into new areas of the yard despite their efforts. Finally, Coy concluded, "We're gone," and Weyerhaeuser sent him home to look after his family.[4]

While Weyerhaeuser, Coy, and their three-man crew were struggling to contain the fire as it entered the Northern Lumber Company yards, several of those people who had fled their farms on the Fond du Lac reservation came down from the Indian Village into the North End. William Wiselan came through the village and down the hill into the yards of the lumber company. Neither the village nor the Holy Family Church had burned when he passed by, although there was fire on the road south of him and there were many sparks and firebrands in the air. Moments later Joseph Petite and his wife walked down into the company yards toward town, but they met his sister and turned and headed north once again. At that point Petite saw fire enter the yards near the lath mill, so they again turned back to town. Petite talked with Weyerhaeuser, who wanted to know if the upper yards were burning by then. The Petites went on into Cloquet, past Weyerhaeuser's house, to Pinehurst Park. As "the fire was coming right along, coming over that hill," Wiselan and his family made their way east along the tracks into Cloquet. Anton LaFave, who had gone to find his daughter in the Indian Village, returned to Cloquet just as the fire appeared. Standing on the railroad track between the planer and the water tower in the upper yard, LaFave, like Coy and Weyerhaeuser, saw the fire coming "over the hill, down over the hill."[5]

Rudolph M. Weyerhaeuser

The wind was then blowing at least sixty miles an hour, and the fire had entered the lumberyard at what was called Bottle Alley. When the fire entered the piles of drying lumber, enormous amounts of fresh fuel were added to the intensity of the heat. The cut boards, neatly stacked in rows, were driven into the air by the rising heat and wind and blown burning across the city, starting fresh fires in advance of the main fire. Commissioner Campbell, who drove back and forth between Cloquet and Carlton several times during the night, reported that when the west end of Cloquet was engulfed in flames at about 10:00 P.M., fires, or spot fires, were breaking out as far east as Tenth Street.[6]

The citizens of Cloquet were not doomed even if the city was. The railroads provided the avenue of escape, and certainly trains saved the people of Cloquet. It is difficult, however, to piece together from the available documents the story of how the several trains were arranged. Local tradition holds that Lawrence Fauley, the Cloquet Union Depot agent, took action on his own responsibility and during the course of the day ordered trains from nearby rail centers into town, to be held for a possible evacuation. George Stewart, the Great Northern superintendent in Superior, however, was thought to be responsible for holding the four trains in Cloquet and the one in Brookston. The files of the Great Northern and the Northern Pacific explain little. The Northern Pacific's superintendent in Duluth reported to his supervisor that he ordered a switch engine to stay in Cloquet on October 12 in case of need and that this engine pulled a train of mixed freight cars out of the city. A Northern Pacific passenger train of twenty coaches was sent to evacuate Carlton during the night, but it arrived in Carlton after the fire crisis had eased, and so took Cloquet refugees into Duluth.[7]

What is clear is that there were four trains available in Cloquet as the crisis developed: a Northern Pacific passenger train of three coaches (known locally as "Gilbert's train" after George Gilbert, the conductor) that made a daily trip from Cloquet to Duluth and back and that was held at the depot after it completed its run; two empty Great Northern ore trains, which had been upbound for the iron ranges but that were held in Cloquet because of the fires at Brookston and beyond; and a mixed freight train of boxcars and gondolas, pulled by the Northern Pacific switch engine. It seems clear that Fauley and Mayor John Long were responsible for assembling the freight cars from the rolling stock in the Cloquet rail yards during the afternoon and getting them unloaded for possible emergency use. Any cars ordered into town by Fauley would have been used for this train. In any case, by nightfall the four trains were available, and they rescued between seven thousand and eight thousand people from almost certain doom.[8]

Several other efforts were made during the afternoon to prepare the city for possible disaster. Telephone operators remained at their switchboards to attempt to phone every number in the city if the fire came. Mayor Long arranged for runners, including the police, to be sent through the streets of the city to carry information or to order people out of their houses and toward the relief trains, if it came to that. The local American Red Cross was alerted, although the focus was on aid to the Brookston refugees rather than on the situation in Cloquet.[9]

With the sirens and whistles, the alarm went out across the city. Just as the sound of the mill siren was heard, Orlo B. Elfes, the editor of the *Pine Knot*, "wild-eyed and puffing," came running into his house on Third Street, calling to his wife, "Ada, get the girls . . . we have got to get out of here. This whole town is going and it is going fast, the fire is already in the upper mill yards." Anna Dickie Olesen, the wife of Cloquet-schools superintendent Peter Olesen, was the host for Dr. Mabel S. Ulrich, the speaker that evening at the Cloquet Mothers' Club meeting in the new high school. Mrs. Olesen and Ulrich were just finishing their coffee when Mr. Olesen rushed in and said there would be no meeting because the fire was coming across the hills. Police chief John McSweeney, his whole force of four men, all of the runners organized by the mayor, the telephone operators, and people shouting from automobiles spread the order to get out of town and the news that there were trains waiting. John Blomberg, who ran a general store on the east end of Cloquet Avenue, kept phoning Fauley at the depot during the evening for reports on conditions in the west end of town, while one of his customers, old Johnny Bull, sat eating a pie with painful slowness and declaring, "This town ain't gonna burn." By 9:00 P.M. Blomberg was not so sure. When no one answered at the depot, he decided it was time to leave.[10]

From all parts of the city and the outlying region, from as far away as people could walk or ride in an hour's time, a newly created community of refugees made their way to the depot, the rail yards, and the rail crossings in Cloquet. William Wiselan and his wife and two children, who had been almost chased down the old tote road by the fire, walked right through the Northern Lumber Company yards, past the burning planer, past the now-burning Wright Hotel, and right onto one of the ore trains. The Elfes household walked down Broadway past Avenue C, where they saw that "a shower of burning boards was flying around" in the next block. Young Kathryn lost her hat, her mother did not want to go, Hilda the maid was separated from the others, but in the end they all made it to the trains. When they found an empty boxcar, Ada R. Elfes said to her husband, "But Orlo, I can't get in that! I've never been in a box car!" Kathryn remembered that her exasperated father "picked her up and threw her in with more speed than grace." The Olesens, their daughter Mary, and Mabel Ulrich all made their way to the relief trains, the fierce wind blowing smoke and sand in their faces.[11]

People streamed down toward the tracks: toward the depot in the west end, toward Johnson's Crossing in the east end, and toward various mill crossings elsewhere. Some went in automobiles or horse-drawn wagons, but most walked; several invalids were pushed in wheelbarrows, including a young woman who had given birth that day. Although by 9:00 P.M. there were burning boards flying through the air and landing in the streets and small fires breaking out in various buildings, there seems to have been no panic. People plodded along steadily against the very strong winds. Lines of men steered people toward the waiting cars at the depot. The streets were cluttered with abandoned automobiles and wagons. Anna Olesen had a lasting memory of numerous empty baby carriages that had to be left behind at the depot platform. As the trains stood waiting to go, people watched the city begin to burn. Orlo Elfes saw his *Pine Knot* office go up; others remembered watching the Young Men's Christian Association (YMCA) building, the Cloquet Hotel, the Methodist church, and the high school in flames. Eventually, the trains began to leave.[12]

The passenger train was loaded with women and children only. This decision split up many families (which created problems because the trains did not all go to the same destination), and in the crisis some families chose to stay together in a freight train rather than risk separation. All the passenger train's aisles were filled with people standing, and people sat three or four in seats that were intended for two; no luggage was allowed on board. This three-car train carried well over 1,000 people and was the first to leave for Carlton and Duluth. Then the two Great Northern ore trains, made up of seventy-five cars filled with about 4,700 people, left, bound for Superior. The mixed freight train pulled by the Northern Pacific switch engine, with about 2,000 on board, held back until the last possible moment so that no one attempting to leave would be left behind, no matter how late in getting to the tracks. By 10:00 P.M. the west end of the city was burning in earnest, as those in the boxcars watched anxiously. When the depot and the last two boxcars caught fire, the train was moved a short way up the tracks. No more people arrived to get on the train, leaving only the unreal spectacle of frightened and thrashing horses, empty burning streets, the wail of steam whistles, and the continuing roar of the fire. Perhaps at the insistence of Chief McSweeney in the engine cab, the train pulled slowly out of the yard at about 10:30, with depot agent Fauley on the cowcatcher holding a lantern into the smoke. Kathryn Elfes Gray remembered that "as the last box car swung past him, Mayor John Long . . . jumped aboard."[13]

The trains took their passengers to safety, but the journeys were not without perils as well as discomfort. They left the depot very slowly, stopping at every crossing and junction to pick up more people. Those in the east end of Cloquet who hoped to take the trains had fled to Johnson's Crossing at the foot of Fourteenth Street, so there were many passengers there. The cars themselves were crammed with people, all tired, many frightened, some sick. Willa M. Spoor rode out of Cloquet in the baggage car of the first train, sitting on a milk can and holding her sleeping baby in her arms, while her two other children leaned against her. Evelyn Elshoss, who got on a train at Johnson's Crossing, remembered, "In retrospect, I can see myself sitting in a corner of the boxcar. Bodies are packed together all about me. My nostrils are filled with the stench of the barnyard, of too permeating perfumes, of unbathed bodies, of garlic, and of tobacco. Above the murmured prayers and childish whimperings, I can hear the voices of men fill with a bravado that tends to cover any weakness they might have shown earlier in the evening."[14]

Fires were burning in many places along the tracks on the way to Duluth and Superior, so there was a fear that the trains themselves might run into as big a fire as that burning Cloquet. Every bridge and trestle had to be checked by trainmen with lanterns. Pearl Drew remembered the tension: "We passed through Carlton, came to the high tressle [sic] in Jay Cooke [State] Park, and stopped right in the middle of it. Of all places we had stopped, this seemed the worst. Fire was everywhere — flames licking from the deep gullies to the very tracks we were on. This was the end — we were sure of it." Rumors spread through the trains, fear rose, but in every case the trains started moving again.[15]

Not everyone left by train, although the vast majority did. Allan G. and Laura Wight had escaped with their young son, Lloyd W., from the Hinckley fire of 1894 on a train that passed over a burning trestle. They now buried their valuables in their back yard and started

Refugees waited for a train in the ruins of the Union Depot, Cloquet, about October 16, 1918 (Olson)

walking toward the open fields south of town. Mayor Long had sent his family to Duluth earlier in the day, with his teenage son, Leonard, driving the automobile. Ranger Vibert got his wife out of the city hospital, put out a grass fire near his home west of town, and around 8:00 P.M. drove to Carlton, as he put it, "just as fast as I could." Sherman Coy, after leaving Rudolph Weyerhaeuser in the Northern Lumber Company yard, went home, packed a few valuables, and drove his family and several neighbors (ten in all) to Carlton. The automobile had just been made operational that afternoon. Guy Smith drove his family to Carlton in their brand-new Ford; but after listening to reports there, they decided to take the Northern Pacific relief train to Duluth later in the night, abandoning the new automobile at the depot. Lester J. Blomberg, the fifteen-year-old son of store owner John Blomberg, drove a delivery truck laden with the family possessions while his older brother Raynold drove a neighbor's automobile loaded with people. The road to Carlton was filled not only with automobiles but also with people walking and begging for rides. Ruby H. Spurbeck wrote years later, "Traffic was so congested that it took about two hours to reach Carlton. We had to stay in line as people were walking, carrying what they were able to and using such conveyances as wheelbarrows, baby buggies, etc. Some were leading cows."[16] The visibility was very bad and some automobiles did not have lights, but there were no bad crashes or pile-ups such as at "Dead Man's Curve" near Moose Lake.

When the fire entered the city, the fire department members began a losing battle. Although they had attempted to get into the Northern Lumber Company yards, they had not been able to bring their equipment to the site of the early fire. Firebrands from the lumberyard sent the department back into the city. The department, with about fifteen men, had more than one thousand feet of hose and a big Seagrave pumper truck that could draw water from the river or from hydrants and shoot a stream of water at 250 gallons per minute. But it was not capable of fighting fire across the whole city. With Chief George Mayhan blinded by smoke, the fire fighters fell back to Carlton sometime after midnight. There, led by Assistant Chief Archie Lessor, they hooked on to the Carlton water mains to help hose down the area, and worked to set the backfires that helped to save Carlton.[17]

Hundreds of people streamed into Carlton on foot, in automobiles, and even from the trains. Many intended to travel on to the homes of friends or family in Barnum, Moose Lake, or Duluth, only to find that the roads were closed or at least dangerous. There was little choice but to stay the night or take the relief trains. Carlton opened its doors to the Cloquet refugees. It was said that every home and business made room for people to come in out of the night. The Elfes family heard their name called from the depot platform as they sat in a boxcar on a relief train. It was an invitation to stay with stationmaster Lee Brower's family. Some fifty people stayed in the large brick home of Henry Oldenburg — the Coys, Belle M. Hornby (wife of Harry), Clarence I. McNair and his family, Hugo Schlenk and his family, Dr. James Fleming, and several others. Twelve-year-old Maurice H. Haubner, who lived south of Carlton, drove the family automobile into town to see what was happening, and took back about twenty refugees to stay with his parents or with neighbors. There was a danger that Carlton might burn as well as Cloquet, and people were prepared to flee to Thomson Lake or to take one of the trains. Fires north and west of Carlton earlier in the week, however, had created some-

Sherman L. Coy

thing of a firebreak. With the help of at least two hundred people putting out spot fires and backfiring, together with the efforts of the
Carlton volunteer fire department, the Cloquet fire department, and
the Northern Pacific pump engine, the city was saved.[18]

The fact that the Carlton road remained open allowed Commissioner
Archie Campbell to travel back and forth three times during the
night, monitoring the plight of Cloquet. Campbell probably saw
more of the city burn than anyone else, and he was later able to report
the capricious behavior of spot fires, which burned well in advance
of the main fire, and the fire pattern in the houses on the crest of the
hill. The first houses that he actually saw burning were in the west end
at Avenue D and Arch Street, sometime after 9:00 P.M. By the time
he had driven to the east end of town, he found houses burning on
Thirteenth Street between Carlton and Selmser avenues. Very
quickly, houses along the high ridge between Avenue F and Carlton
Avenue, from Third Street down to about Thirteenth Street, were

House ruins, Cloquet, October 1918 (McKenzie)

"catching the brunt of the fire first," Campbell observed. "The houses that was up on the hill, they caught fire before the flat." The commercial buildings along Cloquet Avenue were burning by 10:00 P.M. but as late as 2:00 A.M. Campbell was able to travel down by the railroad tracks past the Cloquet Lumber Company. He reported to anxious listeners in Carlton that it looked as if the east end of the city might be saved; but between 3:00 and 4:00 A.M. the winds shifted, and the east end went as well as the rest of the city. "At four o'clock it was practically all burned," he reported. Campbell picked up people on his return trips, and collected food from the doomed stores for the refugees in Carlton.[19]

Nor was Commissioner Campbell the only person to travel back and forth from Carlton. Sherman Coy, having got his family to safety, returned to Cloquet on several trips, along with a number of others. On his last trip, however, Coy was unable to get beyond the Garfield School, and had a number of close calls. At one point a burning telephone pole fell right where his automobile had been.[20]

Not everyone chose to leave the city while it burned. Joseph Petite, who had come into Cloquet from the reservation, did not follow the streams of people to the depot, but went instead to Pinehurst Park and spent the night in one of the small lakes there, together with his wife, his sister, and a fair number of other people. When asked what he saw of the fire as it burned around him, he replied, "I didn't pay no attention even when we stayed in Cloquet, I didn't pay no attention to the fire. I was all the time dipping water and wetting these people that was with me." L. A. Hanson put his family on the relief trains and then went home to try to save their house. When it became too dangerous for him to persist, he fled to Pinehurst Park, where he spent the night in the lake with Joe Madwayosh and several other Ojibway who had come in from the reservation. Madwayosh, a medicine man and future world logrolling champion, was nicknamed "Joe Mud" by other Ojibway after his night in the lake.

Anton LaFave stayed down by the river and the islands all night. He came through the Indian Village just ahead of the fire and went down into the mill yards. He crossed the river several times during the night on the bridges to and from Dunlap Island and the old bridge across the river from Posey's Island. At one point early in the night, LaFave and Frank Houle helped Father Simon Lampe, O.S.B., the priest in charge of the Holy Family Church, and his niece carry his bags across the river, and they assisted several others as well. When one of the bridges caught fire, LaFave and a small group spent the rest of the night in a building on the north bank.[21]

In another part of the city, Elise Wenzel and her family — her husband, two sons, and mother — decided to stay and try to save their house rather than take the trains as did most of their neighbors. She put tinned food in a large boiler of water; one son buried some supplies and valuables in the back field; her husband cleared away some dirt in a ditch, put up a tent in the cleared space, and then put dirt on the tent. When the fire came her husband and the elder son fought to save the house, but when a neighbor's place caught fire the Wenzels' could not be saved either. They were so cramped in the tent that they could hardly straighten their limbs, but she remembered, "In the early morning, before daylight, we could hear other people over in the field beyond us, so we knew we were not alone." They had survived.[22]

At least seventeen, and perhaps as many as fifty, men stayed and fought to save the mills and Dunlap Island. In this they were incredi-

The Cloquet company sawmill and burners (left center) and Johnson-Wentworth sawmill and burner (center) still stood along Cloquet Avenue after the fires, October 1918 (detail of panorama by Olson).

bly successful, although the direction of the wind may have been instrumental. Indeed, in saving some of the mills they saved the future of the whole city. After Rudolph Weyerhaeuser left the burning hill behind his house, he went down into the Northern Lumber Company yards, which were directly in the path of the fire coming out of the northwest. By the time he got into the mills, now abandoned, the lumber (some sixty-five million board feet) drying in the several yards was already burning. Weyerhaeuser and Joseph Wilson went to the barns and got about one hundred horses out and across the river to safety, Wilson getting kicked by a horse for his efforts. With several of the few remaining workmen they returned to the pump house, which was still in operation, to attempt to hose down the lower sawmill. The heat from the upper yard and the upper sawmill was too great, however, and the water failed to protect the buildings; all of the Northern's facilities were consumed. Also destroyed were the

Duluth and Northeastern Railroad depot and roundhouse and the buildings of the St. Louis River Mercantile Company, both on the western end of Dunlap Island. The rest of the island, with its bridges spanning the St. Louis River, its hotels, and its saloons, was spared.[23]

At the Cloquet Lumber Company, farther downriver, manager Harry Hornby and a handful of others were able to keep hoses in operation, wetting down the big sawmill on the river and several other structures; but they were unable to save their planing mill, much of their cut lumber (forty million board feet), or their barn and horses, all of which burned after 2:00 A.M. The Johnson-Wentworth Lumber Company, which was farther downriver still, was virtually undamaged. It seems clear that the fire came quite steadily out of the northwest; the Northern Lumber Company, the western end of Dunlap Island, and the western and central parts of the city bore the full brunt of the heat and flames. Farther east along the south bank of the river, the crest of the opposite bank, which was as high as 120 feet, provided natural protection that helped to save not only those plants mentioned but also the power plants along the river, the Cloquet Tie and Post Company facilities on the north bank of the river, the Northwest Paper Company, the Berst-Forster-Dixfield toothpick factory, and the Rathborne, Hair and Ridgeway Company box plant, all in the east end of town. In some ways this seems almost miraculous. Only a handful of other buildings survived the fire: the Garfield School, five or six houses, and the buildings on Dunlap Island, previously mentioned. Could the whole city have been saved? Rudolph Weyerhaeuser, though perhaps a bit optimistic, thought another one hundred men might have done it.[24]

The real miracle of the Cloquet fire was the successful evacuation of about eight thousand people by trains. Stephen Pyne noted that in most of the great forest fires in the upper Midwest the railroads played a major, and often heroic, part in rescuing the inhabitants. The Cloquet fire was perhaps the ultimate example, with trains carrying to safety the vast majority of a very large population. Deaths in the city were few (probably fewer than six) while the number of people killed in the rural areas near Cloquet was estimated by Herbert Richardson to be more than one hundred. The other miraculous aspect of the Cloquet fire was the survival of substantial elements of the city's industrial complex along the riverbank. This critically important industrial base made possible the almost immediate commercial revival of the city, and perhaps the region. Many of the people saved by the trains had lost their homes and possessions, but they had not lost their future.[25]

CHAPTER FOUR

The Fires above Duluth

That is what we consider a real forest fire.
Clarence H. Barnes

It was roaring . . .
I thought all was the end of the world.
Daniel Willeck

The great fires of October 12 burned almost the entire countryside from Milepost 62 to the eastern edge of Duluth, a distance of twenty-nine miles. Only occasional green areas existed, and these were not extensive. Moreover, the fires that burned up to Duluth ranged much farther north and south than this simple east-west line. The northern boundary of the Duluth fires was near the villages of Alborn and Independence, and the southern boundary near Harney and Nopeming.

Just as with the Cloquet fire, the fires that burned into the outskirts of Duluth were held to have had several sources. In the Cloquet fire, both survivors' accounts and the physical evidence, such as windblown trees and the shape of green areas, reinforced the contention that the fire came out of the northwest. In the Duluth fires, the eyewitnesses were less consistent. The wind was out of the west; it was out of the northwest; it was out of the southwest. The fires seemingly jumped ahead to consume victims before burning the intervening territory. Green areas pointed in one direction; the wind was observed blowing in another.

Were the survivors' accounts accurate descriptions of what happened, or were these people so utterly terrified as to be confused and to exaggerate in their own minds the events that they had experienced? How could the contradictions exist?

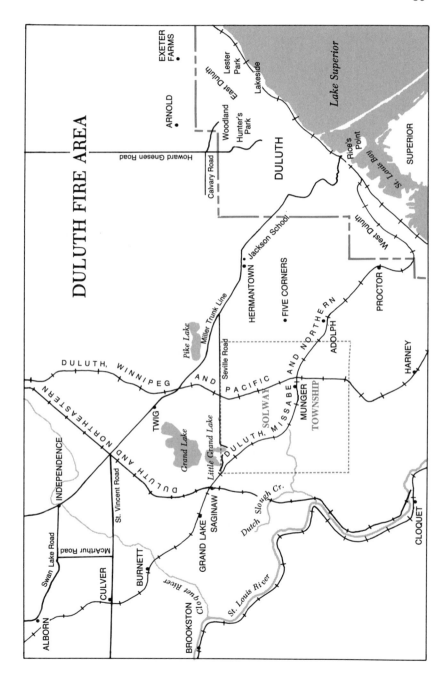

DULUTH FIRE AREA

Certainly the dynamics of huge fires were not very clearly or scientifically understood. Perhaps only after studies of the fire storms in Dresden and Hamburg in World War II, of the nuclear and thermonuclear explosions in the 1940s and 1950s, and indeed of large forest fires themselves in the last thirty years, could the contradictions and fantastic descriptions be seen in a more sympathetic context. In short, the confusing facts of the fires are perhaps less troublesome today than they were in 1918.

A main source of the Duluth conflagration was the Milepost 62 fire west of Brookston. The huge explosion of heat and wind, of sparks and burning brands, generated by the four hundred to six hundred carloads of dry timber ignited at Milepost 62 must be seen as a primary cause for the destruction of much of the region. Matt Miettunen and his son Earl, who had fled from Brookston sometime after 3:00 P.M., crashed their automobile in the fire and made their way to the waters of the St. Louis River below Flint pit. From there they saw the fire jump across to the east bank of the river shortly after 4:00 P.M. When they saw "chunks of fire flying right over us across the river right up in the air," it appeared that the woods on both sides were burning as far as they could see, north or south.[1]

North of Brookston, in the Alborn and Independence areas, the situation became more complex. A gravel train on the Duluth, Missabe and Northern tracks, traveling north at about 2:00 P.M., started fires along the roadbed between Culver and Alborn and beyond. Railroad workers and local people attempted to put out the fires there, and a further effort was made to stop the fire at the Stony Brook road that ran north and southeast of Alborn. But in the atmospheric conditions that prevailed that Saturday, the fires quickly got out of control all along the tracks and began burning into the farms to the east of first the rail line and then the road.

Oscar Marklund saved his house on the north side of the Swan Lake road just outside of Alborn, but Sivert Holten, who lived a half mile from the Missabe tracks on the south side of the road, had trouble keeping the fire from his farm. The family worked with wet gunnysacks to put out fires on and around the house, but lost the other buildings. Meanwhile, Pete and Alvar Holten were caught in the fire while coming from the Alborn station. They found shelter in a ditch beside the Lind road until the fire burned past them. Alborn historian Jacqueline Moran wrote, "The family slept in the house that night, but they were afraid to undress, in case the fire should swing back." Carl Nordin and Andrew Hoiem had farms about a mile east of the tracks and south of the Swan Lake road. They and their families fled. The Hoiem farmhouse was not burned but all of the family possessions, which had been put in the root house, and all of the outbuildings were destroyed. The Nordins lost everything — animals, crops, and buildings. Harry and Bill Hovis were caught in the fire on the Swan Lake road. They abandoned their automobile and attempted to make their way on foot, but it became impossible: "It was mighty hot, let me tell you, but we made it for about a mile before the heat became so intense that we couldn't take it any longer, so we threw ourselves face down in the middle of the road. As we lay there, two or three rabbits bounded out of the burning woods and laid close beside us. Several holes were burned in our clothes from sparks and we were afraid that burning trees or branches might fall on us, but, lucky for us, they didn't."[2]

Although the fire burned north of Alborn too, the greatest danger was from its movement in the direction of the increasing winds to the east and southeast. Thus Independence, the Miller Trunk Line, Twig, and Grand Lake lay in the path of this fire.

South of the Swan Lake road was a large farming community that was badly overrun by the fire. G. A. Ringquist and his family, who lived about three miles east of the tracks, escaped without injury, but their homestead was destroyed; their neighbors Ole Olson and his wife, whose farm was also destroyed, both died of burns suffered in the fire. Farther south, at the corner of the McArthur and St. Vincent roads, the Industrial Evangelical Lutheran Church and the school were burned, and the people seeking shelter in Jack Kerr's blacksmith shop barely escaped when fire blew up the gasoline tank. People in the Burnett area, to the south, took refuge in the Cloquet River. The Milepost 62 fire had earlier jumped the St. Louis River north of Brookston and burned in an easterly direction. These two fires may have joined together at any point from Burnett or the Cloquet River to Grand Lake. They blew up into a large major fire, burning at an intense heat and moving at great speed before a driving wind. Fires

were also burning north of Grand Lake, to the southwest along the
Duluth and Northeastern tracks, and to the east along the tracks of
the Duluth, Winnipeg and Pacific Railway Company. These fires too
probably joined with the Milepost 62 fire. All of the fires together
formed an irregular front ten miles wide, parts of which may have
surged forward as fast as fifteen to twenty miles an hour under winds
gusting from eighty to ninety miles an hour at the site of the fire itself.[3]

Not only had the Milepost 62 fire been driven straight east of Brookston across the St. Louis River by about 4:00 P.M., but it had also
spread across the river between Milepost 62 and Brookston and carried on east, crossing the Cloquet River, which enters the St. Louis
just below Brookston. Ida W. and Frank A. Thorwall had a cottage
not too far from the Cloquet River, where they had come to harvest
potatoes from their garden that Saturday. They had seen smoke in the
morning, but Ida's first realization that there was any danger came
sometime after lunch, when she heard the window glass shattering
from the heat and wind on the west side of the cottage. When she
looked out she saw the fire in the tree tops about "two blocks" away
and she heard a great roar. Ida fled first to the cement root house for
shelter, but as the fire came across the grass in the open fields surrounding the cottage, she ran to join her family at her sister's house,
which was spared. When the Thorwalls returned to their burned cottage the next day, they found among the ruins the clock on the stone
mantle, stopped at 3:30.[4]

Edward F. Gill, a superintendent at the Duluth Universal Milling
Company, had come up from the city on Friday with his nine-year-
old daughter to have a week's hunting at the logging camps owned by
his brother H. P. ("Harry") Gill a few miles west of Grand Lake (or
about four miles east of where the fire crossed the St. Louis River). By
noon on Saturday he began to notice the smoke and heat. The sun,
when it could be seen, looked "like a moon at midnight." Edward and
Agnes L. Gill, Harry's wife, decided to bury some household goods for
protection. Then, carrying the guns and a lunch, they left for Harry
and Agnes's new and still uncompleted house northeast of the camp,
across the Albert road. Once they reached the road they found the fire
perhaps one hundred feet high, burning through the timber on either

Burned telephone pole bearing campaign poster for St. Louis County Sheriff Frank L. Magie, October 1918 (McKenzie)

side of them with a powerful wind and great roaring noise. Cinders and sparks stung their faces. A school and one house along the road had already burned when they got there. Edward described how he understood the fire to burn: "You see, the worst fire — I don't imagine we could have gotten through that fire if we had started while the fire first went through, because the first fire is always the worst. It gets the largest brush and dry grass. But when we went through, why, the trees were all afire, but the fire was not so bad but what we could get through on the road and not get burned."

When they got to the new house about 4:15, Agnes cried that the building had just caught fire. Getting pails of water from the well, they put out the fire and then worked to put out the sparks that were driven by the powerful west wind through the open windows and doors of the uncompleted house. That saved the house, but not the new barn nor a pile of lumber. They all stayed at the new house for the rest of the night; at about 1:00 A.M. Harry, who had been cut off at Grand Lake, made it through to them with a team of horses. Surprisingly, neither the new house nor the logging camps were burned.[5]

When the fire reached the Grand Lake area, it was moving fast (fifteen to twenty miles per hour, with faster surges of flame), under the driving force of a powerful wind (from sixty to ninety miles per hour) and was spread along a broad front. The people who witnessed the fire in this sector were remarkably in agreement about the fire conditions, the direction of the wind, and the time of the fire's arrival. It was quite simple, noting the times, to plot the movement of the fire on a map.[6]

Sometime after 4:00 P.M., the fire, burning on quite a broad front, reached the Grand Lake station on the Duluth, Missabe and Northern Railway, and shortly after that it reached Saginaw junction, where the Missabe and the Duluth and Northeastern Railroad tracks crossed. Daniel Willeck, who had a farm just south of Saginaw, had gone to a store at Little Grand Lake on Saturday morning, but had hurried home along the Seville road about 2:00 P.M. when he saw clouds of smoke blowing in from the west. By the time he got home, Willeck had concluded that he and his family would have to abandon their farm. The Willecks hitched up the horses, gathered their belongings and left for Cloquet. The wind was blowing down trees around them, and they first confronted sparks where the Seville road crossed the Duluth and Northeastern tracks. When they got to Hans Blom's house at about 4:00 P.M., they saw the main fire west of his place. Blom told Willeck to put his team in the barn, but almost immediately the barn and the wagon loaded with clothes caught fire. Willeck then tried to help Blom put out the sparks that were landing all about, but they had no success: "You put one out, another one catch right by you." Sparks and fine sand hit them in the face, and then the big fire caught them. "Well, it coming so fast I didn't know when it get there," Willeck remembered. "It was roaring. . . . I thought all was the end of the world; the roaring scares you more than the fire." All of them ran to the milk house, which was made of concrete, and sought protection there.[7]

While the Willecks had been deciding to head south to Cloquet, eight-year-old Viena Hill's family hoped to escape the fire by traveling northeast to Saginaw. The Hills lived about two miles southwest of the Blom farm along the Duluth and Northeastern tracks, above Dutch Slough creek. Viena had been picking vegetables in a neighbor's garden when she first saw the fire coming up from the St. Louis River, no more than a mile and a half away. The family "sprinkled the house" and put some of their clothes and possessions in the creek, by which time the fire "was coming pretty fast." They started up the railroad track toward Saginaw, but they only got as far as the Blom farm. Within minutes of their arrival the "terrible fire," with heavy smoke and burning leaves blown by the powerful wind, was on them. The Hills found shelter with the Willecks and the Bloms in the milk house, where they stayed until 2:00 or 3:00 A.M. Willeck recalled later, "And in the morning when I got out and went off to my place to look at it what was left there, there was nothing but black stumps and ground. That is about all the fire left. And the country was burned all over." The same dismal sight greeted many other people throughout the region.[8]

Some were luckier. Eleven-year-old Katharine Luomala lived on a farm farther south of Saginaw with her father and mother, John E. and Eliina F., and her brothers and sisters. Eighteen years later, in a contest sponsored by the Women's Friday Club of Cloquet, Katharine won first prize for the best essay on the fire. She wrote that John and the hired man had gone off to fight the fire in the afternoon, and by early evening had not returned. There had been smoke in the air and an increasing wind throughout the afternoon, but nothing alarming. Things seemed more ominous, however, when her nineteen-year-old sister, Mamie S. Luomala, came back from Cloquet with the news that Brookston had burned and that a relief train had taken the survivors out — and especially when neighbors to the north came running into the Luomala house telling how the fire had burned their farm. Eliina offered them coffee.[9]

Other neighbors rushed in to say that "fires were coming down the hill." Eliina Luomala seemed in a daze, but Mamie got the horses hitched to the potato wagon, and the family, with one or two possessions, started climbing aboard. When Eliina declared that she would

stay at the farm until her husband came home, Mamie pushed her
into the wagon and they started south for Cloquet.

> Even when we had left the yard, there had not been much fire
> about us, but now it suddenly swept about us until the whole
> world was on fire. Every tree on both sides of the road, every
> fence post, every stump, and every blade of grass was ablaze.
> Red flashes of flame skimmed up the trees and jumped across the
> branches which fell crashing to earth. The fence posts were rows
> of burning torches. The thick underbrush of the roadside was
> burning fiercely, and brands of fire fell into the road. The ter-
> rified horses dodged around them and galloped on. I expected
> any minute to be swept heavenward in a blazing wagon drawn
> by two snorting horses.

Mamie, her long brown hair streaming in the wind, drove the team
with a reckless determination. Within a year and a half, Mamie had
died of tuberculosis; Katharine always remembered her as she looked
that night: "a goddess of some mythical, thundering chariot in
Hades."

When the Luomalas got to the top of the hill at Sunnyside above
Cloquet, they heard the mill whistles begin to blow throughout the
city. They realized that the town was on fire, and they turned north
once again. Although they had to drive through more flames and
swirls of sparks, they found a green area where many people had
taken refuge, including several who had been burned or had lost family members. Later, a man told the Luomalas that he had gone by
their farm at 3:00 A.M.; it had burned and John Luomala and the
hired man were dead. While the family silently absorbed this stun-
ning news, John rode up on a horse; his eyes were red and puffy, but
he was very much alive. Their house was safely standing but was filled
with hungry refugees who needed their help.

At about 4:00 P.M., Clarence H. Barnes, the school superintendent at
Eveleth, was attempting to drive back home from a day trip to Duluth
with his wife and another family. When they got to the Twig railroad
depot, they could see fire crossing the road just beyond the store. They
turned back a short distance to eat a lunch and wait for the fire to pass.
When they started out again, however, they found the fire had worsened, so they decided to return to Duluth for the night. The Miller

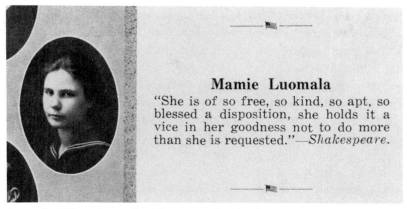

Mamie Luomala

"She is of so free, so kind, so apt, so blessed a disposition, she holds it a vice in her goodness not to do more than she is requested."—*Shakespeare.*

From the White Pine, *the Cloquet High School yearbook, 1918*

Trunk Line angled more or less southeast below Twig, bending around the west end of Pike Lake. Through this stretch, which was a major green area, they encountered only heavy smoke and strong winds, but when they reached the Jackson School, north of Hermantown, at about 5:15, they found themselves in a fire coming from the west and burning on both sides of the road. "The fire was crackling in some tree tops as we passed by, getting close to the road," Barnes recalled. "I think the big fire was coming from the west. There was a little fire on both sides of the road, just below the school there, and there appeared to be a sort of swirl or a little like a wind storm, you know."

They raced as fast as they could until they were out of the fire, which was almost to the crest of the Duluth hill. They reached the city at about 5:45 P.M. and stayed in a hotel for the night. "That is what we consider a real forest fire," Barnes declared later.[10]

While the Barneses and their friends were returning from Twig, almost straight south in Solway the Hanson family saw the first flames come out of the west. "In the afternoon there was all kinds of smoke, and then we heard roaring just like thunder. We thought it was thunder when it was roaring like that, but when we looked out we saw the flames in the tree-tops," Anna Hanson remembered. A little after 5:00 P.M. she and her husband, John H., and their five children got into their Ford automobile. With the fourteen-year-old son driving, they attempted to flee to Duluth by way of the Seville road and the Miller

Trunk Line. At about 5:30, just past the Jackson School, the Ford was engulfed in flames and they ran into the ditch. They abandoned the burning automobile and attempted to make their way back about three blocks to the school. "There was fire there all round us. It was raining on us — fire raining on us. When we went to the Jackson School it was storming and knocked the children down in the road." They stayed outside while the buildings around were burning, but after the fire subsided they went into the Jackson School and stayed there until about 2:00 A.M., when the Minnesota Home Guard came and took them to Duluth. They were lucky. No one was hurt in the crash; only one child was burned, because she did not have a coat on; the Jackson School gave them shelter and did not burn.[11]

Victor Leslie, a widower who lived on a farm south of the Miller Trunk Line and west of the Jackson School, saw the fire about 5:00 P.M. He had planned to go into Duluth on Saturday to sell a load of wood, but because of the fire danger he did not want to leave his children alone. Leslie stayed on the farm hauling stones to clear land and doing other chores. By late afternoon he went to telephone around to find out if the fire had blown up. He also went south about a half mile on the Ugstad road, where he met Mrs. Charlie Anderson and two children. She was crying because the fire was approaching her house, and he went to see what he could save. When the fire came right up to the house, he had to leave. As he put it, the "fire came just as fast as we could run," and the "sparks and the flames was all over us." He had to hurry home to save his children. Leslie had been a sailor about forty years earlier but he had never seen such a fierce wind. The flames were right over his buildings, coming out of the northwest, when he left. Leslie made his way north with his family, his horses, and his cows to the green area along the Miller Trunk Line below Pike Lake. By 5:30 or 5:40 they were safe, but all of his buildings and those of his neighbors were destroyed. At night, after the main fire had passed, Leslie went into Duluth.[12]

Pike Lake was a popular resort area for Duluthians, and there were many fine cottages and summer homes along its shores. In view of the good weather on Saturday morning, many people had gone out from Duluth to spend the day or the weekend. In the late afternoon, as conditions deteriorated, some people simply packed up and drove

Automobile wrecks on the Pike Lake road, probably with photographer's
automobile at far left, October 21, 1918 (McKenzie)

back to Duluth. Others waited too long; they either tried to reach
Duluth and were caught in a pileup of automobiles on the Pike Lake
road, or decided to stay and attempt to avoid the flames by taking to
their boats out on Pike Lake. In the waves churned up by the sixty-to-
ninety-mile-an-hour winds, many boats capsized, throwing the passengers into the water. Several families drowned in these circumstances. Charles A. Marshall, the president of the Lyceum Theatre
Company in Duluth, first attempted to drive back to town, but
returned to his cottage, hoping to find safety on the lake. Marshall,
his wife, and their small son were drowned when their boat overturned. Others on land sought safety in ditches or gravel pits. Generally, the loss of life in the Pike Lake area was particularly heavy.[13]

    Farther to the southeast, the settlement of Hermantown was
badly damaged. Almost every farm in the township was at least partially burned. This was prosperous dairy farming country, with herds
as large as fifty head. Much of the livestock was killed, and those that
survived could not be fed, because most haystacks burned. Of four
buildings at the Hermantown corner — the Hermantown School, the
Woodman Hall, the town hall, and the Hermantown church — only
the church burned. The Maple Grove community, just east of Proc-

tor, was destroyed. Only six of the forty-seven buildings in Maple Grove survived the fire. The railroad town of Proctor suffered no damage, and was able to take about 1,200 refugees from the area in the aftermath of the fire.[14]

As the fires began to reach the Duluth area, refugees poured into the city and the news spread of dangerous fires to the north and west. Captain Henry L. Tourtelotte, the commanding officer of the Duluth District of the Fourth Regiment of the Minnesota Infantry National Guard, was on duty at the Duluth Armory about 3:00 P.M. on Saturday when he received a telephone call that automobiles were needed on the Rice Lake road, north of town, to take people out of danger. Captain Tourtelotte and another officer left in an official automobile. When they reached the fire they found Clarence R. Magney, the mayor of Duluth; Robert D. McKercher, the chief of police; members of the Duluth fire department; and eight or ten private citizens with automobiles. Refugees were picked up and brought back into the city. The National Guard and the Home Guard were mobilized later in the afternoon, and when a request came for assistance in fighting fire near Hermantown at about 7:00 P.M., the Fourth Regiment was driven there by the Minnesota Motor Corps (an adjunct of the Minnesota Home Guard) and civilian volunteers. They were instrumental in saving both lives and property in the Hermantown area. Between about 6:00 and 7:00 P.M. the Third and Seventh Battalions of the Home Guard were dispatched to assist the fire department in defending the suburbs of Woodland. Other units were sent to different areas with members of the Third being sent to evacuate patients at the Nopeming Sanatorium (the county-run tuberculosis hospital) and to fight fire there. Herbert Richardson estimated that thousands of volunteers worked to fight fire with the troops and the fire department and to rescue people, particularly those without transportation.[15]

In at least one instance the big fire came upon the Duluth fire department while it was working on a small fire. Captain Wallace A. West had a brigade of firemen working on a bog fire on a lettuce farm just off the Hunter road at about 3:30 P.M. They did not have enough hose to put the fire out, but it was in no danger of spreading or becoming a menace to the neighborhood. At about 7:00 P.M., however, the big fire swept down on them from the west: "Fire rolling hundreds of feet high, roaring, and wind coming like a hurricane." West, who had worked for the fire department for twenty years and put out fires in grain elevators and lumberyards, said it was "the biggest I ever saw. . . . We ran for our lives and took our equipment and saved it." Even a trained force of fire fighters could not cope with this fire at its height, but some people were lucky and kept it at bay with a garden hose. Edward L. Kimball, a lawyer who lived on East Anoka Street in Woodland, was talking on the telephone about 7:00 P.M. when his wife noticed sparks flying past the house. Kimball, who had been aware of smoke and high winds throughout the afternoon, rushed outside, hooked up the garden hose, and began putting out the sparks and wetting down the sides of the house. Fortunately, the house was partially sheltered on the west side by a hill, and Kimball found that he could keep water playing over the whole of the west side of his house, as well as the roof and sides. He did this for about two hours, during which time he noticed that the wind, while generally out of the west, veered somewhat around to the north.[16]

About a half a mile northeast, Harry E. McCool and his neighbors on West Faribault Street were burned out. McCool, a draftsman for the Duluth and Iron Range Railroad Company, spent the afternoon working in his garden about a quarter of a mile from home, harvesting rutabagas, potatoes, and cabbages. By 5:30 the wind, smoke, and cinders in the air had made things so disagreeable that he went home. He and his family had supper. After the children had been put to bed, Harry and his wife, Zillah, saw fire to the north along the Calvary road. People were going down the street, fleeing from the fire and carrying their belongings with them. The McCools invited ten to fifteen people into the house to rest. "They were old people, tired out, carrying bundles," Harry remembered. Conditions got worse, however, as the smoke thickened, the wind shifted out of the northwest and north, and sparks and embers began landing around the house. Harry thought he could put out the fire with wet sacks; but about 7:00 P.M., with the sky glowing red to the north, the McCools got their children out of bed and dressed, and they started to walk to the Woodland streetcar line. Zillah carried the youngest child, while Harry carried the second and led the eldest son. The smoke was so dense that they could not see well, but by the time they got to the stop they had seen

*View of Duluth with the Union Depot at center left and the Spalding Ho-
tel behind it, about 1912 (probably by McKenzie)*

two houses burning south of theirs. Zillah and the children were given
a ride in an automobile going into the center of the city and Harry got
a lift in a truck about fifteen minutes later. The McCool home and
much of the neighborhood were destroyed.[17]

Not everyone found the crisis to be traumatic. Mildred Washburn, a young woman who lived with her parents, Jed L. and Alma
P., in Hunter's Park, drove the family automobile up to the Howard
Gnesen road to try to help. She thought to herself, "This is the next
best to being in France," and she congratulated herself on the wisdom
of learning to drive. "I wish you could have heard that wind," she
wrote to a friend. "It seemed just like the work of the devil that there
should be a wind like that — 60 miles an hour — the very night we got
the fire." She went back home and, fearing that their neighborhood
would burn also, loaded the automobile with family and friends, babies and servants — thirteen in all and several on the running

Rails dangled from the ruins of a Soo Line railroad trestle between Duluth and Superior, October 1918.

boards — and drove to the Spalding Hotel, where they spent the night wondering if the whole city would burn. When they went home the next morning, however, they found everything as they had hurriedly left it, or almost. "All the dishes were unwashed, the lights on and some prunes still cooking burned to pieces."[18]

The Washburns and their friends were not the only ones who worried that Duluth itself would burn. The roads out of town were blocked, the waters of Lake Superior were too cold to allow people to find refuge there, and the high winds whipped up such waves that few boats could ride out such a storm. The constant wail of fire engines and ambulances through the night heightened the general anxiety.[19]

As the evening wore on, the fires around Duluth began to burn themselves out. The winds reached their greatest intensity (fifty to sixty miles per hour) in Duluth between 4:15 and 9:00 P.M., and they decreased to around forty miles per hour until 2:00 A.M., after which they subsided sharply. In East Duluth the flames burned through Lakewood, Lakeside, and Lester Park right down to the shores of Lake Superior. One of the easternmost properties to be destroyed was the farm of Theodore Hollister, a lawyer who later represented the fire sufferers in court. At the height of the blaze, when the streetcars were unable to handle the volume of refugees, the Northern Pacific sent a relief train out to Lakeside on the Duluth and Iron Range tracks to bring people back to the city. In the western part of Duluth, the fires around Nopeming were brought under control by about 3:00 A.M., reducing the danger in that sector. Along the crest of the Duluth hill, over much of the length of the entire city, the Duluth fire department, various troops, and thousands of volunteers worked at backfiring and putting out spot fires throughout the night. They were largely able to keep the flames from reaching down into the city, although many farms, dairies, houses, and even such landmarks as the Northland Country Club were destroyed. Perhaps one of the freaks of the fire was the burning of various structures well into the city or near St. Louis Bay, a great distance from the fires up on the hill. Presumably through a great leap of heat and flames, fires broke out in the Northern Pacific's yards both in West Duluth and on Rice's Point, destroying a number of railroad cars and burning the roof of a roundhouse at the latter. The Alger-Smith Lumber Company on Rice's Point also caught fire, and sparks and firebrands from the lumberyards set fire to the Interstate Bridge connecting Duluth and Superior. The Great Northern Railway bridge was also burned for about two thousand feet, causing $85,000 worth of damage and putting it out of operation for about thirty days.[20]

Most important, however, the city itself was saved. The burning of Duluth would have been a catastrophe of unimaginable proportions.

CHAPTER FIVE

The Tragedy at Automba, Kettle River, and Moose Lake

It seemed like a week while I was in that fire.
Arthur C. Russell

We were going right through a big red wall of fire.
Irving B. Phelps

Dead Man's Curve. This ominous name describes a part of the road that is present-day Minnesota State Highway 73, about two miles south of Kettle River and a little more than four miles west of Moose Lake. It looks harmless enough today. Indeed, the curve is itself now obscured by the straightening of the road. No doubt this "improvement" was done more to protect today's young people on Saturday nights than to erase the memory of the events of the tragic Saturday in 1918 that gave the bend its name. At Dead Man's Curve, and in the region around it, the most disastrous episodes of the great fire took place. The stories of the fires in Cloquet and Duluth are of danger and escape, but the stories of Lawler, Automba, Kettle River, and Moose Lake are of tragedy and death.

There were five major fire areas in this region. The largest fire included Moose Lake and Kettle River, and it burned in Carlton, Aitkin, and Pine counties. Its northern border was roughly the Northern Pacific tracks between McGregor and Tamarack, and it burned southeast to just beyond Moose Lake and Sturgeon Lake. The railroad tracks of the Soo Line, crossing the region diagonally from Moose Lake to McGregor, were at the heart of the fire area. The next largest

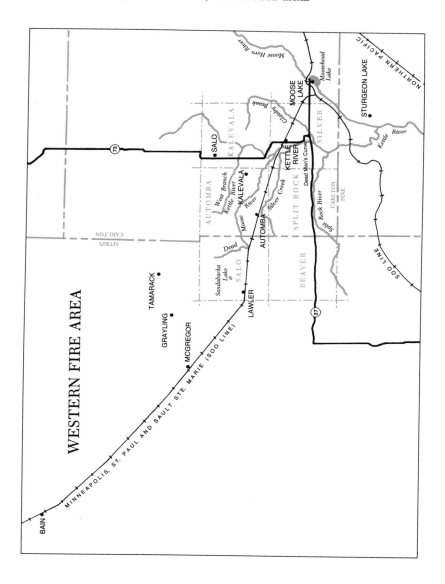

fire was farther northwest up the Soo Line tracks, in Aitkin County, with the community of Bain roughly in the center. The third largest fire was south in Pine County, stretching from Willow River, along the Northern Pacific tracks, to Bruno, along the Great Northern tracks, to the outskirts of Cloverton. Somewhat smaller fires burned just to the west below Sturgeon Lake, and farther west still in the White Pine–Arthyde region. Numerous smaller fires burned close by, but independent of these fires. Because the region was crisscrossed by three railroads and because numerous railroad fires were positively identified, the popular view has always been that responsibility rested with the train companies.

The topography of the Moose Lake–Kettle River area was different from that of the Cloquet-Duluth area in several important respects. One was the presence of peat bogs. Peat is a common fuel in some parts of the world, and it burns well when dug out of the bog and dried. When the bogs were drained, as had been done in this region to create new farmland, or when the summer was particularly dry, as in 1918, peat-bog fires presented a distinctive problem. Once a brush fire or a railroad fire got into a peat bog, there was almost no way it could be put out. It simply smoldered indefinitely, even into the winter, often without any particular harm to surrounding property. But in conditions of falling humidity and rising wind, the relatively quiescent peat-bog fires could flare up, burn much more rapidly, contribute to the heat and wind, and in a short time ignite farmland or forests on the border of the bog.

A second characteristic of the area traversed by the Soo Line was the virgin pine forests, which were substantial enough to sustain numerous small sawmills. Lawler, Automba, Kettle River, and Moose Lake each had at least one sawmill, and several smaller operations were at river sites or crossroads. Each mill was accompanied by the usual sawdust piles and lumberyards.

Finally, there were no large bodies of water — no large rivers, such as the St. Louis or the Mississippi — which might have acted as firebreaks. It is probable, however, that the chain of small lakes from Moose Lake to Sturgeon Lake contributed to stopping the fire at its southeastern extremity on the night of October 12.

After following a laborious grade up the hill from Duluth, the Northern Pacific railroad main line headed almost straight west from Carlton as far as Wright before it began to angle gently to the southwest, through Tamarack and McGregor and on to Brainerd and the west. The Soo Line was built out of Superior in a long curve that swept through southern Carlton County and northwest into Aitkin County, passing through the towns of Moose Lake, Kettle River, Automba, Lawler, and McGregor on the way. Along these Northern Pacific and Soo Line tracks the worst fires in the western region had their origins.[1]

Throughout the summer and early autumn the Northern Pacific maintained a fire patrol along its tracks. The railroad sent George Brand from McGregor along the tracks in a speeder to Tamarack and back again two times a day, following the major trains on the line. His job was to inform the section crews of any Northern Pacific railroad fires. During the summer and autumn of 1918, although he had seen smoke to the north all season, Brand had reported only one fire, which was burning on the north side of the tracks between Grayling and Tamarack on the morning of October 4. Brand was taken off the fire patrol at that point and assigned to work on the section crew. Not until October 9, when his crew got a note from a locomotive engineer that this fire had crossed the tracks and was threatening the stockyards west of Tamarack, did he deal with the fire again. The section crew prevented the fire from burning into Tamarack, but they were unable to put it out because of the tall, dry grass.[2]

On October 12 the humidity dropped, the wind increased, and this railroad fire as well as bog fires north of the line flared up. By 1:00 P.M., E. R. Jacobson, the township road overseer, got a message to come into Tamarack to fight fire in the area north and south of the town. The smoke was very thick and a sizable fire had blown up. J. P. Brenner, the cashier at the First State Bank in Tamarack, went back to his farm north of town for lunch. His two daughters remained working at the bank, but because of the ominous situation he telephoned to tell them to put all the papers in the vault, lock up, and come home as soon as possible. The fire burned both north and south of his buildings, but it was moving in a southeasterly direction before a strong northwest wind. Brenner fought fire with his neighbors from after lunch until 3:00 A.M. the next morning.[3]

In Tamarack itself, Mrs. Marcus Nelson shut down the family sawmill early in the day and sent the workmen to make firebreaks with plows on the outskirts of town. She also telegraphed for help from Governor Joseph A. A. Burnquist, who sent Home Guard troops from Aitkin to assist. Her son, Orvis Nelson, remembered years later that the troops arrived on the afternoon train and "their presence that night undoubtedly saved the town."[4]

The Northern Pacific ran two relief trains into the area as far as Tamarack, picking up refugees. By 6:00 P.M. one train lost two cars to the fire, but the crew got them onto a siding, where they burned harmlessly. The remainder of this train then made it back to Carlton. The second train moved back and forth between Cromwell and Tamarack throughout the night and the next day.[5]

Dennis Carr, a farmer who lived south of Tamarack, had successfully fought fire on a neighbor's farm on Friday, but he went into town on Saturday morning. When he returned home for lunch he saw fires burning in the direction of his place along the roads leading south. He and his neighbors waited for the fire to approach. As the wind increased, the fire spread across the roads and into one farm after another — the Douglas place, the Friestad place, Black's land, King's land. In the early evening, the fire reached Carr's farm from out of the woods. At this time the wind was blowing very hard, fire was in the air, and sparks started to land on the ground. Carr sent his daughter and her children to a neighbor's, and he then attempted to save his buildings. When the buildings caught fire, however, he retreated to a clearing south of his house. The fire was burning fiercely and moving toward the southeast.[6]

Farther south, in the area between the Northern Pacific and Soo Line tracks, particularly in Salo Township, serious fires developed on October 12. Under the conditions of falling humidity and rising wind, bog fires flared up and burned into the adjacent fields and woods, and many also joined with the numerous fires burning along the Soo Line tracks. A major contributor was a railroad fire that started at Milepost 263, beyond Lawler. Here farmers and their families had no time to get away as the fires blew up in the late afternoon and bore down on them from the northwest. The wind, rising to between sixty and one hundred miles per hour, not only drove the fire before it but also

Dead farm animal near fence, Moose Lake, October 1918 (Irish)

knocked over trees, picked up stones and boards, and hurled haystacks through the air.

One of the many farmers who had been fighting fire since early morning was Uno Lake. At about 5:00 P.M. the fire got out of control, and he and the others fled to try to save their homes. With the wind at his back, Uno bicycled home as fast as he could and got his wife, Mary, and their two children. They abandoned the farm and made their way to a freshly plowed field two miles away. There, under cover of wet blankets and rugs, they attempted to save themselves from the heat and firebrands. Their blankets and clothing caught fire, and Uno actually had to take off all his clothes, but the Lakes survived.[7]

Edward Rosbacka, overseer of the Salo Township roads, had been out working on the fire all day, too, but retreated for home when the fire blew up. He got home about 5:30 P.M., minutes before the fire reached the farm. The family tried to save the buildings with potato sacks and buckets of water, but, as Aili Rosbacka Field, Edward's daughter, remembered, "There was fire everywhere — the sky, air, ground — everything appeared to be on fire." The roofs of the buildings started burning, her mother collapsed, and all the property was lost. They made their way to a plowed field, where they suffered burns but survived. The Henry Maijala house, the Alex Illberg house, and several others escaped the flames, and many of those who had spent the night in fields or stream beds found shelter there as they ventured out through the blackened landscape to see if anyone else had survived. Miriam Sanda Shilston remembered that when the fire came her mother took five-year-old Miriam and her four sisters and brothers from their house and out onto Sandabacka Lake. Seventeen children spent the night in boats on the lake, where buckets of cold lake water were thrown on them when their clothes were in danger of burning. Ironically, the Sandas had been invited to seek shelter with friends in their root cellar; the only deaths in Salo Township were those of Carl and "Mamma" Koivunen and two others, who suffocated in that cellar.[8]

These fires cut telephone and telegraph connections along the Soo Line tracks in eastern Aitkin County, but shortly before 5:00 P.M. a train crew at Riverton got telephone orders from the Soo Line office in Minneapolis to take their train into Lawler. Picking up empty boxcars, flat cars, and a water tank, this relief train started southeast, stopping to put out small fires along the way, saving two bridges that were on fire. When they got to Lawler about 6:00 P.M. they found many people from the town and the countryside and the families of several of the train crew waiting at the depot. C. A. Hanna, a brakeman on the train, remembered years later that just after the train was loaded, as it pulled away, the station "burst into flames and exploded." The crew took the passengers up the track, left the women and children at East Lake, and then returned to Lawler to see if there was anything that could be done. The whole town had burned, except for the brick school, the hotel, the telephone exchange, and the Spicola brothers' store. The train returned to pick up the women and children and proceeded to Aitkin.[9]

The area's earliest fire for which there were eyewitness accounts was a railroad fire started along the Soo Line tracks less than a mile west of Moose Lake. Because of the grade and the curve in the tracks, west-bound trains labored to get up speed along this stretch, and in the process they belched out a lot of smoke, steam, and sparks. Gilbert Buxter, who had forty acres south of the right-of-way, saw a passenger train heading west out of Moose Lake one afternoon during the first week of August. Within ten minutes of the passing of this train, Buxter saw smoke rising from the bog near the tracks. Not until four or five days later did a section crew attempt to put out the fire. Following requests from Perry W. Swedberg, the state district forest ranger, section crews continued to work on the fire periodically throughout August and September, but without success. On September 27 the fire flared up and threatened the property of Jacob Anderson on the north side of the tracks. His wife telephoned the Soo depot in Moose Lake, and a section crew came out to help them and their neighbors keep the fire from burning the Anderson buildings. They saved the buildings, but were unable to put out the bog fire.[10]

About two miles west of Kettle River, farther up the Soo Line tracks, Fred Maunula, a section hand on the railroad, saw trains ignite two fires along the roadbed, one on September 30 and the other on October 3. The latter burned north into the Joseph Winquist farm and could not be extinguished. The Reverend Matt Reed, who had a farm just east of the Finnish community of Automba, saw a Soo Line locomotive start a fire near his property on October 1. During the first week of October, Gust Sahlstrom observed a fire along the Soo Line tracks near the Dead Moose River bridge, about one and a half miles west of the Aitkin County border. This fire, he noted, burned about three miles north and was never extinguished. In fact, Ranger Swedberg later reported that he knew of thirteen dangerous fires burning along the Soo Line tracks, west of Moose Lake for twenty-eight miles. On October 9, Deputy Ranger Frank Ronkainen was ordered by Swedberg to gather a crew to fight these fires, and perhaps more than a hundred men were on the fire lines.[11]

On Saturday, October 12, Gust Sahlstrom, who had a farm about three miles northwest of Automba, went down to Charles Jokimaki's sawmill on the Dead Moose River to check on some lumber that he was having cut. A big fire had burned near the mill that week, and Sahlstrom said that on Friday night "the heavens were aglow, red" in the direction of the mill. When Sahlstrom arrived about 3:30 on

Saturday afternoon, the fire was coming into the lumberyard, burning the sawdust, and it was clear from the strength of the wind and
the intensity of the flames that the mill and his lumber were going to
burn. Staying no longer, he returned north to his farm, reaching it by
about 4:00 P.M. There he found that the wind was much stronger
than when he had left and fire from the south and west was bearing
down on his farm. Sahlstrom managed to save his house and the
northern portions of his property, but his possessions, which he moved
out into a field, were destroyed. For the town of Automba, "there was
no avenue of possible escape except the railroad," concluded Ranger
Swedberg. Although a relief train had been requested from the Soo
Line as early as 3:00 P.M., none arrived.[12]

The fire along the Soo Line tracks and the Dead Moose River
"slowly inched its way toward Automba" to the southeast. The efforts
of the many men fighting the blaze were futile, especially as the wind
rose during the afternoon. Steve Tomczak tried to convince William
G. Young, a lumberman whom he was helping on Saturday, to flee
south with him to the Polish settlement at Split Rock. Tomczak last
saw Young standing on the depot platform with his bicycle. William
Maki, who with his partner Charles Jokimaki owned two sawmills
and a store in town, remembered that until the flames actually entered Automba, people were confident that the fires could be controlled: "Some people started to leave right away but most did not become alarmed and didn't start to flee until the lumber yards caught
on fire. The intense heat and flying burning boards from the lumber
yards turned the little town of Automba into an island of flames in a
matter of minutes. When the fire hit the lumber yards, it seemed as
if they exploded."

Maki, his wife Olga, and Charles Jokimaki drove south toward
Split Rock along the dirt tote road as fast as they could. "As we raced
down the road with my Dodge car, we saw this French family following us out of town in a wagon with a team of horses," Maki recalled.
"The fire caught up to them in a matter of minutes and we never saw
them alive again." The last image he had of his store was one swept
by flames, and he was sure they were the last people "to get out of Automba alive." At that they did not get very far before they found the
road blocked. When their automobile caught fire they fled to an open
clearing, where they stayed until the fire passed. Automba, which

had a population of about 350, was completely destroyed; twenty-three residents were killed attempting to escape.[13]

North of Automba, and perhaps four miles east of Sahlstrom's farm, other members of the Maki and Jokimaki families found themselves caught in the fire sometime after 4:00 P.M. Aina Jokimaki Johnson remembered that the cows had been milked and the daily chores completed when the fire reached the Jacobson brothers' sawmill, with about a million board feet of lumber in the yards, near the Jokimaki home. "Suddenly," she recalled, "the flames hit the lumber yard and one board took off in the air like a flaming arrow and landed on a hay stack about ½ mile away and the hay exploded in flames." Each member of the family was given something to carry, and they all set off for a swamp east of the farm. But in what seemed like an instant, "the terrifying inferno was over and above and all around us." In the confusion the family got separated. Aina burned her legs walking between red-hot logs. "Imagine yourself, a terrified young girl in shock, under these conditions," she said years later. "I was wearing stockings and high top shoes, but although none of my clothes burned, my feet actually baked inside my shoes and stockings, something I did not realize until later. I still have scars to remind me of that night. I will have them to my dying day."

Aina made her way to a stream, where she found her painfully burned father, William Jokimaki. The next day she and William were taken to St. Mary's Hospital in Duluth. Dead were her mother, Suoma; six brothers and sisters; one cousin; and many neighbors who farmed and worked in the sawmills.[14]

Fourteen-year-old Fred Maki was telephoned by his brother, William, from Automba and asked to take the children of William and his business partner, Charles Jokimaki, out of the path of the fire north of Automba. Fred made two trips to the fire front in his family's Model T Ford, rescuing first the Maki and Jokimaki children and then fourteen people from the Lambert Hendrickson farm. Two trips were all he could manage, because "by that time, the fire was rapidly moving like terrific clouds of lightening [sic], in a leap frog fashion through the air." Their escape was doubtful in the slow-moving and vastly overloaded automobile, but they got as far east as Highway 73. When its canvas top caught fire, they abandoned the automobile.

*Aina Jokimaki Johnson with bandaged hands and legs, October 1918
(photograph by William Bull)*

Fred Maki and a young girl from Crosby spent the night in a culvert
under the road. When he emerged after the fire had passed, Fred
found the automobile was still operable; he drove home to find that
his own family had survived (his mother in a field with a deer), but
two children from other families had been lost.[15]

Farther south along Highway 73 the fire swept across the road,
burning almost all the farms and homes in the area. The Kalevala
Finnish Evangelical National Lutheran Church, some four miles
north of Kettle River, was spared by the flames. Erick Westerback,
the church's pastor, fled with others to the West Branch River; survivors long remembered his praying for the Lord to destroy all of them
because they were all sinners. They survived, however, and made
their way back to the road, to find the church still standing. In the
morning many survivors walking along the road found shelter and
rest in the church. For some weeks after the fire, the Kalevala church
was used by the Red Cross and the National Guard; as the influenza
epidemic worsened, it was also used as a hospital.[16]

Driven by winds out of the west and northwest, the fire burned beyond Automba toward both Split Rock and Kettle River. Many of
those fleeing Automba to the south were pursued by the flames. Mr.
and Mrs. Whiting and their five children died on the road, in the company of several other families. William Maki's path was blocked and
his automobile burned. Mr. and Mrs. Leo Soboleski and their family,
who lived about two and a half miles south of Automba, found shelter
with several neighbors in the Soboleskis' well (the stronger men cling-
ing to ladders to make space at the bottom). Sparks flew in the opening but were extinguished, and all fifteen people survived. All the
members of the John Homicz family were killed nearby, some in a
root cellar and some in a well. Andrew and Frances Homicz and their
ten children survived the night in a plowed field, and Mrs. Benjamin
Butkiewicz and her children joined them. They all walked around in
a circle so as to keep awake. One small child was lost in the darkness
and smoke, but was blown into a creek bed, perhaps unconscious, and
was spared. In the morning the Homiczes found their farm burned,
but the Butkiewicz farm was saved; they all went there for rest and
food.[17]

Farther south, near present-day Minnesota State Highway 27, the
160-acre farm of Peter and William Suchoski burned twice. The two
brothers completed the major work on a new barn that afternoon and
then went straight to work fighting fire, trying to save their property.
One fire burned through the southern part of the property at about
7:30 P.M., and a second fire, even hotter and more violent, destroyed
the rest at about 8:00. Years later Clara Suchoski Caskey, Peter and
William's younger sister, remembered, "The flames were rolling
through the air like huge clouds of flame. Whenever they landed on
any building, the entire structure seemed to explode and in minutes
the entire building was in flames. The entire area was virgin balsam
and pine timber, combined with the fierce 70 mile-an-hour wind. It
seemed as if we were surrounded by a raging furnace." In the end Peter and William, fourteen-year-old Clara, and their widowed mother
fled with their automobile, cattle, and horses into the Split Rock
River. They used wet sacks to keep themselves from burning. Crouch-
ing down in the river, the brothers were sure this was the end of the
world, but their mother told them all to have faith. After the fire

passed, they all made their way a half mile to St. Joseph's Catholic church, which had not burned.[18]

The northeast corner of Split Rock Township, Section 1, was crossed by the Soo Line tracks. The fires along the tracks, whipped up by the great fire that swept through Automba, spread southeast through the northern part of the township toward Kettle River. The Reverend Matt Reed, who lived about two miles east of Automba on the south side of the tracks, had sent his wife, Edna, and their two sons north to stay with Edna's uncle, William Jokimaki, while Reed and John Luoma, his hired hand, attempted to save the farm. The fire came so quickly, however, that the two men did not even have time to get the horses harnessed, but simply fled east down the road. They got the horses and several other people into an open field and "a miracle happened," Reed said. "The flames parted and went to either side of us."[19]

By a little after 6:00 P.M. the fire burned southeast into the Joseph Kologe farm, about four miles from Automba. A curious set of coincidences put Lillian Peterson of Pine City down in the middle of the fire. Peterson, the new local schoolteacher, had been picked up at about noon at the train station at Moose Lake and driven to the Kologe farm, where she was to board. A boy went to fetch her trunk, which had been sent on to Kettle River by train. Meanwhile, she was introduced to the Kologe family, shown some family pictures, and made comfortable in her room. By late afternoon the smoke in the air got thicker, and around 5:00 it began to get dark. Peterson was called to look at the smoke, and she could just see some flames beyond the schoolhouse. The cloud of smoke was moving "as fast as an automobile. As that came nearer, kept coming nearer all the time, seemed to be coming quite fast, and all of a sudden the whole cloud of smoke turned red; and after that it was all fire to me." While the older members of the family attempted to fight the fire, Peterson took the several little children out into the adjacent plowed field. When she left the house it was just after 6:00 P.M. Very shortly they were joined in the field by all the adults, and they watched the house, the barns, and Peterson's trunk burn.[20]

One of the fires that was a serious threat to the area was the fire started along the Soo Line tracks on September 30. This fire burned into the

Joseph Winquist and Charles Nikkila farms on the north side of the tracks, about three-quarters of a mile from Kettle River. Frank Williams and Charles Silverberg had for several days been in charge of directing the men who were attempting to keep this fire from getting out of control. By Saturday, October 12, the fire had spread to both sides of the tracks, and several firebreaks had been made from the tracks north to the Dead Moose River and from the tracks south to Silver Creek. Word spread throughout the region that more help was needed, and men from all over came to fight the blaze and maintain a firebreak. Walfred Westholm, the cashier at the Farmers State Bank in Moose Lake, his brother Moritz, and several others drove out to Kettle River at about 1:00 P.M. to volunteer to help. They were sent up the tracks to where others were working on the firebreak. By about 3:30, they had seen no fire, although there was lots of smoke, so they went back to Kettle River for lunch. When they returned to the stream later, the fire blew up. Walfred Westholm recalled that they "immediately ran into the fire across the river, just dropping into the brush and grass. . . . The smoke was quite thick there at that time. And I just ran into the brush and tried to stamp it out; saw we could not do it; and turned around and went for town."[21]

Westholm mentioned at least twenty men who had been working on the fire at this point, but they were powerless to stop it or to control the spot fires ignited by firebrands. At about 5:00 P.M. Williams and Silverberg ordered their men out. George Maijala and his father left then and got as far as Highway 73, where they turned north, before the fire caught up with them. But between fifteen or twenty were trapped and perished when the fire blew up. Others, witnessing the blowup, simply fled to try to save their own families and farms. Gust Granrose remembered that "we could hear some terrific explosions to the northwest and realized that fire was approaching us from that direction at a terrific speed." As he put it, "We all took off for home, concerned with the safety of our families." Frank Ronkainen, later praised by the state Forest Fire Investigation Commission, stayed as long as he could, but finally had to abandon the fire, not to mention his sawmill and farm near Kettle River, and make his way to Moose Lake.[22]

Several men — Walfred Carlson, who had been working on road repairs farther south on Highway 73, Charles Eckman, and others —

set off during the afternoon to help fight the fire on the south side of the Soo Line tracks. By late afternoon, many were turned back by the smoke and flames on the road. Fire fighting there simply broke down. They all attempted to return to their homes as fast as possible to look after their own families.[23]

Walfred Westholm and his companions ran east through the woods for Kettle River, passing a farmer crying for help. Westholm attempted to telephone his home in Moose Lake from the farmhouse, but could not get through. He talked to the phone operator in Kettle River and tried to alert her to get everyone out of the town. The fire broke through the trees behind the farm while he was talking on the telephone. The farmhouse clock read 6:00 P.M. as Westholm fled out the door and across an open field to a road leading south to Kettle River. He and several others jumped on a farm wagon galloping past, which took them to the town.[24]

Panic gripped Kettle River. Black smoke billowed in from the northwest. The wind was very strong. Embers and rubbish were blown through the air. Arthur C. Russell, the manager of the Hart Brothers Lumber Company, sent his wife and two children to Moose Lake with businessman Albin Odberg's family at about 5:00 P.M. The Soo Line depot agent packed up his family and his belongings in his automobile, placed another family on the running boards, and headed south. Sixteen-year-old Ailie Leppa Nikkila worked as an operator for the Kettle River Telephone Exchange, which had set up a switchboard in her home. All afternoon she was "swamped" with calls from people seeking information or asking for help. By about 6:00 P.M. John H. Mattson, the cashier at the Farmers State Bank, called to inform her that he had a truck to take people to safety in Moose Lake. Ailie and her mother, Hanna Leppa; Ida Hiipakka, a schoolteacher; Stella Paapanen; Mr. and Mrs. Reino Aho; and several others climbed on board Leonard Lofback's truck and headed down Highway 73.[25]

The Soo Line, which according to Ranger Swedberg had been notified as early as 3:00 P.M., sent a relief train up from Moose Lake just after 6:00. The engine had been put away for the day, but the crew was reassembled and a train made up of an engine, tender, and caboose. They were to make a run to Kettle River, Automba, and Lawler. The trip out was uneventful, but when they arrived in Kettle

*Child refugees in
schoolhouse, Moose Lake,
October 1918 (Irish)*

River it was clear that the town was in imminent danger and that the
train could not go any farther west. The engineer ran the locomotive
out onto the wooden railroad bridge west of town and attempted to
wet it down by opening the blow-off cocks. When this operation became dangerous he backed into town, picked up people at the station,
stopped again at the section house, and halted a third time at the road
crossing to take on more people. Engineer Ernest Vandervort described the situation at about 6:45 as the train left: "Well, just as I
pulled away from the depot at Kettle River the fire had struck the
town, and the stores north of the crossing were . . . all afire, and
also the section house was afire." With its whistle tied down, the train
backed caboose first toward Moose Lake. The caboose was packed so
tightly with men, women, and children that the brakeman, Irving B.
Phelps, could hardly move. When possible, he kept the door open so
that no one would suffocate. About two miles east of Kettle River they

encountered a big fire among the trees on both sides of the tracks. To Phelps it looked as though "we were going right through a big red wall of fire." The paint was blistered on the locomotive and fire broke out on the cab's running board, but the train made it through to Moose Lake, arriving at 7:05, about a hour after it had left.[26]

The fire burned into the lumberyards on the west side of Kettle River, into the Soo Line railroad property, and then into Michaelson's store on the north side of town. In fact, fires, perhaps spot fires, seemed to have swept past the town both to the north and to the south. Arthur Russell, together with brothers Richard T. and Charles Hart (who had come up from Moose Lake earlier to look after their lumber company), started to drive south along Highway 73, but fire had crossed the road and it was now impassable. They then drove east on the Barnum (or Brown) road, hoping to get to Moose Lake by this alternative route, but they discovered fire coming onto that road from the northwest. With fire in the ditches, the six or seven passengers simply lifted the automobile and turned it around, and they retraced their tracks into Kettle River. They drove through fire to the west side of town until they got to the river. Russell estimated that it was only ten minutes from the time they left the lumberyard until they got to the river, although he said, "It seemed like a week while I was in that fire." The river varied in depth from several inches to four or five feet, and the water was very cold and was covered with ashes, but they found many other people there. They plunged into the water to wet their clothes, and Russell splashed water on the children when the big fire came. "Well, it was just a wall of smoke and seemed like flames all mixed up with it," Russell described, "and it was rolling just like a cyclone."[27]

Most people in Kettle River and the surrounding area attempted to escape from the fire by going south on the road to Moose Lake. The road south in 1918 was not the later broad, asphalt-surfaced Highway 73, but rather a small dirt road between trees and fields. It was so narrow, in fact, that when automobiles met they had to drive up onto the grass with their right wheels in order to get past each other. The hazards of this situation were further complicated by the timing of the fires burning Kettle River, which were slightly later than the fires burning into Silver Township from farther south in Split Rock Township. The result was that when people started leaving Kettle River in large numbers as the fire descended on the town, it was almost too late to make it safely down the road south to Moose Lake. The possibility of entrapment in the narrow confines of the road was compounded by the sharp bends in the road, which in the dark and heavy smoke resulted in a pileup of automobiles at Dead Man's Curve.[28]

Walfred Westholm, who had fled from the fire on the banks of the Dead Moose River, just made it into Kettle River. He heard the whistle of the relief train, but it was just passing out of town when he got to it. Nevertheless, he was able to jump on the running board of a southbound automobile that was already packed with people. The smoke was thick and visibility was extremely poor, and the automobile went off the narrow road. Fortunately, it did not crash, and Westholm told the driver to follow him while he walked on ahead. Within minutes, however, the automobile passed him, missed the sharp turn in the road at Dead Man's Curve, and tipped over in the ditch. When Westholm got to the corner, two more automobiles missed the turn and tipped over. Westholm helped a woman out of the wreckage of one. They made their way to Glaisby Brook, a short distance to the southeast. Leonard Lofback's truck, filled with a terrified Ailie and Hanna Leppa and several others, crashed and rolled on its side. Ailie and those in the back were thrown out, but Hanna's hand was pinned under the truck in the burning brush. Some men helped Hanna, screaming in pain from her burned arm, get free. Now in the midst of the large fire, the Leppas were protected somewhat by their winter coats and hoods. Stella Paapanen and Ida Hiipakka, their clothes burning, were last seen alive as they ran off into the woods. Paapanen's body was identified after the fire and buried in the mass grave at Moose Lake, while Hiipakka's remains were not found until 1920. Ailie and Hanna walked down the road until they were helped by three young men to Glaisby Brook, where many people in the area found safety.[29]

Although some automobiles drove through the perils of Dead Man's Curve without accident and some people walked through the burning area without mishap, about fifteen or sixteen automobiles, most of them overloaded with terrified people, went off the road into the rocks and burning brush. Years later Celia Kowalski described the crash of an automobile loaded with a family of children: "They hit the curve, careened off the road into the rocks and burning stumps and overturned. I will never forget the terrible screaming of those poor souls slowly burning to death." The carnage was incredible. Although accounts vary, between seventy-five and one hundred people died at Dead Man's Curve, some pinned under wrecked automobiles, some in the woods, some on the roadside. Survivors told of the horror of the burned bodies along the road, some dead and others dying. Many were so badly burned as to be unrecognizable, and those who survived, like John Michaelson, the owner of a store in Kettle River, were forever scarred by the burns they received.[30]

Ailie and Hanna Leppa, Walfred Westholm, and many others watched the fire pass around them from the safety of Glaisby Brook. Because of the cold night air, Henry Baakari took the wet women and children to a coal fire at a nearby road-repair shed he discovered. Westholm climbed out of the stream and back onto the road to continue his way to Moose Lake. He found many figures lying along the road, some dead, some alive and in great pain. He met a friend searching for his children and helped to look for a while, to no avail. Westholm continued east down the road to the unburned Charles Eckman house, about three miles from Moose Lake.[31]

The fire had burned fiercely around "Eckman's corner." Walfred Carlson estimated that more than sixty people died within the two-mile radius of Eckman's corner and "Haikola's hill," including people in both the old West Side church and the Eckman School. Charles Eckman, having got away from the fire in Kettle River, attempted to drive his family to Moose Lake in their Model T Ford, but crashed in the ditch. His wife was injured and his leg was broken when he was hit by another automobile. The Eckmans were given a ride by a friend, but that automobile also went into the ditch. After both automobiles started to burn, the passengers finally found safety from the fire in an open field. The Eckmans' house, however, survived, and in the early morning people attempting to make their way to Moose Lake found shelter there. Arnold Lund, then a nine-year-old boy, remembered as many as a hundred people, many suffering badly from their burns, crowded into the house. Dr. F. R. Walters from Moose Lake came early in the morning to provide what medical assistance he could.[32]

Relief workers with bodies removed from a root cellar, October 1918

Although many people had attempted to flee to Moose Lake, others were not able to do so and sought shelter on their own farmsteads. It was possible to survive in open fields, streams, and even culverts and ditches, but some of the worst tragedies were deaths by suffocation in root cellars and wells. Almost all of the Soderberg family of fourteen, the Ivar and Ainio Jalonen family of three, and Saima Williams and her three children were trapped in root cellars as the oxygen was drawn out to feed the surrounding fire. Perhaps the most pathetic story was that of Nick and Hulda Koivisto and their children of Silver Township. When the fire hit them at about 7:00 P.M., Nick and Hulda took seven of their eight children to a neighbor's root cellar. There sixteen people crowded in amongst the potatoes while Nick, Hulda, and John Niemi stayed outside in the wind and heat, pouring water on the cellar door to keep it from burning. Even so, they could not protect their families, as Hulda related: "Every root cellar had an air vent and finally in all of the confusion, it dawned on us to call down this vent to inquire about the welfare of the people inside. Upon receiving no answer, we opened the door, and you can imagine the horror when we discovered all of the people we had so desperately tried to save, were dead, suffocated from lack of oxygen."

Only one of the Koivisto children survived the fire. He had been taken by his grandfather, Henry Portinen, earlier in the afternoon. Portinen died at his own farm gate, and his wife was so badly burned that she died later in St. Mary's Hospital in Duluth, but seven-year-old Arnold and several other children survived with an uncle in a low spot in an open field. Arnold remembered years later that his mother refused to permit the National Guard to bury her seven dead children — Leonard, Wilbert, Ellen, Elsie, Evelyn, Ethel, and Esther — in the mass grave in Moose Lake. The officers finally relented, and an army truck took all the coffins back to St. Peter's cemetery near Highway 27.[33]

Moose Lake lay directly in the path of the oncoming fire. When the fire burned through Kettle River at about 7:00 P.M., it formed an irregular fire front, extending about seven or eight miles from Kalevala Township south into Silver Township and moving at speeds of between fifteen and twenty miles an hour. The Soo Line relief train sent up to Kettle River had encountered no serious fires on the way out, just after 6:00 P.M. When it returned about an hour later, spot fires had ignited in the swamps, and the Buxter fire, which had been smoldering for weeks, had blown up and was burning out of control. The train passed through flames for a good part of the trip back to Moose Lake, the brakeman said. Even before the crisis arrived, the Northern Pacific railroad made three trains available for relief work: two sent north from Hinckley, stopping at Sturgeon Lake and Moose Lake, and the third southbound from Carlton. Together these three trains took more than three hundred people out of the two towns. At about 7:30 or 8:00 P.M., fires reached Moose Lake and Sturgeon Lake.[34]

An effort was made to save the town of Moose Lake, but fire fighting collapsed when the electrical power failed and the pumps were rendered useless. The waters of Moose Head Lake became the refuge of most of those who remained in the town. Walter and

Matt O. Wilson drove in from Kalevala Township with an automobile filled with at least ten people, having successfully threaded their way through the congestion of Dead Man's Curve. They were sent to the lake by Frank Ronkainen and Charles F. Mahnke (editor and publisher of the town newspaper, the *Star Gazette*), who were directing traffic even while the business section of Moose Lake was starting to burn. The old Mitchell automobile stalled just after they crossed the Northern Pacific tracks, and they had to walk the rest of the way. Fourteen-year-old Tillie Odberg Westman from Kettle River was just sitting down to dinner with the Reverend L. J. Sundquist and his family when the minister's son ran into the house crying that the town was burning. The family loaded up their automobile and they too headed for Moose Head Lake. Unfortunately, they collided with another automobile, and Tillie was thrown out. The machine could not be restarted, so Tillie caught a ride on the running board of yet another automobile, which took her to the lakeshore. Mrs. Jack Kohtala, a nurse in Moose Lake, told of Dr. Walters, who attempted to drive his family and two patients from the hospital to Sturgeon Lake. The fire burned across the road and the automobile itself caught fire. Dr. Walters then drove the burning automobile right into the lake, where his family and the two patients, one of whom had been operated on shortly before the fire, stayed until the fire died down.[35]

Those who spent the night in Moose Head Lake had the unique experience of watching the town burn. Matt Wilson found a bucket for his aunt, Linda Peura Martilla, to sit on, and kept splashing water on her to keep her clothes from catching fire. Tillie Westman ran into the water among the hundreds of people in the lake. She tried to breathe through a tiny handkerchief she had with her, but Gladice Hart Williams (Richard and Charles Hart's sister) gave her a towel, which was much more effective. Years later Tillie recalled, "It seemed like every soul from Moose Lake was there, in or near the water. Soon the cottages at the resort started burning, and we actually saw the flames leap over the lake and ignite buildings on the opposite side. The entire heavens were a huge ball of flame and within minutes, the entire city was blazing."

Strange sound effects were created when ammunition in a hardware store exploded as the store burned. By about 10:00 P.M., although individual fires were still burning, it was safe to come out of the lake and to try to get warm. Mrs. Kohtala and several other nurses went to the east side of the lake and watched "the town turn from a smokey grey to a bright glowing red and then to black dotted with spots of flame." She noted, "The fire swept mainly from the south-western part of the town burning everything but a few buildings on Soo Hill and the brick school building." When the smoke cleared they could see a farmhouse nearby, so they all went there to spend the rest of the night. Meanwhile, in the woods outside of Moose Lake, George Vader, a Northwestern Telephone company lineman, attempted to maintain contact with Barnum. His voice faded as the connection deteriorated, and Vader died at his post. His body was found in the woods.[36]

Richard Hart, the mayor of Moose Lake and also one of the owners of the Hart Brothers Lumber Company, spent the first part of the night in the Kettle River with his brother, Charles; Arthur Russell; and a dozen other people, just west of the town of Kettle River. After the main fire had burned over them, he made his way back to Moose Lake during the night, through Kettle River, Dead Man's Curve, and Eckman's corner, surveying the death, injury, and damage. Although Hart's own house near Moose Head Lake was still standing, almost all of the town of Moose Lake had been destroyed, including the railroad offices and telegraph facilities. Hart walked down the Northern Pacific tracks to Sturgeon Lake, another six miles, where he telegraphed Governor Burnquist in St. Paul:

> WE MUST HAVE FOOD AND CLOTHING FOR
> THREETHOUSAND [sic] PEOPLE AND THREE HUNDRED
> CASKELS [sic] AT MOOSELAKE AT ONCE[.] ENTIRE
> COUNTY BURNED AND PEOPLE SUFNERING [sic.] ALL
> COMING TO MOOSELAKE FOR AID[.] WE MUST ALSO
> HAVE FINANCIAL AID[.] THIS APPEAL IS URGENT[.][37]

If the Cloquet and Duluth fires were the most spectacular in terms of property damaged or numbers of people involved, the Moose Lake and Kettle River fires were the most tragic because of the desperate plight of the people and the incredible number of deaths in the region. While it is impossible at this date to determine the exact numbers, the Minnesota Forest Fires Relief Commission report estimated that at least half of the 453 people killed in the whole fire perished in this re-

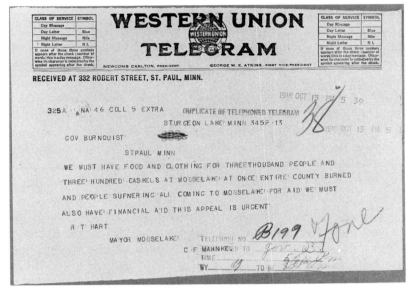

Telegram from Mayor Richard T. Hart of Moose Lake to Governor J.A.A. Burnquist

gion: fifteen to twenty volunteer fire fighters west of Kettle River; seventy-five to one hundred at Dead Man's Curve; sixty-seven near Eckman's corner; sixteen in a root cellar with the Koivisto children; almost fourteen in the Soderberg root cellar and seven in the Williams root cellar; many others in wells, buildings, streams, fields, and woods.

Unquestionably, the fire hit hardest and dealt the most devastating psychological blow here. The region did not die, but it was staggered. Many towns came back, led by Moose Lake and Kettle River. But many other settlements just withered — Automba, Split Rock, Lawler, Bain, and others never recovered.

Most of the people in the area held the railroads responsible for the fires. Even a superficial examination of a map of the fire area will show the tracks of the railroads, the Soo Line and the Northern Pacific, to be in the center of the burned districts. While there were certainly many circumstances beyond any human control — the drought, the fall in the humidity, and the wind (the synoptic weather pattern) being the most important — the railroads in the end bore the

Ruins of business district, Moose Lake, October 1918 (Irish)

responsibility for the disaster. The report of the state Forest Fire Investigation Commission singled out the fires along the Soo Line as a determining element in the region between Automba and Moose Lake. Perry Swedberg, the district forest ranger who felt that the Soo Line officials had refused to take his advice all autumn, concluded dramatically in his annual report that the railroad was "Guilty of Criminal Negligence of the highest class."[38]

PART THREE

The Aftermath of the Great Fires

Relief workers lined up for food with refugees, including a man wearing a donated Northern Pacific jacket, Moose Lake, October 1918 (Irish).

CHAPTER SIX

Relief Operations

I cannot urge too strongly upon the people of the State, the immediate necessity of large funds to care for the personal needs of those suffering and to aid in restoring the settlements that have been destroyed.
Governor J. A. A. Burnquist

The fires created a crisis for which there was almost no warning: no steadily rising flood waters, no new rumblings from a seemingly dormant volcano. Within hours a pleasant and utterly typical October Saturday had become a regional catastrophe, with many people injured or dead and much of the population uprooted. The first need after rescue from the flames was medical help and shelter for the survivors. State and national agencies quickly expanded the providing of these necessities into a major relief project that encouraged the recovery and reconstruction of the region. Although the damage done by the fire seemed almost overwhelming, the burned-over region was, with great effort, reoccupied and rebuilt. The credit for the area's revival belongs not only to the people who were determined to come back and start again but also to the organizations and individuals who, almost in the midst of the flames, began the relief and reconstruction operations.

Relief efforts began in Duluth on Saturday afternoon, even before the extent of the fires was fully known. Captain Henry Tourtelotte and Lieutenant Karl A. Franklin of the Fourth Regiment, Minnesota Infantry, National Guard, received a call at 3:00 P.M. to assist north of Duluth along the Rice Lake road, where automobiles were needed to pick up people who were fleeing the flames. There the two officers conferred with Mayor Clarence Magney, Chief of Police Robert McKercher, and others. Captain Tourtelotte drove back to Duluth (taking with him an elderly woman and eight children) to mobilize the units under his command. By 5:00 P.M. the two companies of the National Guard in Duluth were ordered to report to the armory in old clothes, ready to fight fire. Within two hours they set out, equipped with fire tools from the city supplies, to the farm land around Hermantown, northwest of Duluth. They found the situation there too far out of control for them to contain the flames, and they quickly turned to rescuing people who had been cut off by the fire or who were helpless and without transportation.[1]

Meanwhile, Major Roger M. Weaver, the commanding officer of the Third Battalion of the Minnesota Home Guard, concluded that a serious emergency was developing. He offered the battalion's services to Chief McKercher and conferred with Captain Tourtelotte. By 5:40 the fire chief requested Major Weaver's troops, and the mobilization procedures were set in motion. Within about an hour, seventy men had assembled at the Duluth Armory and were dispatched to fight fire, the first group being sent to Woodland, a suburb in the east end of Duluth. As additional troops reported to the armory, they were sent to various fire fronts. In the evening, a major effort up on the hill west of Duluth saved the St. James Catholic Orphanage and the Nopeming Sanatorium. More than two hundred patients and employees were evacuated and transported to the Denfeld and Irving schools in western Duluth, some eight miles away. Later in the night the fire seemed to threaten the buildings at Nopeming once again, but the flames were eventually brought under control, and the $350,000 institution was saved.[2]

By great good fortune, two of the Minnesota Home Guard units in Duluth were companies of the Seventh Battalion, Motor Corps, under the command of Major Henry J. Mullin. Their early involvement provided a high degree of organized mobility to both fire-fighting and rescue operations. The Motor Corps was able to deliver both National Guard and Home Guard troops quickly and in large numbers at various fire sites around the Duluth area. Its members also performed the even more critical task of taking fire victims away from the fire scene and into the Duluth Armory. The Corps ferried refugees from the train stations to the armory and to various hospitals, and it served as an essential courier service. Indeed, transportation became so critical that the Motor Corps accepted local citizens as drivers; when that proved inadequate, it pressed private automobiles into service. The Standard Oil Company stations in Duluth stayed open all night and made no charge for the gasoline dispensed, to facilitate the transportation needs of the emergency. One volunteer driver, who had seen the fire come within a half a mile of where he was staying, brought three loads of people into Duluth on Sunday morning, October 13, and then from noon to 10:30 P.M. moved supplies to the hospitals. For the next several days after the fire the Motor Corps remained the primary means, especially in the Duluth area, of moving relief goods into the fire district, rescuing survivors in remote areas, searching for bodies, and making preliminary assessments of the damage. Both Major Weaver and Governor Burnquist singled out the Motor Corps for high praise after the fire. They concluded that the death toll in the Duluth area would have been higher but for the heroic services of these volunteers, who provided their own vehicles and uniforms.[3]

When Major Weaver found that the fires near Nopeming were successfully contained, he decided to travel "by machine" to Carlton and Cloquet to assess the situation. In Carlton he found a large number of refugees who had fled from Cloquet. Weaver was asked for food and supplies; he immediately passed these requests on to the Duluth Chapter of the Red Cross, which belonged to the organization's Northern Division, headquartered in Minneapolis. Making his way to Cloquet itself, the major found the destroyed city almost completely deserted and many fires still burning. Surveying the smoldering city, he concluded that the ruins, including bank vaults and many store safes, and the remaining buildings and mills would need immediate military protection and that substantial relief facilities would have to be created.[4]

Weaver returned to his headquarters at the Duluth Armory and conferred again that night with Captain Tourtelotte. Lieutenant Franklin and fifty National Guard troops who had been fighting fire all night were called for immediately, and by 8:30 on Sunday morning, October 13, they were taking up their stations in Cloquet. Property was to be protected: no one was allowed to return without some proof of ownership, a measure that eliminated sightseers and souvenir-hunters. Sanitary regulations were posted and enforced, and

Breaking open a safe, Cloquet, October 1918

public latrines were provided. Unburned buildings on Dunlap Island in the St. Louis River became the headquarters, and within a matter of days a barracks, called Camp McDonald, was built for the soldiers at the corner of Cloquet Avenue and Second Street. Sergeant Gus Apel set up a dispensary in the old Northeastern Hotel, where for thirty-six hours without rest he looked after refugees, administered first aid, and put dressings on burn victims. The National Guard also ran a mess service for several days, serving hot food to refugees returning to Cloquet to inspect their losses.

The troops made themselves generally useful to the returning residents. A guardsman instructed John Blomberg and his family about the procedures of returning to their property and later broke open the safe at the family store when no one could remember the combination. The possibility of looting was a real concern. When Allan Wight returned to Cloquet early on Sunday morning, he found someone digging up the valuables he had buried in his back yard before he and his wife, Laura, had fled.[5]

Troops moved to several other towns in the aftermath of the fire. First Home Guard and later National Guard units served in Carlton, assisting Sheriff Harry L. McKinnon by patrolling the town, keeping watch for fires, and regulating traffic into Cloquet. Major Weaver

Minnesota Home Guards arrived for relief work at Moose Lake, October 1918 (photograph by Fred Levie).

sent Home Guard troops into Barnum and Moose Lake by train on Sunday morning, and they were later joined by troops from southern Minnesota under the command of Colonel LeRoy D. Godfrey. What time troops actually arrived in the Moose Lake area is unclear, but numerous survivors' accounts agree that quite early on Sunday morning guardsmen were in Moose Lake dispensing first aid. They quickly moved out along Highway 73, picking up bodies of victims at Dead Man's Curve and around Kettle River. Hulda Koivisto remembered that the "dead bodies were piled like cordwood" for survivors to identify at Moose Lake's Elm Tree Hotel, which had not burned. Even more important, the National Guard shuttled burn victims and injured people into Moose Lake. Although a temporary hospital was set up first in a railway car and then in the unburned high school building, the serious cases were sent right off by train to hospitals in Duluth. Twelve-year-old Matt Wilson had his eyes treated and then was given some coffee and doughnuts, which after a long and stressful night "were the best I have ever tasted, and that delicious aroma still comes back to me after almost 60 years." Soup and sandwiches were served to all who got into Moose Lake.[6]

A Duluth detachment also traveled to Brookston to take charge of relief operations and to establish military protection until normal civilian control could be resumed. Smaller groups of soldiers were posted to places like Floodwood and Brevator. To relieve the Duluth troops, many of whom had been on constant duty for longer than thirty hours, soldiers were mobilized from Two Harbors, Grand Rapids, Bemidji, Eveleth, and several other cities on the iron ranges. They also worked to suppress fires for several days after October 12. The troops were the initial agency for dispensing medical and relief supplies and for protecting property. A variety of work required immediate attention: roads to be cleared and in many cases rebuilt (wooden culverts burned out during the fire, causing the road surfaces to collapse); a pontoon bridge to be built across the St. Louis River at Brookston to reach areas almost inaccessible by any other route; livestock to be rounded up and fed; both living and dead fire victims to be sought out in remote rural areas; coffins to be provided; and dragging operations to be undertaken in lakes where people had taken refuge, only to drown.[7]

In short, until civil authority was restored and until some of the normal population returned, the troops performed whatever tasks were asked of them. Walter F. Rhinow, the adjutant general of the Home Guard, established his headquarters at Moose Lake, and operating out of that town in almost continual use were some 275 National Guard troops, thirteen army trucks, twelve civilian trucks, and twelve Motor Corps automobiles. Home Guard Captain Frederick L. Smith, a physician at the Mayo Clinic, ran a hospital in the repaired Moose Lake high school. The military operations were large and involved a substantial number of people drawn from the volunteer ranks of both the National Guard and the Home Guard. Generally, the relations between the troops and the communities they served were excellent. Certainly in the Moose Lake–Kettle River area the troops were greeted with desperate thanks and were warmly remembered years later. Gradually the number of troops involved was reduced as things began to return to normal and civilian groups moved to take over the tasks of relief operations. On December 13, 1918, General Rhinow was asked to withdraw troops from Moose Lake. This final process took much longer than was expected, in Moose Lake and in several other communities, with the result that the previously good relations were eroded a bit. By the end of January

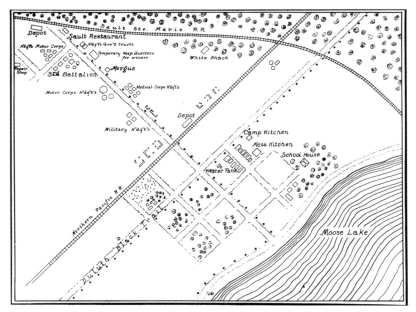

Relief operations in Moose Lake, October 1918 (Irish)

1919, however, all troops in the Cloquet and Moose Lake districts had been sent home.[8]

The Red Cross in Duluth, like the troops, mobilized quickly on Saturday. A number of Red Cross women volunteers were working at the Duluth Armory on Saturday afternoon, when it became clear that a disaster was in the making. Major Weaver asked Kathleen W. (Mrs. W. Sumner) Covey to take charge of establishing an emergency hospital in the National Guard dormitory in the armory building. Covey, who worked without rest for the next twenty-four hours, earned warm praise for her organizational skills in anticipating the needs of the fire victims and in getting all of the facilities ready. After the Brookston relief train stopped in Cloquet at 5:00 P.M., local Red Cross worker Lucile Booker Watkins telephoned William A. McGonagle, the chairman of the Duluth Chapter, to inform him that refugees

Relief workers at the Duluth Armory helped refugees, many wearing influenza masks, to fill out forms and obtain donated clothing, about October 14, 1918 (McKenzie).

would be coming to the city. Both the Red Cross women and the medical corps of the Home Guard worked as hospital and dispensary staff. Thus, when burned or injured people began to arrive at the armory, the facilities were set up and ready to receive them. Even these preparations were soon overwhelmed, however, by the number of refugees. Additional cots were brought into the temporary hospital, raising the number of beds from fifty to seventy-five, and then cots were set up in long rows on the drill room floor of the armory. At the same time the medical staff was expanded to handle the number of sufferers. Doctors and nurses in the city were requested and volunteered readily. John B. Adams, the manager of the Duluth Chapter, undertook to get medical supplies, cots, beds, and bedding from city hotels and stores.[9]

When it was learned that Cloquet had burned and that there would be many more refugees from there descending on Duluth, the Red Cross made arrangements to place them at the courthouse, the Masonic temple, the Shrine auditorium, the YMCA buildings, and several centrally located churches and hotels. Each building was assigned a doctor and several nurses, together with bedding and medical supplies. The figures vary, but it seems that within the first twenty-four hours approximately 438 serious injury cases were treated. From the armory's mess facilities, Home and National Guard cooks, who worked for two days without rest, continuously served hot food all night Saturday and all day Sunday to nearly three thousand refugees. Frank Murphy, a volunteer driver, wrote his mother several days later, describing the scene: "I will never forget the sight at the Armory. The main floor was filled with Cots and people sleeping there[,] some of them not knowing where the rest of their families were or whether they were alive or not." Mrs. W. H. Slavel, who had struggled to get all of her family on the relief train in Cloquet, saw her daughter, who had just that day given birth to a child, put in an ambulance and sent to a hospital. Slavel, another grandchild, and the rest of the family were taken from the depot to the armory, where they received influenza masks, a hot lunch, and cots on which to sleep. Guy and Tena Smith and their three children, also from Cloquet, just went up from the Union Depot to the Spalding Hotel and slept on cots on the top floor. Murphy's own conclusion was appropriate for the whole experience: "It was one wild night."[10]

The most serious burn and injury cases were moved to St. Mary's and St. Luke's hospitals under the supervision of the doctors who had first treated them. The drill floor of the armory was emptied in order to convert that area into the operations headquarters for the disaster relief effort. As quickly as possible, the organizers attempted to administer first aid and burn treatment to people in areas outside Duluth. In Cloquet a dispensary opened on Sunday morning, and teams of doctors and nurses went as soon as they could from Duluth into the outlying districts. During the next few days doctors and nurses went into rural areas on day trips, giving follow-up treatment to patients.[11]

In the western fire district, a Red Cross headquarters established in Aitkin's Willard Hotel on October 13 provided one hundred refu-

Nurses in disaster area, Moose Lake, October 1918 (Irish)

gees with medical aid and shelter. Many people in the western reaches of the fire were also sent south to Sandstone, Hinckley, Minneapolis, and St. Paul. The onset of chilling rains on October 18 further compli-cated the general medical situation by weakening survivors' resistance even more and contributing to the local spread of the worldwide in-fluenza epidemic. Major E. L. Paulson, the National Guard's chief medical officer who was traveling with General Rhinow after the fire, ordered all people in the fire district to wear influenza masks. One hundred six deaths in the area were attributed to influenza and pneumonia.[12]

By early November the number of people who had been looked after at the armory and other Duluth facilities numbered 761, and countless more were served in the outlying districts. The medical officer of the Duluth Home Guard battalion reported that twenty-nine physicians, fifteen nurses, and twenty-one helpers gave their ser-vices. Eventually a Red Cross hospital built in Cloquet served 1,445 patients over the following year: 375 bed cases, 1,000 clinical cases, and 70 maternity cases.

In addition to providing medical care, the Red Cross brought into the area fifty-one trained social workers, who assisted the refugees in locating family members and getting back to their homes, and who kept records of each of the fifteen thousand families registered. The Red Cross urged refugees to register, and lists of names and temporary addresses were published in the newspapers in order to facilitate the reunification of families. Because one train took only women and children and some trains went to Duluth and some to Superior, many families were split up and spent the next several days anxiously uncertain of the fate of those missing. Fourteen-year-old Walter Hanson's mother and sister went on one train and he on another, and his father stayed in Cloquet. It took him two days to find his mother and four days to get together with his father. Rosella Singpiel Harney's family took a week to be reunited. These were common experiences.[13]

The Red Cross also opened a Bureau of Legal Advice at the armory on Tuesday, October 15, and published in the Duluth newspapers immediate and direct appeals for specific contributions of clothing and farm equipment, such as women's dresses, children's clothes, wagons, and harnesses. On October 31 William G. McAdoo, who was both the secretary of the U.S. Treasury and the director general of the Railroad Administration, stopped in Duluth to inspect railroad ore dock facilities. He visited the armory and praised the Red Cross work of Jessie B. Raisky and others for their efforts in the fire crisis.[14]

Superior, Wisconsin, was not directly in the path of the fire, as was Duluth, but it became a major center for Red Cross relief. Superior's strategic position in relation to the fire grew out of the fact that the Great Northern and Soo Line railway lines that passed through the western fire district ran into that city. Thus, trains loaded with refugees from Brookston, Cloquet, Carlton, and Moose Lake unloaded their passengers in Superior. George Stewart, the Great Northern superintendent in Superior, had been able to monitor the fire situation from reports by station agents along his rail lines. Learning that Brookston had burned and that Cloquet was threatened, Stewart convened a meeting of about twenty-four businessmen in his office in the early evening to make preparations for the arrival of large

Appeal for aid to fire victims, Duluth
Herald, *October 15, 1918*

numbers of refugees. Subgroups were organized to make arrangements to provide shelter, food, and medical assistance and to receive
and transport the refugees.[15]

By the time the Brookston relief train arrived in Superior at 11:30
P.M., some facilities were ready, and throughout the night, as the four
subsequent trains came into town, the injured and burned were taken
to hospitals and others were sheltered in churches, schools, stores, the
YMCA, and club buildings such as the Masonic temple — some eighteen places in all. Later, many people were housed in private dwellings. By Sunday morning the Red Cross began providing hot meals for
the refugees at one of the central churches.

Pearl Drew of Cloquet was taken first to a home for the night, but
she was too nervous to sleep, and went to the YMCA: "I went to the
'Y', where volunteers were making thousands of sandwiches and gallons of coffee. There was plenty to do here. Mattresses were spread
over the large 'gym' floor, each one haven of a foreign family. They
would not be separated for a minute. With their few belongings in a
sack, the mother clutched it firmly and would not budge. The family
moved as a whole, or not at all." On Sunday Drew went back and
worked on the refugee lists, trying to reunite families separated by the

confusion of the fire or by the fact that some trains had gone to Duluth and some to Superior. Anna Olesen and her daughter, Mary, had taken the train for women and children, but they got off at Superior with many others, "and there we waited for our men," Anna Olesen said. "We waited hour after hour, and finally the trains came in bringing our men, and I saw the families that were united." She and her family had a fitful night's sleep; and on Sunday morning, without benefit of comb or toothbrush, she went to the Red Cross headquarters and asked if there were anything she could do. "They did not, perhaps, recognize that I was a fire sufferer; and I stood behind the table and helped pass out clothes to our people who the day before were happy and comfortable with this world's goods." People were asked to work as volunteers at refugee centers or to contribute clothing or to provide housing. Years later, Iva Andrus Dingwall recalled being told of the relief needs by a neighbor whose automobile had been used all night to shuttle refugees around Superior. By 11:00 that Sunday morning she was at the Red Cross headquarters "with a parcel of clothing," and she volunteered to house three people in her home.[16]

The Superior Fire Relief Committee, with Thomas B. Mills as chairman, was formed in the early hours of Sunday morning from the ad hoc group still meeting in George Stewart's office. Committees of finance, housing, clothing, food, health, labor, and registration were created, and $3,500 was immediately allocated to the finance committee by the Superior Chapter of the Red Cross, which belonged to the organization's Central Division, headquartered in Chicago. Mayor John Long of Cloquet worked closely with Mayor Fred D. Baxter of Superior and with the Superior Chapter. Several social workers were sent from Chicago to assist, and by the end of October Governor Burnquist was informed that of 8,375 refugees taken care of in Superior, 3,685 had left and 4,690 remained. There had been 295 cases of influenza, with two deaths, and there were 110 refugees still in the hospital, suffering from burns or injuries. The people of Superior had privately housed 735 refugees, organized their own fire relief committee, and raised a fund of $126,819.33. Burnquist sent his thanks to the State of Wisconsin.[17]

Governor J. A. A. Burnquist (hatless, at center back) watched Minnesota Home Guards and other gravediggers at work, Moose Lake, about October 14, 1918.

On Monday, October 14, Governor Burnquist, his wife Mary Louise, State Forester William Cox, General Walter Rhinow, and a number of other state officials came north to inspect the fire district. Much needed to be done. The National Guard troops brought into Moose Lake the bodies of those people killed at Dead Man's Curve, Kettle River, and Automba and in root cellars and wells throughout the area. These bodies had to be disposed of immediately. The governor himself oversaw the burial of some two hundred fire victims in a mass grave in Moose Lake. While Mrs. Burnquist helped with relief work in Moose Lake, the governor and his party traveled on to Cloquet and Duluth to view the devastation and to talk with the fire sufferers. After what he saw, Burnquist was convinced that the dimensions of the disaster required special measures by the state government.[18]

The first major step was to create a committee authorized by the state government to deal with the situation and to coordinate the relief efforts of the several groups who had stepped into the emergency. This was done on October 16, when members of the Minnesota Commission of Public Safety (MCPS) met in special session in Moose Lake at the governor's request. They created the Minnesota Forest Fires Relief Commission, which was empowered to take over all responsibility for relief operations in the fire district. The MCPS also authorized both St. Louis and Carlton counties to spend all the available moneys in their general revenue fund for immediate relief. Later in the month the MCPS placed $300,000 at the disposal of the relief commission, and somewhat later the state legislature formally authorized the commission. The legislature also appropriated $1,850,000 for the commission on February 7, 1919, but only after debating the issue and sending the relevant legislative committees on a visit to the fire area.[19]

The members of the commission were appointed with a view to both the relief experience of the individuals and representation of various involved parties. The chairman was William McGonagle, who had had relief experience in the Baudette-Spooner fire of 1910 and was chairman of the Red Cross chapter in Duluth, as well as president of the Duluth, Missabe and Northern Railway. Colonel Hubert V. Eva of Duluth was the commission's secretary and general manager. A long-time member of the Minnesota National Guard, Eva was a veteran of the Spanish-American War and World War I. He had also served on the Baudette-Spooner relief commission and had been on military duty at the Virginia, Hinckley, and Chisholm fires of 1893, 1894, and 1908, respectively. Mayor Magney and Charles A. Duncan represented Duluth (when McGonagle resigned later in 1919 for health reasons, Duncan succeeded him, and Hiram R. Elliott, a Duluth meat packer, was added to the commission). The commission also included Clarence McNair of Cloquet, Charles Mahnke of Moose Lake, Ben R. Hassman of Aitkin, and George H. Partridge of Minneapolis. Emil G. Steger of St. Paul coordinated the affairs of the commission with those of the Red Cross's Northern Division.[20]

On Thursday morning, October 17, the commission met in Moose Lake. As the new group was to assume responsibility for the kinds of work that the Red Cross, the military, and the private groups had been carrying out, a considerable amount of organization was necessary. Both short-term and long-term emergency relief and long-term reconstruction had to be planned and coordinated. The armory in Duluth, which was already serving as a center for relief operations, became the headquarters, and several departments were created to

Colonel Hubert V. Eva

carry out the organizational and administrative task. Men were placed in charge of departments of purchasing and supply, legal aid, auditing and finance, general replacement, building, and survey. The committee work eased the confusion of the immediate crisis and made the work of the commission more efficient.[21]

The commission gradually assumed a larger share of the burden of both expense and manpower from the Red Cross, the military units, and the various private groups. The commission worked with those bodies, however, until their jobs were done rather than simply replace them, so that first aid, food, shelter, and the like continued to be handled through the same people who had served on the first Sunday morning after the fire.

The commission decided at its first meetings that some long-term or permanent relief measures were necessary if the region was to recover and return to some semblance of normal prefire living. The commission's philosophy was to "help every man to help himself," and to that end it formed a Central Replacement Committee with four district committees in St. Louis County, northern and southern Carlton County, and Aitkin County. These district committees, made up of local people, scrutinized applications for assistance and listened to appeals. The committee members were expected to know the local situations and to be able to act more fairly and confidently than strangers or professional social workers. To this organization were added local committees from the destroyed communities. Offices and warehouses were established in eleven towns, and in twelve smaller communities temporary distribution centers were operated. Swiftly implemented procedures allowed refugees returning to the burned-out areas to go to a relief commission representative, identify themselves, and describe the dimension of their losses and the scale of their needs. The commission, through these local committees, would then dispense relief as it felt fitted the circumstances of the particular region.[22]

Emergency relief work had gone so well that by October 23 McNair, the commissioner from Cloquet, could write to Governor Burnquist, "It gives me great satisfaction to report, that owing to the generous relief poured into this district from all sections, there has been no suffering from want of food or clothing, and that this relief thus far has been wisely and effectively locally administered, by the Committees named." McNair went on to say that the dimensions of the disaster were such that, although the immediate crisis was being met, relief needs were elaborate and would continue for some time. Several days later, Chairman McGonagle was able to make a similar report to the governor for the whole commission.[23]

The refugees fell into two broad categories: urban workers or businesspeople, and rural farmers. Both groups required food, shelter, and clothing. The commission provided food rations, which enabled people to do their own cooking rather than be dependent on public mess halls run by the military or the Red Cross. Refugees also received the lumber, hardware, and furnishings to make a small shelter. Plans were immediately drafted for two styles — a twelve-by-sixteen-foot structure for small families and a twelve-by-twenty-foot one for larger families. Those applying for help had to fill out elaborate forms to prove loss and show that they had no significant resources, but the supplies to construct the shelters were quickly forthcoming, so that people returning to the area in October and Novem-

Minnesota Forest Fires Relief Commission
AMERICAN RED CROSS

No._____   Date_____

Surname   Nationality   Citizen Yes No

Permanent Address   Map Description

Present Quarters   Phone No.

Title of Property in Whom   Acres Cleared   Unc'l'd

Nearest Ry. Station   Auto Road   Wagon R'd

Two Nearest Neighbors

	Age	Occupation	Wages	Disability	Insurance
Man's Name					
Woman's Name					
1					
2					
3					
4					
5					
6					
7					

Relief assistance form, 1918

ber were able to have a structure to call "home" within a few days of their arrival. One newspaper reported that by November 15 more than 250 such shelters had been constructed in Cloquet, and by the end of December, most of those who had returned to the burned-over area were living in some kind of shelter of their own. To be sure, these were crude and sparse, but they were intended as temporary quarters that would at least enable people to get through the winter. The commission spent $872,706.65 on building materials for fire victims, $263,941.97 on hardware, stoves, and implements, and $161,306.75 on furnishings and bedding. This was an incredible undertaking.[24]

Later in 1919 state appropriations enabled people to put siding on the shelters and to make them more comfortable (many of these structures survive in the Cloquet area today as rather elaborate garages on the lots of older houses). Then more permanent houses began to appear. The lumber mills in Cloquet furnished $175.00 worth of rough

Home Guards distributed donated clothing, including St. Paul Winter Carnival costumes, to refugees, about October 14, 1918.

lumber to each of their employees and many others and allowed the employees to build their houses and to help their neighbors while on company time.

Clothing was also distributed. Most of the fire sufferers fled on October 12 with little more than what they could carry, if anything at all. There was a major and immediate need for warm clothing as winter came on. The commission spent $184,599.68 on clothing and shoes, but it also assigned a great deal more that had been contributed from around the state.[25]

The commission soon decided that farmers would need even more help than the urban residents if they were to get back on their feet. Farmers, it was reasoned, required shelter not only for their families but also for farm animals and crops. The commission therefore provided lumber for the construction of barns and outbuildings appropriate to the kind and size of farm that had been destroyed by the fire. Lost farm implements and equipment also had to be replaced. Furthermore, the surviving farm animals had to be fed; where the hay and feed had been destroyed by fire, these too were provided by the commission. For those who had lost all of their animals, the relief groups attempted to make a start at replacing them. The United States Department of Agriculture, the University of Minnesota, the Minnesota Guernsey Breeders' Association, and the Minnesota Holstein-Friesian Breeders' Association helped in this by giving assistance and lending prize animals to reproduce decimated herds. The commission also provided the seeds for various crops in the spring of 1919 so that the whole farm economy could begin functioning again. Indeed, when hail destroyed the entire crop of the Sturgeon Lake and Split Rock areas in 1919, the commission furnished food for the farmers and feed for their livestock during the winter; it also supplied fresh seed when the abnormally wet spring of 1920 destroyed the potato crops in the burned district. Altogether the relief organization spent $172,036.55 on farm wagons, harnesses, and implements; $52,281.71 on livestock; $118,112.45 on seed; and the large amount of $807,422.95 on hay and feed.[26]

The fact that farmers got more assistance in dollar terms, and generally over a longer period of time, did not pass without comment or controversy in the burned-over district. Many people felt that while the fire had destroyed equally the entire worldly possessions of urban and rural dwellers alike, the commission had attempted relief and reconstruction on a far grander scale for farmers than for city dwellers. Others in the towns argued that relief should be distributed on an equal basis. They maintained that it was unfair that one family got a rude shelter, some old clothes, and a few weeks' worth of food, while others were supported for almost a year and were virtually reestablished in their former agricultural occupations. These feelings naturally gave way to accusations of bad faith and favoritism.[27]

Supported by the Red Cross, the commission claimed that the inequality of relief distribution for rural and urban fire sufferers was necessary because there were fundamental differences in the two situations. The urban worker or business owner who obtained food and shelter could go back to work or reopen the business, the commission argued. (To be sure, the surviving lumber companies in Cloquet resumed production in October 1918, but they neither operated at capacity nor employed as many people as before the fire.) To assist local businesses, the commission attempted by 1919 to buy all of its needed goods from merchants in the fire-stricken area rather than buy in large quantities from some metropolitan center.

Farmers, the commission held, had no alternative source of income until their next year's crop came in or until their livestock could begin producing again. Not only their homes but also their incomes had been destroyed by the fire, and at a time of year that gave them no other resources for many months. Rural areas, therefore, needed greater assistance; and the commission argued that in a disaster where only limited relief could be extended, need rather than equality was the overriding consideration.[28]

The commission was convinced that only its promises and relief program brought 95 percent of the burned-out farm settlers back to the land in the aftermath of the fire. Yet rural people complained too, particularly those whose equipment or livestock feed had been confiscated in order to fight fire or facilitate relief efforts. Compensation did not come quickly enough, and they argued that they would have been self-sufficient but for the need to get back what they had sacrificed. Disgruntled letters continued to flow to various authorities into 1919. The commission defended itself in its report, saying that "mistakes have been made. . . . but if we did not make mistakes we would be really inactive" in the distribution of relief; any errors were minor in view of the scale of the relief effort. The Moose Lake–Kettle River area survivors' accounts seem to agree. The medical aid, the tents, the lumber for shelters, the feed for animals were gratefully remembered years later.[29]

The commission also had to deal with special situations. Many people who were burned or injured remained hospitalized for prolonged periods of time. Directly fire-related injuries were almost immediately overtaken by the influenza epidemic, which fell particularly hard upon an area where people were living in crowded and inadequate circumstances at the onset of a cold and rainy autumn. Many elderly people who were dislocated by the fire were too infirm to return to their farms or to undertake any form of reconstruction. Some of them were placed in homes for the aged, and others were settled in towns untouched by the fire. The commission allocated money for grants to take care of these people. Similarly, orphans and widows with children received funds that would, in the words of the commission, "insure a bare livelihood."[30]

The relief organization had taken on a prodigious task. Within five days of the fire it had assumed responsibility for fifty thousand people or more, and it would continue to function for the next several years. Although it had the help of the Red Cross and the military — both of which paid their own expenses — the commission had the immediate task of raising funds to carry out its mandate. When Governor Burnquist announced the creation of the body, he also issued an appeal for public support, asking people to send money to either the MCPS or the relief commission. "I cannot urge too strongly," he said, "upon the people of the State, the immediate necessity of large funds to care for the personal needs of those suffering and to aid in restoring the settlements that have been destroyed." Those who had survived and lost homes or family needed the support and sympathy of the rest of the state, the governor pleaded; and the state responded to the governor's appeal. By October 15, clothing and supplies for the fire victims were being collected at five different locations in Minneapolis, and this work continued until the middle of November. Voluntary contributions of money reached $1,101,310.75, from towns, clubs, churches, schools, and merchants, and from every part of the nation. Most of the checks were accompanied by expressions of sympathy and encouragement. Plain citizens, touched by the tragedy, dug into their pockets with gifts of money that ranged from fifty cents to a generous one thousand dollars (the latter from a man in Olmsted County). The governors of other states sent official condolences and offers of help, frequently adding their private contributions. Even Prince Axel of Denmark conveyed his concern to Governor Burnquist less than a week after the disaster. By February 1921 the Forest Fires Relief Commission had raised and disbursed $3,145,840.60 (a sum that included the contributions of the Minnesota legislature) in the form of assistance.[31]

Efforts outside the machinery of the commission were significant also. The railroads were of critical importance. Not only had they been instrumental in taking people out of the fires on October 12 but they were also vital to the relief effort. The Great Northern, Northern

Pacific, and Soo Line railroads and the Chicago, St. Paul, Minneapolis and Omaha Railway Company all ran numerous special trains into the devastated areas in the days following the fire. These trains carried National Guard and Home Guard troops, fire fighters, search parties, doctors and nurses, relief supplies, and eventually, returning refugees. The railroads charged a fare only for the troops, transporting refugees and relief supplies free throughout the crisis. Company representatives meeting on October 15 with state officials — urged on by the regional director of the United States Railroad Administration — developed a joint policy that was designed to be as helpful as possible in moving people and goods.[32]

State Superintendent of Education Carl G. Schulz took the initiative in mobilizing public and private school systems to collect clothing from all over the state to be channeled into the relief area through the Junior Red Cross of the Northern Division. Clothing was to be brought to the schools from October 23 to 25, sorted and labeled on the weekend, and sent to the fire area on the following Monday. Much of this clothing was disbursed from a remaining school building in the fire area, the Garfield School in Cloquet. The *Duluth News Tribune* began receiving money for a relief fund before any of the agencies could get their programs started. This fund ran for only a week but collected more than $40,000.00. The Superior Fire Relief Committee in Wisconsin raised and dispersed $128,177.36, and the Northern Minnesota Finnish Relief Society raised more than $36,000.00, some of which it turned over to the commission and some of which it distributed itself. Private organizations such as the Masons, the Shriners, and the Independent Order of Odd Fellows made extensive efforts to look after fellow members. Through the organizational facilities of the Red Cross, many skilled carpenters and builders donated a day's labor to build shelters in the fire district in the weeks after the fire. Clarence W. Wigington, a St. Paul architect who was with the city's department of parks and playgrounds and the captain of a Home Guard company, offered his services. In a letter to the governor Wigington stated that "as a citizen and architect" he would be "pleased to be called at any and all times." When the employees of the Marshall-Wells Company in Duluth each donated one day's pay — a total of nearly $8,000.00 — to the relief fund, the company managers contributed from $25.00 to $200.00 apiece, and the firm added

$5,000.00. Many other people made generous voluntary contributions.[33]

Special provisions were made for the relief of the Ojibway from the Fond du Lac reservation. The fire had scattered and separated many of the families from the affected areas of the reservation. Homes and farms were destroyed, livestock killed or left without feed. Red Cross facilities in Superior, Duluth, and Cloquet were immediately made available to Fond du Lac Ojibway, along with other refugees. Many of the Ojibway who spent the night of the fire in Cloquet or who found safety in the lakes on the reservation went later to the Indian Hospital, which had not burned. Some sixty people were fed and given shelter there, in addition to those treated for burns or injuries. The nearby Indian Farm, which also had survived the fire, was made available for holding and feeding the Ojibway livestock. At the request of George Cross, the agency superintendent, the Office of Indian Affairs provided $5,000, with which Cross purchased flour, groceries, beds, mattresses, blankets, and other emergency supplies. He also bought fifty thousand board feet of rough lumber so the homeless Ojibway could build twelve-by-twenty-foot Red-Cross-style shelters. These were just the first steps to be taken in the situation, in Cross's estimation; by October 18, 1918, he requested another $5,000, although the release of that amount does not seem to have been authorized. Cross attempted to find work for those Ojibway whose farms had been destroyed. "We are placing all the Indians we can in Duluth and Superior and finding employment for them," he reported to Washington. A number of Bois Fort Ojibway from the Nett Lake reservation lived near Brookston, on the northern region of the Fond du Lac reservation, and Cross attempted to help them as well. To help raise immediate cash for Ojibway fire sufferers, Cross also obtained special permission from the OIA for timber cutting on reservation allotments, if the value of the trees cut did not exceed $100. These efforts, together with those of the Red Cross and the relief commission, gave the Fond du Lac victims some immediate assistance.[34]

Superintendent Cross concluded that to reestablish the Ojibway on the reservation, their homes, at least, would have to be rebuilt. He estimated that the replacement cost of all of the destroyed houses would average about $1,000 each, and roughly an additional $500 was needed for burned barns and outbuildings. Cross urged that the OIA arrange for between $75,000 and $100,000 to be appropriated to build new structures for the fifty or so families whose homes and farms had been destroyed. Cross was supported in this when the executive committee of the Chippewa Council of Minnesota authorized the expenditure of $100,000 from the tribal fund, subject to congressional approval. E. B. Merritt, the assistant commissioner of Indian affairs, did not recommend asking Congress for such a large expenditure. On June 30, 1919, Congress authorized the appropriation of $60,000 for the construction or purchase of houses for those Indians whose dwellings had been destroyed in the fire. The request for funds to rebuild the barns and outbuildings was refused.[35]

Nothing was done during the summer of 1919 to make the money available, and anxious letters and telegrams were sent by Leo S. Bonnin, the new Fond du Lac agency superintendent, pointing out to the OIA that the Ojibway wanted to begin construction on their houses before the weather turned cold. It was not until October 17, 1919, that Selden G. Hopkins, the assistant secretary of the interior, authorized the release of the funds to Superintendent Bonnin. The number of Ojibway actually eligible for this money worked out to forty-seven, and in late 1919 and 1920 funds were made available to build the houses on the reservation or to purchase houses in town. Although the process was not without difficulties and frustrations, eventually substantial amounts of money were made available to the Fond du Lac fire victims.[36]

The enormous efforts of all of these groups — the National Guard and the Home Guard, the Red Cross and the Minnesota Forest Fires Relief Commission, the governor and the legislature, the OIA and the railroads, and private individuals — culminated in a major sustained effort at relief and reconstruction. The devastated region could never be fully restored, nor could the suffering and damage be altogether eased. Nevertheless, the fact that relief of some kind was available and that local authorities, the state, the Red Cross, and numerous other institutions and individuals encouraged the refugees to return and

*American Red Cross and Home Guard members assisted fire victims,
Carlton County, about October 15, 1918 (McKenzie).*

worked to assist people to get a new start provides much of the expla-
nation for the eventual recovery of the area. The relief effort was a
monumental task, one for which there was no practical planning or
anticipation in those years before civil defense programs. The problem forced the creation of a solution.

CHAPTER SEVEN

Fire in the Courts

We find no difficulty in assigning the origin of the fire at Mile Post 62 to the defendant railway company.
Judge William A. Cant,
Eleventh Judicial District

I have always understood that the administration had as good a defense in the Cloquet cases as would probably arise on most of the claims.
James C. Davis, *General Counsel*
United States Railroad Administration

The fires that swept northeastern Minnesota were hardly extinguished before people began asking who was responsible. Almost everyone in the region had opinions about how and why the fires had started, why they raged out of control, and who should be held accountable for the damage. Public opinion demanded that there be some kind of official inquiry, and after a fashion there was one. The inquiries, however, left many unanswered questions, and they were particularly vague as to who caused the fires and who was responsible for all the destruction.

In the minds of the public, the railroads were responsible. District Forest Ranger Perry Swedberg believed the Soo Line to be responsible for the fires from Lawler to Moose Lake, and he stated this in his annual report. On October 25, 1918, the *Pine Knot* published an article reporting that the fire that destroyed Cloquet started at the little station of Mirbat, thirteen miles west of Brookston on the Great Northern tracks. Countless others, living in different areas, believed that the railroads had started the fires that destroyed their property. Thus, early in 1919, suits against the railroads were launched in the Min-

State Forester William T. Cox (right) and Forestry Board member Milton M. Williams, Itasca State Park, possibly 1915

nesota courts. These suits eventually involved millions of dollars, a partial settlement authorized by President Warren G. Harding, and a legal battle that lasted until 1935.[1]

The official who was clearly charged with responsibility for controlling forest fires and for monitoring forest conditions in general was William Cox, the state forester. Cox submitted his own report on the fires on November 1, 1918, two and a half weeks after the event, as an adjunct to the Minnesota State Forestry Board's annual report to the governor. Cox, who obviously did not have much time for either investigation or deliberation, was bland in his conclusions. He asserted that "in the main" the great catastrophe had been the result of "slow-burning marsh or bog fires, the number of which had been increasing as the fall season opened up." He went on to say that careless travelers, railroad locomotives, and landowners had, in violation of the law and in the face of fire restrictions and severe drought conditions, started numerous fires in the district. These circumstances, cou-

pled with the insufficient number of forest patrolmen, rangers, and
trained fire fighters, were the primary causes of the unusual destruction. Cox's real message in the report was that the calamity might
have been prevented if the state legislature had appropriated the
funds the Minnesota Forest Service requested to maintain a reasonable level of fire protection. This was a theme that the forestry profession would later develop more fully. Cox was also reported in the *Pine
Knot* as saying that, considering its limited resources, the forest service had done everything possible.[2]

At Cox's urging, Governor Burnquist appointed a Forest Fire Investigation Commission, to be chaired by Jed Washburn, a Duluth
corporation and railroad lawyer, and to include six others: two forestry professors, a state forest ranger, and three local people. The
commission was instructed to do two things: to "make a thorough investigation of the facts" in order to "locate the responsibility" for the
fire, and to "secure information" that would enable the state to eliminate "a repetition of the awful catastrophe." Burnquist was able to
prevail upon a reluctant Washburn with the argument that "we owe
the settlers in the burned district . . . the proposed investigation for
the purpose of doing everything possible to prevent a repetition of the
disaster."[3]

Beginning on November 14, the commission held hearings in
Duluth, Moose Lake, and Cloquet and traveled throughout the fire
district. But it did not use its powers to subpoena witnesses or to take
testimony under oath, nor did it regard its mandate to be to collect
evidence with a view to initiating legal proceedings. As a result, the
commission's report, which was sent to Governor Burnquist on
November 26, was also bland and unspecific. The season was dry, the
rainfall short; the swamps had been drained and the slash accumulated; clearing fires and bogs had been burning for some time; railroad operations, specifically the Soo Line northwest of Moose Lake
and the Great Northern west of Brookston, were responsible for some
fires. The report, however, did not attempt to single out specific
blame or responsibility for the massive destruction. If a finger was
pointed anywhere, it was at the wind, which, in the words of the report, "arose and increased in volume and velocity until it was little less
than a tornado and whipped all these numerous fires into a great
conflagration." In short, the catastrophe was an act of God.[4]

Even though state officials and forestry professionals were hesitant to name individuals who might be responsible for the damages created by the fires, the railroads almost immediately began to make preparations to defend themselves against the charge of having started the calamity. In many ways the railroads had been the heroes of the fire, having rescued thousands from Cloquet and Brookston, having struggled to get through to Moose Lake and other towns, and having put on numerous special trains for relief operations after the fire. But both the Great Northern and the Soo Line had also been singled out by the state Forest Fire Investigation Commission, and the railroads generally felt themselves to be vulnerable, in the early years of the twentieth century, to damage claims in suits that went to jury trials. Even with expensive corporation lawyers, a railroad often had difficulty successfully defending itself when a verdict was determined by a jury of local people. Several of the railroads, therefore, began to take precautions. Because of the publicity it had received about the fires along its tracks, the Soo Line almost immediately began its own investigation about the nature of the fires and the damages suffered in the Soo Line's district.

The Railroad Administration started its investigation along the Great Northern line northwest of Cloquet, near Milepost 62, in January 1919. A special train, equipped with sleeping cars, diners, and accommodations for a substantial number of people, provided a base from which two groups of investigators obtained statements from the fire victims about the fires that they had witnessed and the property that had been destroyed.[5]

By early February 1919 the Railroad Administration lawyers began to show alarm at the situation. On the one hand, they felt that railroad investigations tended to "attract attention to the matter [of possible railroad responsibility], and in effect invite such claims"; on the other hand, they were increasingly concerned about local lawyers taking the initiative and soliciting suits against the railroads on a contingent-fee basis that was rumored to be as high as 40 percent of any settlement. It was not a comfortable position for the railroads. Eventually all the railroads operating in the region sent investigators into the fire district to take verbatim statements from the survivors about the characteristics of the fire in their area and the property destroyed. These statements were subsequently gathered into reference books that were brought into the trials and used when those same people testified in the lawsuits. If the testimony given at the trial varied from that taken down by the railroad investigators, the defense lawyers had the earlier contradictory statements read out to the court.[6]

The situation was complicated also by the fact that during World War I most of the railroads in the country had been nationalized by the federal government. In order to coordinate rail traffic across the nation during the war, Congress had created the Railroad Administration. One of the provisions of the legislation was that rail lines submit themselves to the laws and the courts of the states in which they operated. The actual operations of the lines were left in the hands of the original management, even if technical ownership and responsibility rested with the federal government through the administration. Thus, the suits that were initially taken out against the local railroads eventually named as the defendant in the suit the director general of the Railroad Administration, as agent of the president. The legal office of the administration continued to operate into the 1930s, although the railroads themselves were restored to the original companies in 1920.[7]

Years later, testifying at congressional hearings, N. B. Arnold of Duluth told how he had become involved in the fire cases as a lawyer. A former client of his from Eveleth owned eighty acres of land along the Duluth, Missabe and Northern line; the land had burned in the fire, and the client asked Arnold in late 1918 to investigate. Arnold found that several farmers who had been burned out had "banded together," and his former client asked him to represent them if they had a case. As he began investigating along the Great Northern line in the Brookston area, Arnold found more farmers who had evidence that the origin of the fires could be traced to the railroads. They wanted to go to court to recover their losses if they were entitled to do so. N. B. Arnold and his brother, John B., took the cases and began initiating suits in January 1919. Their firm, Arnold & Arnold of Duluth, became a major participant in the suits. The first case, which went to trial in May, dealt with the suit of Carl Nordin, whose property was in the Alborn district on the northern perimeter of the fire, near the Missabe tracks. Nordin's farm was just a mile from the alleged origin of the fire. The trial lasted about a week, and the railroad won the case. The railroad also won a second case, *Sivert Holten v. Duluth, Missabe & Northern Railway Company*, in the same district. A third case started against the Missabe in the Alborn district involved the destruction of the property of G. A. Ringquist, who lived about three miles from the source of the fire. The trial went on for two weeks, but in this instance the jury disagreed. A new trial was ordered for September, and that too resulted in a disagreement: the jury at the second trial stood ten to two in favor of the plaintiff.[8]

Despite the lack of success in the first several court cases, increasing numbers of fire sufferers began to initiate suits to recover damages for the loss of property. Within the next several years a staggering 15,003 cases were brought against the various railroads in the region and against the Railroad Administration. This extraordinarily large number of cases convinced the officials of the administration that they were being made the victims of unscrupulous northern Minnesota lawyers who had traveled through the burned-over country drumming up business. The officials drew particular attention to the fact that local lawyers had taken most of these cases on a contingent-fee basis.[9]

This meant that the lawyer was paid for representing the client with an agreed percentage of the amount of damages awarded if the suit was won. The practice was contrary to the English common-law tradition and not permitted in some American states. Conditions in the fire district were desperate, however, when these cases were launched. Generally, in those areas in which the fires burned, the destruction was complete. Fire sufferers lost everything — their homes and all of their possessions. Farmers lost their harvested crops and their livestock; town dwellers lost their jobs or businesses, either permanently or temporarily. In short, the economy of the fire district was crippled, and much of the population was either on relief or close to it. Paying the lawyers on a contingent-fee basis, rather than in cash before the trials, was a necessity — as a group, the fire victims had no cash.

The cases involved an enormous amount of legal preparation. The lawyers hired timber cruisers from 1919 to 1921 to inspect the areas burned and to estimate the value of the timber and land destroyed by the fires. At one time the paperwork involved in compiling evidence, filing suits, and corresponding with litigants required the assistance of twenty-three clerks and stenographers in Cloquet and fifteen in Duluth. N. B. Arnold reported that he had spent $30,000 on expenses before he was in a position to recover any payment, even for cases that he already had won. The Northern Minnesota Fire Sufferers Association, which eventually numbered some seven thousand members, was created in 1919. The organization served as a clearinghouse and lobby group and it raised money to pay plaintiffs' legal fees before settlement. The Railroad Administration officials never seemed to take into account the extraordinary conditions that prevailed in the burned-over district or the vast number of people who had lost property through these fires.[10]

The first case a fire sufferer won in the courts was *Jacob Anderson v. Minneapolis, St. Paul & Sault Ste. Marie Railway Company and Others.* This case involved the loss of property in the area west of Moose Lake as a result of fires along the Soo Line tracks. The trial opened in Duluth on November 19, 1919, and finished on December 29, the longest of the early suits. The plaintiff argued that Jacob Anderson's barn had been destroyed by a fire started by the Soo Line in early August, a fire that the railroad had been unable to put out during August and September and that flared up on October 12 to destroy the property. The railroad did not deny the existence of the fire started by its locomotive in August. But the railroad argued that the plaintiff's property was destroyed in part by other fires of unknown origins, which joined with the railroad fire, and that these independent fires would have destroyed Anderson's barn whether there had been a railroad fire or not. Anderson's lawyers, cross-examining the defense witnesses, were able to show, over the objections of the defense attorneys, that the so-called fires of unknown origins had also been started by the Soo Line farther up the tracks. The railroad lawyers relied, as had lawyers in the earlier cases, on the precedent of *Cook v. Minneapolis, St. Paul & Sault Ste. Marie Railway Company.* The Wisconsin courts in the *Cook* case had reasoned that if a fire of known origins merged with a fire of unknown origins, the liability for the new combined fire could not be traced to those responsible for the known fire. The *Cook* case had been a powerful ally for the railroads in early suits.[11]

Unquestionably, an important element in the verdict in the *Anderson* case was Judge Herbert A. Dancer's charge to the jury. Judge Dancer told the jury that the defendant might be held liable for damages even if the fires that destroyed the plaintiff's property had several origins, only one of which could be traced to the defendant's railway. "If you find," Judge Dancer said, "that other fire or fires not set by one of the defendant's engines mingled with one that was set by one of the defendant's engines, there may be difficulty in determining whether you should find that the fire set by the engine was a material or substantial element in causing plaintiff's damage. If it was . . . the defendant is liable." These instructions meant the plaintiff had to show only that the railroad fire constituted a "substantial element" in causing the damage, rather than that it was the exclusive source of the damage, as the *Cook* precedent demanded.[12]

This charge from the judge opened the door to other verdicts in favor of the fire sufferers. When the *Anderson* case went to the Minnesota Supreme Court, Judge Dancer's instructions to the jury, as well as the verdict for the plaintiff, were affirmed. In so doing the court held, "If the fire started by the railroad united with a fire or fires of other or unknown origin, it was a question of fact for a jury to determine whether or not the fire started by the railroad was a substantial element in creating the damage, and if so, the railroad was liable for the entire loss." The Supreme Court decision on September 17, 1920, also affirmed the points that neither unusual weather conditions, such as drought or violent winds, nor an independent concurrent fire that might be termed an act of God, nor the combination of other fires with the defendant's fire, could "relieve the railroad company from liability." The *Anderson* case was a major legal victory for the fire sufferers.[13]

The next important case was *Hans J. Borsheim v. Great Northern Railway Company*. Borsheim owned property about a mile and a quarter south and east of Milepost 67 along the Great Northern tracks west of Brookston. It was shown at the trial that a fire had been started by a Great Northern engine along the tracks near Milepost 67 on October 10, 1918. Railway crews attempted to put the fire out, but it smoldered on during the next day and then flared up on October 12. At that time it joined with other fires in the area and swept over Borsheim's property. As in the *Anderson* case the railroad was held liable under Minnesota law for damages caused by a fire that had several sources, only one of which was traceable to the fire started by the Great Northern. The *Borsheim* case was also appealed to the Minnesota Supreme Court, which, citing the *Anderson* case, affirmed the lower court's decision on June 3, 1921. On a reargument of this case, as with a second appeal on the *Anderson* case, the defendant railroad company was dismissed and the director general of the Railroad Administration, as the agent of the president of the United States, was substituted.[14]

Perhaps as a result of the first defeat in the courts, but also in response to the Northern Minnesota Fire Sufferers Association, Max A. Thelen, the director of the legal division of the Railroad Administration, prepared two long memoranda for Walker D. Hines, the director general, on January 3 and 7, 1920. Even before the *Anderson* case was started, George Schlecht, the president of the association, had written to Hines, urging that the administration, in view of the number of cases, undertake an "independent and neutral investigation of the responsibility for these fires and the losses sustained with a view of eliminating as much delay and litigation as possible, thereby assuring earlier relief to the sufferers." The association also complained that the railroads seemed to have embarked on a policy of "harassing" the people and undertaking "defensive litigation carried on for the sole purpose of discouraging the now too-much discouraged fire sufferers." Congressman William L. Carss of Proctor, Minnesota, had joined with the fire sufferers in early December 1919 in urging that the Railroad Administration set up some kind of an "investigation" commission, with the view that such a body would be empowered to arbitrate and settle claims, the alternative being to channel every claim through the courts in the form of a suit.[15]

Of course, by early 1920 the administration, together with several of the railroads most vulnerable to suits, had conducted investigations in the burned-over district, but with the purpose of collecting evidence that could be used in court to deny the claims of the fire sufferers. The administration's legal division, which saw the fire sufferers association as simply the tool of the unscrupulous Minnesota lawyers, therefore recommended that no such investigation commission be created. In providing background information to the director general, these reports described the 1918 fires and the destruction they wrought and then focused on the causes of the fires. To explain the causes, the legal division relied heavily on State Forester Cox's report of November 1, 1918, and the state Forest Fire Investigation Commission's report of November 26, 1918. Cox had attributed the fires to a multitude of general causes; the commission had taken a similar view, indicating specific railroad responsibility only in the case of the Great Northern west of Brookston and the Soo Line west of Moose Lake. In these circumstances, Thelen recommended that the Railroad Administration "pay promptly the entire loss in those cases in which [railroad] investigation shows that the loss was due to railroad operations." He thought that the director should make a clear public statement of the administration's intention to accept responsibility where blame was demonstrated and to fight in the courts those cases where blame was in doubt.[16]

These recommendations provoked a considerable discussion among members of the Railroad Administration. Some members felt that in cases where railroad investigation showed railroad responsibility prompt payment should be made. As Director General Hines wrote to the general counsel of the administration, "I do not see how we can justify a refusal to pay a claim when our own investigation shows clearly that the Director General of Railroads is liable therefore."[17] But on the other hand, there was also the view of members of the administration's legal division that the "local legal representatives of the R. R. Administration are declining settlement of any claims, on the ground that settlement will lead jurors to assume the R. R. Administration has assumed responsibility for all of them."[18] These two positions summarized the dilemma of the administration, and in the end this dilemma inhibited any action. LaRue Brown, the general counsel, reported on February 5, 1920, that the lawyers of the Great Northern had as a matter of policy settled claims where liability was clear and that the Northern Pacific had made one settlement to date. Neither the Soo Line nor the Duluth, Missabe and Northern had made any settlements. Whatever the intentions of Hines or Thelen, the actual settlements were so small in number, compared to the volume of suits involved, that the public impression remained that the Railroad Administration would fight every case in the courts.[19]

All of the cases tried thus far had represented the claims of farmers in various outlying parts of the burned-over district. Some thirty-six towns or villages, however, had been destroyed by the fire; the largest was Cloquet, with a population of more than eight thousand. Damage claims for the destruction of Cloquet were enormous (between $15 million and $25 million). Therefore, a great deal rested on the outcome of what became labeled the "Cloquet case" — *A. R. Peterson v. Walker D. Hines as Agent of the President under the Transportation Act.* In this suit, A. R. Peterson, a Cloquet homeowner, claimed the fire that destroyed the city and his property had been started by a Great Northern locomotive passing Milepost 62, four miles west of Brookston, on October 10, 1918. This fire first ignited some four hundred carloads of ties, posts, poles, and other forest products stacked in rows at a siding along the tracks. The efforts of the railroad crews to extinguish this fire were ineffective, with the result that winds on the morning of October 12 fanned the flames into an intense blaze, which spread and grew with alarming speed.

The plaintiff's lawyers claimed that this fire burned across the countryside in an easterly and southerly curving direction, following to some extent the St. Louis River valley, until on that evening the fire entered what was called Bottle Alley in the Northern Lumber Company yard at the northwest end of Cloquet, and subsequently destroyed the city. In its defense the Railroad Administration made a major effort. Claiming that because there were some four thousand suits in Carlton County an unprejudiced jury could not be found there, the railroads asked for a change of venue to Duluth. Hibbing, in western St. Louis County, was ultimately agreed upon as the site for an impartial trial. The railroads did not deny that a major fire had developed at Milepost 62, but argued that because the wind on October 12 was essentially out of the west, with only a possible variation south by twenty degrees, this fire would have burned well to the north and could not have reached Cloquet. The fire that destroyed the city, the defendant's lawyers argued, started west of Cloquet in the vicinity of Cress Lakes and burned more or less in a straight line into the city. The trial opened in February 1920 and ran for about two weeks, but it resulted in a hung jury. A second trial was convened almost immediately, but this new jury was also unable to agree upon a verdict.[20]

Courthouse (center) in Hibbing, chosen as an impartial site for the trial of the Peterson v. Hines *case*

Even before the second trial ended, N. B. Arnold, as one of Peterson's lawyers, talked with the leading attorney for the Railroad Administration, Albert Baldwin of the Duluth firm of Baldwin Baldwin Holmes & Mayall. Arnold asked Baldwin about arranging to waive the right to trial by jury and to have the case decided by a judge. Upon consideration, the administration agreed, but under the conditions that there be a panel of five judges from the district court, that the court sit in Duluth, and that all 278 of the Cloquet cases that had been started and for which summonses had been served be grouped together (there was a total of between 2,600 and 2,700 such cases). Other provisions of the stipulations, signed by the lawyers of all parties on April 8, 1920, pertained to fees of the plaintiff's attorneys (a matter of constant preoccupation to the administration), specifying that they be set by the court; the protection of the Railroad Administration from subsequent suits by insurance companies; and questions concerning the admission of evidence. The critical passage in the stipulations, however, read as follows:

> That if it shall be determined upon the trial of said actions that plaintiffs have established defendant's liability for the cause of damage, in such event the questions of title to property and the extent of damages to individual plaintiffs shall be determined by one or more, as the Court may direct, or said Judges.

This meant that if the Railroad Administration lost the *Peterson* case the same court would subsequently establish the damages to be paid. The fate of all the 278 Cloquet cases, and likely all the other cases that had not yet been started, hinged on this trial. The administration felt that it was in a strong position. At this time there had been two trials with verdicts for the defendants, two with verdicts for the plaintiffs (although these two were on appeal before the Minnesota Supreme Court), and four trials with hung juries.[21]

The third trial of the Cloquet case was convened on May 9, 1920, and ran until July 9, during which time the five judges heard all of the testimony and oral arguments and received written briefs from both sides. The judges then considered this evidence for about two months. On September 11, four of the five judges of the court found that the Great Northern fire was the cause of the destruction of Cloquet. In the findings, Judge William A. Cant held that the railroad had allowed large quantities of combustible material to accumulate along its tracks and sidings, that it had insufficient patrolmen, that it had allowed one of its locomotives to start a fire, and "that the defendant negligently failed to extinguish and prevent the spread of the fire so communicated to such material at said Mile post 62, and negligently failed to provide sufficient men for that purpose." In the memorandum attached to the findings, Judge Cant concluded decisively,

> We find no difficulty in assigning the origin of the fire at Mile Post 62 to the defendant railway company and in tracing it in a crescent-like course to sections 4 and 5, 49–17. The testimony of practically all the settlers, the lay of the brush, the northeasterly lines of the unburned areas west of the St. Louis river, and the unburned country east of the river, all confirm this conclusion. We believe the St. Louis river and the fire itself affected the direction of the wind that afternoon and evening.

In short, the city had been burned by the Great Northern fire that began at Milepost 62 and traveled southeast, being influenced by the course of the St. Louis River, and then entered Cloquet through "Bottle Alley and the Upper Planer district."[22]

The Railroad Administration appealed the case to the Minnesota Supreme Court. A. R. Peterson, whose case had led the suit, had left Cloquet to work in Michigan and was by this time effectively out of reach. As a consequence the case that actually went to the supreme court was one of the others originally grouped with Peterson — *Philip Hall v. James C. Davis as Agent of the President under the Transportation Act*. Once again, the administration felt that it had so strong a case that the appeals court was certain to find in its favor. James C. Davis, the general counsel, wrote to one of the railroad lawyers in Duluth on December 7, 1920, before the supreme court had heard the case,

> I have always understood that the administration had as good a defense in the Cloquet cases as would probably arise on most of the claims, and have believed that the liability of the Railroad Administration should be litigated in this particular controversy, upon appeal, to final judgment in the Supreme Court, in order that we may have in this case definite rules of liability determined.[23]

This seems to indicate that Davis was prepared to accept the decision of the Minnesota Supreme Court on the issue of whether the Railroad Administration could be held liable for the destruction caused by the fire that started at Milepost 62. Nevertheless, two days later Davis wrote to E. B. Merritt, the assistant commissioner of the OIA, responding to an inquiry concerning the possible payment of damage claims,

> You are misinformed as to the fact that the Government has agreed to abide by the decision of the five Judges in what is known as the Cloquet case. The truth of it is, the Railroad Administration is not, as yet, prepared to admit liability for this great conflagration, which was occasioned by an unusual hurricane and a combination of a great many fires, some of them set out by irresponsible persons, and of unknown origin, and possibly some fires set out by the railroads. These matters are still being considered by the Courts, and, until there is a final determination, the attitude of the Railroad Administration will not be definitely decided upon.[24]

Thus, despite the stipulations signed by the Railroad Administration's lawyers on April 8, 1920, and the findings of the district court on September 11, and even the possible decision of the Minnesota Supreme Court, Davis was not prepared to commit himself to a decision that went against the government.

*Burned locomotives and repair equipment in ruins of the Duluth and
Northeastern Railroad roundhouse, Cloquet, October 1918 (Olson)*

After examining the evidence, the supreme court handed down a
decision on July 22, 1921, affirming the lower court. Justice Andrew
Holt took special note of the "commendable candor" of the defendant's
"able counsel" in making a concession not to challenge the trial court's
finding that the Great Northern was responsible for the fire at Milepost
62. This allowed the supreme court to focus on whether that fire or the
fires from farther west entered Cloquet first and thus were responsible
for its destruction. Justice Holt stated in the decision, "The nature and
direction of the wind as the fire swept on, and the testimony of witnesses in the path of the most northerly as in the ones to the south
thereof, seem to establish with reasonable certainty that the north fire,
the one from mile post 62, came to the city first." The supreme court
took account of the difficulty of fully consistent evidence concerning so
unpredictable a subject as a forest fire and noted the dissent of one of
the fire-trial judges, but concluded, "We think the findings made by
the court are amply sustained."[25]

CHAPTER EIGHT

The Railroad
Administration Settlement

*I said, "Gentlemen, this is the best I can do; take it
or leave it."*
James C. Davis, *Director General
United States Railroad Administration*

It was a cheap settlement for the Government.
Judge Herbert A. Dancer,
Eleventh Judicial District

The Minnesota Supreme Court decision on the Cloquet case on July
22, 1921, was a smashing legal victory for the Cloquet fire claimants.
Just as the *Anderson* case had established the legal precedent that a
railroad could be held liable even if fires other than those of railroad
origin merged with a railroad fire to destroy a plaintiff's property, so
the Cloquet case established a practical procedure for trying numerous identical cases at once before a panel of judges instead of a jury.
This seemed to promise a much more expeditious processing of the fire
claims, and a similar "Moose Lake case," involving 850 suits, was already underway. This decision also signaled to the Railroad Administration that the several railroads operating under its jurisdiction in
northern Minnesota in 1918 were seen to be responsible for the fires
both by juries of common men and by judges on the district court and
the state supreme court. The courts and the plaintiffs hoped that this
signal to the administration would lead the government to accept
general responsibility and devise a practical, efficient, and fair means
of adjudicating claims and awarding settlements. Events took a sur-

prising turn, however, and although the results were a "settlement," the issue of the fire sufferers' claims was far from settled.

The burden of all of this litigation in the courts in northern Minnesota had been substantial. The few cases that had been tried had taken a long time in the trial courts, and all the cases won by the plaintiffs had been appealed to the supreme court and still were not settled. Members of the court estimated that it would take at least ten years to try singly all of the backlog of cases, and then only if no other ordinary cases were brought to trial. In the autumn of 1920, Judge William Cant, the senior judge of Minnesota's Eleventh Judicial District, began to question whether the court system could cope with this unusual situation. In early January 1921, Judge Cant, on behalf of the five judges in the Cloquet case, and as a result of correspondence with Minnesota Senator Knute Nelson and conversations with Railroad Administration officials, drafted a letter to William D. Mitchell of St. Paul, the administration's regional counsel. After summarizing the fire-case situation, the letter said flatly, "It is quite apparent that in the ordinary course of business the court cannot possibly deal with this flood of claims." The judges proposed that Congress, in cooperation with the Railroad Administration, "provide for a commission, or possibly a few groups of commissioners, who shall take this matter in hand and speedily determine who is entitled to recover and how much." Although this proposal was better argued and more fully thought out, it was essentially what the Northern Minnesota Fire Sufferers Association had suggested in 1919.[1]

Through one of the lawyers, Judge Cant's letter also reached Jacob A. O. Preus, who had succeeded Burnquist as governor in January 1921. Preus indicated his willingness to assist at both the state and federal level. Judge Cant then reiterated the proposal that a commission be created to dispose of the claims against the Railroad Administration. He agreed with the governor that the Minnesota senators be involved, but suggested that the drafting for legislation to establish a federal commission be done by the lawyers for the two parties. He further noted that "the stopping place with all negotiations, however, has been with the Railroad Administration at Washington."[2] In fact, the administration was interested in sounding out opinion in Min-

James C. Davis

nesota, and the director general told E. C. Lindley, vice president and general counsel of the Great Northern, to "get all of the information and 'atmosphere' you can re the Minnesota cases so that you may give me the benefit of your suggestions from time to time."[3]

The Railroad Administration also sent its own lawyers out to seek advice, although it was the opinion of the legal officers of the Northern Pacific that the administration would do nothing until Warren Harding, the newly elected Republican president, was inaugurated and the views of his government made known. Shortly after the inauguration, the Minnesota legislature passed a resolution asking Congress, in view of the prolonged and expensive litigation, to "take such steps as may be deemed best and most expeditious for promptly disposing of said large number of pending cases." This resolution was sent to Congress and to the president, who referred it to the administration.[4]

In late March 1921, James Davis, the former general counsel, was appointed director general of the Railroad Administration. Davis had earlier conferred with Governor Preus, who shortly after Davis's promotion sent both congratulations and a copy of a letter from Judge Cant. The governor wrote to Davis, "I sincerely hope that you will take the matter up and dispose of it along the lines which I felt sure you were inclined to at the time I called on you in Washington and which are very like the suggestions submitted by Judge Cant."[5]

Whatever impression Governor Preus had of Davis's support for Judge Cant's proposal for a commission to settle the claims would seem to have been mistaken. Four months earlier, on December 7, 1920, Davis had indicated to Albert Baldwin that he did not think the creation of a commission to make decisions on legal liability was necessary or advisable, but that the Railroad Administration and its lawyers could deal with those matters. Governor Preus, the courts, and the fire victims looked upon the appointment of Davis as a sign that the new government in Washington intended to move on the fire claims matter. Davis, however, replied to Preus, "I have felt that, before the administration would be justified in considering a liability that aggregates such a vast sum, perhaps another case should be submitted to the Supreme Court of Minnesota, which would more particularly set out some of the questions of law which it seems to me are in doubt." Thus, Davis, too, intended to adopt a cautious wait-and-see attitude, in response to which Preus felt bound to "lie low" for the time being.[6]

When the Minnesota Supreme Court handed down its decision on the Cloquet case on July 23, 1921, affirming the findings of the panel of judges in the lower district court, Preus wrote the same day urging that Davis now act "to establish some machinery by which settlements might be arrived at between the fire sufferers of the Cloquet forest fires and the railroads." He also mentioned that the Minnesota legislature had authorized the appointment of five new judges to expedite the fire cases if the Railroad Administration did not move to settle the matter.[7] Years later this statement would be made to sound like a threat, but for the moment Davis replied to the governor that he was giving the situation "very careful consideration" and that he had a proposition that he hoped he could make public in the near future and that he hoped would meet with the governor's approval. A week later, on July 29, Davis and Minnesota Senator Frank B. Kellogg, himself a distinguished lawyer who before entering the senate had represented both the Great Northern and the Missabe lines, met with President Harding to discuss the matter. Davis wrote an aide-mémoire about the meeting, in which he recorded, "We discussed the matter at some length and the President authorized me to take the necessary steps to adjust these cases. There were no special limitations or conditions. I told him I thought the adjustment ought to be made for about $15,000,000.00."[8] Davis's own account would seem to indicate that he had been given a free hand both on the procedure for making the settlement and on the total figure of federal money to be paid out.

Roughly two weeks later Davis again wrote to Governor Preus to say that he had talked to the president, and although Davis did not outline any specific plan of settlement, he did say that "it has been decided that . . . the Federal Administration will adjust these claims if same can be done on somewhat of a fair basis." Furthermore, he went on to say that in his view the fires were an "Act of God" and that "I doubt if a legal liability was ever attempted to be established under circumstances similar to those presented in these forest fire cases." This was a view similar to what Davis had written to the Office of Indian Affairs in December 1920, and it was a view that Davis held throughout the subsequent years of the controversy. Nevertheless, the Railroad Administration would settle (although the terms were not described), despite Davis's conviction that the railroads were blameless, no matter what the Minnesota courts held. Davis also asked for the support of the governor and other state officials in winning agreement for the yet unarticulated plan of settlement.[9]

The "fair basis" of adjustment that was announced on August 29, 1921, two and a half weeks after Davis's letter to Governor Preus, was not the creation of an independent commission to arbitrate and make awards on individual claims. A blanket settlement was proposed for the Cloquet fire sufferers: a payment of 50 percent of the amount claimed for the 278 litigated cases and 40 percent of the amount claimed for the remaining 2,600 Cloquet cases as yet untried. It was a proposition that stunned the Cloquet claimants.[10]

How these procedures were decided on or how the formula of 50 percent and 40 percent of the claimed amounts was derived (especially when the 278 claimants who won their cases were, according to the trial stipulations, entitled to 100 percent of the judgment settled by the court) has never been made altogether clear. Years later, at the congressional hearings on full compensation for the fire sufferers, Donald S. Holmes, a senior partner in the Duluth firm of Baldwin

Baldwin Holmes & Mayall, which represented the Great Northern and Missabe lines, said that the first suggestion of an out-of-court settlement came from Minnesota. On August 6, 1921, the law firm of Abbott MacPherrann Gilbert & Doan, representing a number of Cloquet industries and their employees, after talks with Albert Baldwin, proposed a settlement of 60 percent of the agreed-upon value of property damages claimed in Cloquet. Holmes also produced at the hearings a copy of a memorandum submitted by Senator Kellogg that, while undated, was presumed to have been written in early August. The Kellogg proposal, which dealt with the whole fire area, presumed that the Railroad Administration would pay 100 percent of the specific judgment issued by the court for the *Peterson* and *Hall* cases and suggested that the administration pay 75 percent of the claims in such key regions as the Cloquet-Brookston-Paupores area, the Alborn-Zim area, and the Moose Lake area and pay 50 to 40 percent of all the other claims. Presumably it was out of these two propositions that the administration put forward the 50- and 40-percent formula.[11]

On December 7, 1920, Davis had indicated to Albert Baldwin that he was thinking about a settlement to follow the eventual Supreme Court decision. He suggested,

> After definite rules as to liability have been determined by the court, and it is concluded that a general adjustment should be made on behalf of the administration, I believe that fairer and more economical settlements can be made, based, of course, on legal liability, by creating some special organization either for each of the three roads principally interested or one that might take up the adjustment of all claims.

Davis dropped the idea of a "special organization" or commission, but the notion of working out "fairer and more economical settlements" seems to have become the principle guiding his handling of the matter following the Minnesota Supreme Court's decision — but "fairer and more economical settlements" than what, and for whom? The inference to be drawn from his later behavior is that the settlements would be "fairer and more economical" for the Railroad Administration than were the judgments ordered by the district court.[12]

The protests by the Cloquet claimants were so great that, at the urging of Senator Kellogg, the administration in a letter to Albert Baldwin on September 22, revised its offer to 50 percent of all the Clo-

Frank B. Kellogg

quiet claims, whether already litigated, as in the Cloquet case, or yet
to come before the courts. (Indeed, in his original August 29 letter,
Davis had admitted, "The city of Cloquet must in reasonable fairness
be considered as a unit.") Davis insisted, however, that all 278 of those
whose cases had been merged with the *Peterson* and *Hall* cases accept
the 50 percent settlement and not continue legal attempts to recover
100 percent of their claims. Other provisions were that insurance company claims and other claims over $25,000 (which was to say, primar-
ily the industries), were to be paid at 40 percent of their claims; the
plaintiffs' lawyers were to be paid a fee set by the courts, notwithstanding any previous contract for payment; court-established interest and costs were to be omitted; and all who settled would waive
the right of further claims or litigation in the matter. Recounting the
circumstances years later, Davis himself described his position: "I said
'Gentlemen, this is the best I can do; take it or leave it.' If they preferred to take 50 per cent in cash, I did not deprive them of any legal
right. They had their choice. If that is coercion, there was
coercion."[13]

Thus, A. R. Peterson, who on August 13 was awarded $24,745.33
and who on August 19 saw a judgment entered against James Davis

for $30,271.91 (the award plus 6 percent interest and costs), ultimately had to agree to a settlement of $11,972.67 on November 14, 1921. (Four thousand dollars paid on his insurance claim was subtracted from the total award; 50 percent of the remainder, or $10,372.67, became the base of his settlement; 40 percent of the insurance paid, or $1,600, was added, making a total settlement of $11,972.67.) Similarly, Philip Hall, who was awarded $7,400.00 plus interest and costs by the court and received a judgment against Davis for $8,679.14 on August 11, accepted $3,470.00 on November 15.[14]

This then was the settlement reluctantly agreed to by the people of Cloquet. It was a bitter and disillusioning experience, which seemed to reveal the iron fist of government exercised against the essentially defenseless citizenry. The Cloquet case had, after all, been fought through three trials; the third of these combined 278 cases, which were tried by a bank of five judges under stipulations that had been signed by all parties. These stipulations said that if the trial decided that the plantiffs had established the defendant's liability, then the questions of property title and the damages to be paid would be determined by these judges. When the court gave a verdict for the fire sufferers, the Railroad Administration appealed to the Minnesota Supreme Court and lost its appeal. After judgments were made by the district court for dollar amounts to be paid by the administration, no move was made to pay them, although the trial stipulations formed an agreement to pay if the administration was found liable. Instead the administration came forward with the "take it or leave it" settlement offer of 50 percent.[15]

§

The Cloquet settlement set the pattern for a resolution of the vast number of claims in other areas of the burned district. Trials for damage claims in other areas were in various stages of progress or completion when the Cloquet settlement was worked out. After two hung juries, the third *Ringquist* trial against the Missabe railroad in the Alborn district had been won on February 13, 1920. The *Borsheim* case against the Great Northern west of Milepost 62 was affirmed by the Minnesota Supreme Court on June 3, 1921. The Moose Lake case, in which 850 cases were grouped in one trial, was heard by five judges sitting *en banc*. This trial went on for more than seven months before

Home Guard camp amid ruins, Moose Lake, October 1918 (Irish)

Judge William Cant dismissed the case when the Railroad Administration made offers of settlement for the Moose Lake area close to the Soo Line tracks. The administration also made a settlement offer for the Brookston, Fond du Lac reservation, and Alborn regions north and west of Cloquet along the Great Northern, the Missabe, and the Duluth, Winnipeg and Pacific tracks. In those regions the administration created two categories of payment — 50 and 40 percent of damages claimed. In burned-over areas where fire sufferers had successfully sued the administration in the courts and where damage from railroad fires was reasonably clear, the government proposed to settle for 50 percent of the claim. In all other areas, where suits had been started but not yet brought to trial and where the Railroad Administration held that the damages from railroad fires were more arguable, the administration offered to settle at a maximum of 40 percent of the property loss.[16]

The formula for calculating the amount to be paid, taking into account any earlier insurance payments, was the same as in the Cloquet settlement, as were many of the conditions and exceptions. As in Cloquet, claimants made protests, which Davis acknowledged, blaming them on the local lawyers. Once again at the urging of Senator Kellogg, the Railroad Administration made some minor adjustments after a meeting in Washington between Davis and thirteen lawyers and representatives of the claimants. In the end, the settlement was largely, although reluctantly, accepted.[17]

Just as these claims appeared to be resolved in the western and southern sectors of the fire district, new suits were launched to claim

damages from the railroads for the fires that burned along the outskirts of Duluth right down to the eastern edge of the city and to Lake
Superior. Several cases went to trial, the most notable being *Harry E.
McCool and Another v. James C. Davis*. McCool claimed that the fire
that started at Milepost 62 west of Brookston had been driven twenty-
eight miles east by the wind and had destroyed his property near the
Woodland road. The jury returned a verdict in favor of McCool, and
the Railroad Administration appealed to the Minnesota Supreme
Court. On February 8, 1924, in a decision with two justices dissenting, the supreme court ordered a new trial. The second trial also
ended with a verdict for the plaintiff, and again the administration
appealed. This time the supreme court, on March 13, 1925, in another
decision with two dissenting opinions, affirmed the lower court. On
March 28, Davis made an offer of settlement for the cases pending in
the region north of Duluth on the eastern perimeter of the fire, with
a maximum payment of 50 and 40 percent in two zones.[18]

Still another problem arose with a series of cases involving Ojibway from the Fond du Lac reservation. In the aftermath of the fires,
lawyers from Cloquet and Duluth hired timber cruisers to examine
the burned-over area between Milepost 62 and Cloquet, with a view
to establishing evidence of wind direction during the fires and of property damage caused by fire. Almost all of the intervening territory fell
within the Fond du Lac boundaries, so the lawyers acquired detailed
information about the losses of people on the reservation. When reservation Ojibway talked with George Cross, the agency superintendent, about damage claims, he advised them to secure legal counsel,
who because of the timber cruisers' survey were well placed to represent the Indians. Not all the Ojibway on the reservation, however,
owned their land through patents in fee (Congress had made provision with the Dawes Act of 1887 for Indians to own individual allotments of land on reservations). A large number of Ojibway still held
their land in allotments under trust patents created by the La Pointe
Treaty of 1854 (which meant that actual title to the land resided with
the federal government, although the person who held the allotment
enjoyed possession of the land).[19]

Of all of the Ojibway who sued for damages, 130 did not have actual ownership of their land. The problem was recognized as early as

October 12, 1920, when J. A. Fesenbeck, one of the Cloquet lawyers, wrote to Cross, then superintendent of the Red Lake Indian Reservation in northwestern Minnesota. Fesenbeck inquired about whether Indians without title could sue in the courts for damages to the land they possessed. The question was eventually referred to the OIA in Washington, which concluded that in the case of Indians without title, only the government could sue on their behalf. By this time all of the Ojibway without land titles had already launched suits, but new suits on their behalf were started by the Consolidated Chippewa Agency, an OIA office in Minnesota that had charge of some of the state's smaller Ojibway bands, including the Fond du Lac band.

In 1922 the OIA hired timber cruisers to examine the country that had been burned over four years earlier. In several instances these cruisers estimated the value of the destroyed timber and property at much less than had the cruisers hired by the lawyers. In the case of Joseph LaVeirge, for example, the Duluth law firm of Arnold & Arnold had filed a suit claiming $4,000 worth of damages, whereas the agency claimed damages of less than $400. Because the Railroad Administration would agree to pay only 40 or 50 percent of the claim, the actual settlement to LaVeirge would be between $140 and $150. The Ojibway stood to get much more compensation if the suit represented by the lawyers was the basis of the administration settlement, and the lawyers would earn a fee as a percentage of their Indian clients' settlements, just as they did with white clients. But when the lawyer-represented cases came up for a hearing, the United States district attorney intervened and was successful in having the cases dismissed by the district court. Joseph LaVeirge appealed to the Minnesota Supreme Court with the argument that any Indian should be free to come before the courts to obtain compensation for damages. The supreme court, however, accepted the view that the property destroyed, specifically the timber, was part of the real estate held in trust by the government for the Indians and was not their property. Indians holding land under trust patents, therefore, had to accept representation by the government, and the lawyers were left to accept an offer of 10 percent of the settlement as partial compensation for their services. The decision on the *LaVeirge* case was not handed down until January 15, 1926, which held up the government payment for a number of Indians until long after the white fire claimants had received their settlements.[20]

Was the Railroad Administration's settlement a good one? In the end, the administration was able to discharge its obligation to the fire sufferers with payments of $12,701,664.67. This figure was well below the figure of $15,000,000.00 that Davis had given to President Harding in July 1921, and it would have been lower still had not the *McCool* case forced the administration to make a settlement in 1925 in the area north of Duluth, where it had previously refused to consider any responsibility. The Minnesota district court had set the total amount of damages at $29,743,416.25, well below the $73,000,000.00 claimed by the plaintiffs. Even then, the large amount of $17,041,752.58 was left unpaid: the Railroad Administration paid 42.7 percent of the amount determined by the courts. Furthermore, the administration held signed waivers from each of the claimants who had settled, which protected it from further suits for recovery. Thus, although the administration had repeatedly lost in the Minnesota courts, as a federal government agency it refused to be forced to comply with the rulings and judgments of the Minnesota courts, though this may have been in violation of the federal legislation creating the Railroad Administration.[21]

To James Davis, who never, either in public or in private, admitted any railroad liability, it was generous in the extreme. To Davis, the people of northern Minnesota never had any question that the fires had been simply an act of God until the local lawyers convinced them (perhaps "duped" is the word Davis would have used) that their losses could be made good through suits against the administration. Throughout the legal battle, and even at the congressional hearings a decade later, Davis belabored the point that the lawyers would be the principal beneficiaries in any successful suit or settlement, and he continued to discredit the local lawyers long after they had agreed to have their fees set by the court. The persistent verdicts for the fire sufferers and against the railroads in the district courts and the state supreme court remained a puzzle to Davis, a sleight-of-hand trick by which legal forms could be used to hold a railroad responsible for an act of God. It was contrary to Davis's logic. To Donald Holmes, one of the railroad attorneys from Duluth, the Railroad Administration settlement was not as unfair as the fire sufferers believed. To the administration, the Minnesota legislature's 1921 bill authorizing the governor to appoint five additional judges for the district courts in northern Minnesota was unfair. These new judges, Holmes felt, were to be put on the bench in order to run the cases through the district courts, where the administration was by 1921 losing case after case. The settlement was the government's only protection from losing more cases. [22]

To the fire sufferers, the settlement was a betrayal. Though many people spoke out against the settlement, few were as knowledgeable, reasoned, or persuasive as Judge Herbert Dancer, when he later testified at the congressional hearings in 1930. Dancer occupied a unique position, which enabled him to see many sides of the issue. He had been a railroad lawyer and a partner in Baldwin Baldwin & Dancer (the firm representing the Great Northern and the Railroad Administration in the trials) before going on the bench in 1912, and he joined the firm of Arnold & Arnold (the firm representing the largest number of fire sufferers) when he retired from the bench in 1925. Judge Dancer presided at three of the fire cases during the trials — including the *Anderson* case and the first *McCool* case — and he was one of the panel of five judges that heard the Cloquet case and the Moose Lake case. [23]

Judge Dancer's testimony made several major points. First, the exigencies of the war, as a result of national priorities, so depleted the manpower of the railroads that they were unable to comply with state regulations for fire prevention. Nonetheless, Minnesota state law was clear about the railroads' responsibility for damage caused by fires originating from railroad sources, as Dancer's instructions to the jury in the *Anderson* case indicated. Second, the agreements embodied in the stipulations of the Cloquet case committed the Railroad Administration to pay the damages awarded by the judgments if it lost the case. The administration, like any other litigant who entered the state courts, could not legally defy the district court and supreme court simply because in the opinion of the director general the railroads were not liable. And finally, Judge Dancer thought, the claimants eventually settled under duress — duress because they could not hold out indefinitely; duress in the Cloquet case because all 278 who won had to settle for 50 percent in order for their neighbors to get 50 percent also;

Herbert A. Dancer, 1930

duress for Jacob Anderson, A. R. Peterson, Philip Hall, and Hans Borsheim, who had won their cases but had not been paid, because they
wanted to get something; and duress for all the others who were told
they could sue individually, because they saw no realistic hope of
recovery even if they were successful in the courts. When asked if he
thought the settlement was a fair one, all these considerations to the
contrary notwithstanding, Judge Dancer replied,

> If this settlement had been made immediately after the fire loss,
> before four years of litigation and before the Government had
> finally conducted the litigation to such an extent [that] there
> were hundreds of adjudications against it; if it had been made
> while there was still an opportunity for fair dispute as to liabil-
> ity, then the settlement of 50 cents on the dollar might have been
> a fair compromise. But after four years of litigation and when
> the absolute liability of the Government to the whole city of Clo-
> quet and various other districts was established by verdicts of ju-
> ries and findings of courts, then, I say, 50 cents on the dollar was
> altogether too low. . . .
>   As I have pointed out, I think that Mr. Davis violated the
> law of Congress under which he was appointed when he refused
> to accept the law of Minnesota and the decisions of the Min-
> nesota courts and compelled these people, by stress of their
> needs, to take 50 cents on the dollar, and I say those people have
> every equitable feature in their favor when they ask the Govern-

ment to adjust this matter. Mr. Davis had the right to criticize the decision of the Minnesota court, but not to disregard it. If the Government does not make that right and pay the balance of the claims, I shall always feel those claimants did not get a fair deal.

Was the settlement a good one? Judge Dancer's withering remark was, "It was a cheap settlement for the Government."

When James Davis offered the fire sufferers 40 to 50 percent of their claims after the Minnesota Supreme Court ruled in their favor, when he said, "Gentlemen, this is the best I can do; take it or leave it," he had not reckoned on the people with whom he had been dealing. These were Indian people, successors of the area's earliest inhabitants; these were immigrants, homesteaders, farmers; these were lumberjacks, log drivers, sawmill operators; these were people who had settled towns and carved farms from the forest, built businesses and industries, risked their lives cutting and moving timber; these were people who had endured the bitter cold of winter and the intense heat of summer to make their homes in the woods. This was a community that, surviving the great 1918 fires, had survived the worst that nature had to offer. These people were too tough to be intimidated by a government lawyer.

CHAPTER NINE

Congress and the Final Claims

We must push now, Yetka—no let up.
We can win this time.
Anna Dickie Olesen

The DEBT is PAID.
Pine Knot, December 6, 1935

After the settlement with the Railroad Administration, and after the failure of two cases in the United States Court of Claims, where were the fire sufferers to turn for a final resolution of their claims? A special appropriations bill in Congress seemed the only effective avenue of relief. In 1928 a new group, the Minnesota Forest Fire Reimbursement Association, was organized to lobby Congress and to bring pressure from all over the United States to support a congressional solution to the problem. Although based in northern Minnesota and led in large part by a young Cloquet lawyer, Frank Yetka, this organization generated membership and support from fire sufferers who had dispersed across the country. A national campaign was started. Congressman William Carss and Senator Henrik Shipstead in April 1928 sponsored the first bill to obtain from the government payment of the unpaid balance of fire sufferers' adjudicated claims against the Railroad Administration. This bill was never reported from committee. When William A. Pittenger of Duluth succeeded Carss in 1928 as representative from Minnesota's Eighth Congressional District, he too, again with the support of Senator Shipstead, took up the fight. It would not be finished until 1935.[1]

The "Pittenger Bill" (H.R. 5660), although ultimately unsuccessful, was the subject of a sustained campaign by the fire claimants' association and the Minnesota caucus in Congress. It resulted in public hearings that gave the fire sufferers access to a national platform to explain the dimensions of the fire and the injustices they felt they had suffered at the hands of the Railroad Administration. Introduced on December 2, 1929, the first day of the session, the bill was referred to the Committee on Claims and further directed to a subcommittee chaired by Robert R. Butler of Oregon. Hearings were held from March 26 to 29, 1930, and James Davis, the director general of the administration from 1921 to 1925, was the first public witness.

Davis began his arguments based on the reports of the state forester, William Cox, and the state Forest Fire Investigation Commission, which concluded that the fires were the result of the extraordinary conditions of nature that prevailed on October 12, 1918 (drought and hurricane winds). He also maintained that the suits against the railroads were to a large extent manufactured by the lawyers in northern Minnesota, who saw this litigation as the opportunity to make their fortunes. As for the cash settlements, Davis insisted that he consulted widely with legal counsel, with Governor Preus, with Senator Kellogg, and even with the claimants' lawyers. As a result of these consultations, Davis said, he made the offers of 50 and 40 percent of the claims. As to whether there was any objection about the settlement offer, Davis exclaimed, "Everybody was delighted with the adjustment. Everybody took the money and accepted the adjustment readily. No attorney made any objection that I know of to this adjustment. The whole thing was open and above board. There never was an adjustment in the world more understandingly arrived at. They knew the nature and effect of the settlement they agreed to."[2]

Davis reasoned that, contrary to the findings of the district court and the Minnesota Supreme Court, the Railroad Administration was not liable for the damages. As Davis put it, "The Government always denied and disputed its liability." Therefore, its settlement offer was generous, and the government's settlement was freely accepted by the claimants. Any dissatisfied individuals could have pressed their cases in the courts. As to any further payment by the government, "If Congress appropriates anything, it would be merely a gratuity. There is absolutely nothing equitable about the case." In other words, the

William A. Pittenger

Minnesotans, victims of a purely natural disaster, had already got more from the administration than they really deserved, in Davis's view, and Congress need not provide them with any further hand-outs. Davis fought a hard line, used every lawyer's rhetorical trick, never weakened, and ended with a slurring attack on the fire sufferers by entering into the testimony the text of a skit performed in Duluth that joked about the legal proceedings in Minnesota and the Scandinavian origins of some of the fire sufferers.[3]

Davis did more, however, than merely testify at the hearings. He used his connections and influence in the White House to undermine the Pittenger Bill. Davis wrote to President Herbert Hoover's secretary, Walter H. Newton, formerly a congressman from Minnesota but no friend of the fire sufferers. Davis recalled the settlement, well known to Newton, denigrated the claims, and voiced opposition to the bill. Newton replied cordially that he had "expressed [his] opinion privately in reference to this matter in no uncertain words," and assured Davis that both he and President Hoover would be "delighted" to talk with Davis while he was in Washington.[4]

At the hearings, Davis was followed by Donald Holmes, one of the railroad lawyers, who, although less aggressive than Davis, also supported the position of the Railroad Administration.[5]

The Minnesota Forest Fire Reimbursement Association sent several people to testify at the hearings. The most powerful supporter was Judge Herbert Dancer, who had been active in several of the key fire trials from his position on the bench. Judge Dancer spoke directly to Davis's remarks about the merits of both the original settlement and the proposed bill for further payments. Indeed, Judge Dancer argued with force and passion, stating,

> I feel a great deal more worked up over these cases now than before I heard Mr. Davis's argument, because I thought it was an absolutely unfair position for him to take, and based upon arguments that we lawyers recognize as entirely fallacious.

The judge's main thesis was that the Railroad Administration had violated its congressional mandate and Minnesota law by ignoring the findings and decisions of the Minnesota courts.

> [Davis] has only been able to say that the Government denied liability by refusing to accept either the Minnesota law or the Minnesota court decisions; and in doing that he violates the law of Congress under which he was appointed agent of the President, because the act of Congress under which Mr. Davis received his appointment and under which the Government took over and operated the railroads during the period of the war, expressly provided that those railroads should be operated subject to all the statutes of the various States through which they pass, and while Mr. Davis might criticize our law and the decisions of our courts — it is always the privilege of an unsuccessful litigant to go outside of the courthouse and cuss the jury and court and criticize the law, and we generally do it amongst ourselves — yet we pay just the same.

In short, Dancer's conclusion was that Davis "had no right to disobey" Minnesota law simply because he disagreed with it. As for the settlement following the *Peterson* and *Hall* cases — where the Cloquet litigants accepted a 50 percent settlement so that those claimants whose cases had not yet gone to trial could also get 50 percent — Judge Dancer said,

> I do not know as I have ever heard of a more general application of the doctrine of brotherly love than that displayed by the 278 claimants in the city of Cloquet, entitled to 100 cents on the dollar, in giving up 50 cents on the dollar in order that the Government might be persuaded to pay 50 cents also to the rest of the

claimants of the city of Cloquet who did not have the technical benefit of the trial before the five judges.

It was an impressive challenge to Davis's testimony.[6]

Three attorneys for the fire sufferers spoke at the hearings. N. B. Arnold, whose firm had handled cases in the Cloquet and Brookston-Alborn areas, told how the suits had been started in 1919 and emphasized the element of a bargain in the Cloquet case to be tried before five judges. He quoted Albert Baldwin, a railroad lawyer, as saying, "We will pay the people 100 cents on the dollar if we lose. If we win, we will not pay one cent."[7]

Victor J. Michaelson, a Cloquet lawyer who had represented cases from both the Cloquet and Moose Lake areas, spoke of the Railroad Administration's refusal to pay the court awards.

> When Mr. [Angus A.] McLaughlin [the administration's general solicitor] was there in Duluth in the fall of 1921, when he made this offer of settlement in September, 1921, we said to Mr. McLaughlin: "We realize what you are doing. You have made this offer, but we realize what you are doing. We have won these cases, but there is nothing else for us to do; you are simply gypping us."
>
> We suggested to him that we would take a certified copy of the judgment to the Treasury of the United States and have it paid. He said: "If you think you will do that, you had better think again, because you will not get anywhere with that."

Theodore Hollister, the principal lawyer on the cases north and east of Duluth, talked about the bitter contest with the railroad lawyers the fire sufferers in his area had in making their cases. In the *McCool* case, he pointed out, the defendants had appealed to the Minnesota Supreme Court twice.[8]

Three fire sufferers, prominent members of the Minnesota Forest Fire Reimbursement Association, came to the hearings to testify. Frank Yetka, a Cloquet lawyer who had not been involved in the original cases but was a claimant, spoke about the bureaucratic difficulties the Railroad Administration placed in the way of making a legitimate claim and about the administration's procedure of depreciating the value of all property listed. Carl D. Ohman, a Cloquet businessman, talked briefly about the fire itself, but his main point was that the claimants wanted what they had won in court, not "charity." Anna Dickie Olesen — a fire sufferer who was also some-

Anna Dickie Olesen, 1935

thing of a celebrity, being a well-known Chautauqua speaker and the first woman to run for the United States Senate from the Democratic party — gave a stirring description of the fire's sweep through Cloquet and her family's escape by train. She lashed out at Davis's accusation that the lawyers stood to make all the money from either the trials or the appeal to Congress. After singling out Yetka and Michaelson, Olesen said, "We turned to them and trusted them, and we never thought that we paid them too much for what they did for us in that fight." She also answered Davis's remarks about the timber interests: "Mr. [Rudolph] Weyerhaeuser, who was one of the head men in the mills there, stayed all night in the city, like a captain staying by his ship, and I respect him for it." Davis's references to the lawyers' fees and the payments to the lumber mills were a crude attempt to direct attention away from the plight of the smaller claimants who had lost everything and were forced to settle at 50 percent or less on the claim they had won in court.[9]

In addition, fifteen members of Congress, including William Pittenger, the author of the bill, and Ruth Bryan Owen, William Jennings Bryan's daughter and Anna Olesen's friend, made statements on behalf of constituents who were fire sufferers.[10]

As a result of the hearings before the subcommittee, reports were made to the Committee on Claims by June 30, 1930. Chairman Robert Butler of Oregon and J. Bayard Clark of North Carolina submitted a report and a statement that, after reviewing the history of the railroad case appeals, recommended that the whole Committee on Claims make a decision on the bill. The outcome was that on the morning of January 16, 1931, the bill came before the Committee on Claims, where the committee members pressured William Pittenger and several members of the Minnesota caucus about the lawyers' fees, the insurance claims, and the problem of claimants' selling their claims to other individuals. After two and a half hours, the chairman referred the bill to an executive session of the committee, to be held the following Monday, January 18, 1931.[11] This meeting produced a report amending the original bill and recommending its passage. Provisions were made to prevent insurance companies (other than farmers' mutual companies) from collecting, to prevent people who had purchased claims from obtaining more than their price of purchase, and to prevent lawyers from obtaining any more than 10 percent of any individual client's claim. In the conclusions the committee report said that the fire sufferers had been "practically forced" to accept the settlement, and that therefore the "Government is still indebted to them." The government expected its citizens to pay their debts and did not accept a percentage of taxes due; when the government owed a debt to its citizens it had to maintain the same standards. "It [the Railroad Administration] recognized liability in making part payment on these claims," the report declared. "The only way that justice can be done is to pass this bill and pay the balance."[12]

Throughout 1930 and 1931 efforts were made to enlist the Hoover administration's support on behalf of the Pittenger Bill. Numerous private appeals, as well as appeals from public figures, were sent to the White House. In February 1930, before the hearings, all of the ten Minnesota congressmen, plus nine from other states, sent a long memorandum to the president, outlining the history of the settlement and asking for Hoover's assistance in passing the claims bill. When no reply was received by April 21, Congressman Godfrey G. Goodwin, who had earlier talked with him, renewed the appeal for Hoover's support. The president sent all of this correspondence to Andrew W. Mellon, the secretary of the treasury and the director general of the now almost completely defunct Railroad Administration. Mellon in turn referred all of this material to Sidney F. Andrews, the assistant director general, who had prepared the administration's brief for the congressional hearings in March. The hearings had only strengthened Andrews's views, and he wrote to the White House on May 26, 1930, that the bill "should not be passed." In his letter to the president he quoted extensively from James Davis's hostile remarks at the hearings. When Minnesota Governor Theodore Christianson telegraphed Hoover for support for the bill on May 22, that message too was sent on the circuit to the Treasury Department and back. Private appeals to the president over the next months met with polite but circumspect replies from the White House staff.[13]

Although the bill was favorably reported by the Committee on Claims, it failed to get the unanimous consent of the House of Representatives and died with the expiration of the Seventy-first Congress. When the House reassembled late in 1931, Congressman Pittenger reintroduced his bill (now H.R. 491) on December 8. It was sent again to the Committee on Claims, now under the control of the Democrats. New hearings were not convened, but the committee looked at the issues and produced a report on February 16, 1932. This report was split, a majority following the favorable conclusions of the earlier Committee on Claims statements, but a minority opposing any further payment. J. Bayard Clark of North Carolina and Robert Ramspeck of Georgia, both Democrats, supported the Railroad Administration's position on the challenge to the point of law in the *Anderson* case and on the absence of coercion involved in the settlement that partially paid the claimants and that released the government from any further responsibility. A parallel bill was introduced in the Senate by Henrik Shipstead, but progress in both chambers ground to a halt.[14]

In April Pittenger reported to Frank Yetka that the Senate and House were both preoccupied with new revenue and appropriations bills, and that the chairman of the Senate claims committee was "a violent antagonist of all claims bills." Claims as large as the fire sufferers' ran headlong into the economy drive with which the Hoover administration hoped to ease the Great Depression. The administra-

Frank Yetka, about 1937

tion was urged by its friends to support the new Pittenger bill, but the White House staff avoided any hint of involvement and Hoover himself never commented publicly on the claims bill or signed a letter himself. On June 1, 1932, on the floor of the House, Congressman Thomas L. Blanton of Texas objected to the bill because, he said, of the expense to the depleted federal treasury. This once again removed the measure from the private calendar, on which bills required the unanimous consent of the House. By late April, Yetka, who had emerged as a leading figure in the Minnesota Forest Fire Reimbursement Association, became increasingly frustrated and annoyed over the delays in Congress. He told Pittenger that he thought, in effect, that some members of the Senate were "playing" with them, and he wrote to Anna Olesen that he was angry at Congress's failure to act. The association and its supporters would have to take a much stronger stand.

> In other words, from now on whether they like it or not, I have made up my mind to get on the offensive whether it hurts or not and if it takes dynamite to loosen some of the obstacles out of our way we will have to do it. (By this I mean verbal dynamite of course.)[15]

Anna Olesen, for her part, wanted to commit the national Democratic party to support the issue of the fire sufferers' bill. Unsuc-

cessful in this, she was able to make her case for a new bill after the
November 1932 elections at the Minnesota Democrats' "Victory Dinner," where she sat next to Einar Hoidale, who had defeated Pittenger
in the eighth district. Olesen thought that with the Democratic party
in control of both Congress and the White House, the fire sufferers
would be successful. "We must push now, Yetka — no let up," she
wrote. "We can win this time."[16]

As the New Deal administration was about to assemble in Washington, Frank Yetka wrote to the entire Minnesota contingent in the
House and Senate on behalf of the Minnesota Forest Fire Reimbursement Association. He reviewed briefly the history of the earlier relief
bills, said that they had requested Einar Hoidale to introduce the new
bill, noted that in the past these bills had had the support of the Minnesota delegation, and urged that the members of Congress support
the current measure. When Anna Olesen returned from the inauguration of President Franklin D. Roosevelt, however, she had some mis-
givings about Hoidale as a dynamic sponsor of the bill in the House.
"Hoidale is not the pusher Pitt was (confidential)," she wrote, and she
thought he had a mind that wanted to "weigh matters" carefully and
not rush. She began to develop the idea that the members of the association "must work from the top" and should try to hire someone in
Washington to represent them.[17]

Olesen's anxiety about Hoidale seemed to have been borne out
within the next months. Senator Shipstead introduced the bill in the
Senate on March 23, 1933, before Hoidale got around to it. Frank
Yetka was in the awkward position of having to urge Hoidale to introduce his bill as soon as possible so that it would not get "swamped"
by other bills. Hoidale introduced his own resolution on April 6. He
wrote to Yetka more than a month later saying that in the emergency
session of Congress called by President Roosevelt the Committee on
Claims had not even been organized and that action on such bills as
the fire sufferers' was not likely.[18]

In the meantime, Anna Olesen's conclusion that new tactics must
be used seemed to be bearing fruit. A letter a poor Minneapolis
woman wrote to Eleanor Roosevelt, asking when the government
would pay the fire claims, was referred to Olesen, who drafted a reply

for Mrs. Roosevelt to send. Describing all of this to Frank Yetka, Olesen wrote, "Now that gives me an *idea*. Mrs. R- is a great social justice person. She has a sense of right. It may be that we should get our plea to Mrs. Roosevelt, too. We could reach her, I am sure. But I would not make any move in the matter till you & I had discussed it at length." How effective this approach would have been is hard to say, but Eleanor Roosevelt was certainly held later to have precisely this sort of influence with her husband. While this avenue was being explored, Arthur Mullen, a Nebraska power broker who had been a key Roosevelt supporter at the 1932 Chicago presidential nominating convention, was hired as a lobbyist in Washington to forward the interests of the Minnesota Forest Fire Reimbursement Association.[19]

Furthermore, delegations went to Washington from time to time to press the fire sufferers' case in various offices. Anna Olesen had gone to the inauguration and done what she could in those circumstances. Governor Floyd B. Olson went to Washington to meet with the president in early May, and Frank Yetka went to the capitol at the same time to be of assistance. Governor Olson was prevented by a special session of the Minnesota legislature from conferring with the president in December, but Yetka and Howard T. Abbott (a Duluth lawyer with the firm of Abbott MacPherran Dancer Gilbert & Doan) drafted a letter to be sent to Roosevelt over the governor's signature. This thirteen-page document retold the story of the Cloquet fire, the court cases, the Railroad Administration settlement, and the four years of legislative struggle, and it urged the president to lend his assistance to the passage of the current measure. Senator Shipstead delivered Olson's letter in person. Roosevelt referred it to Attorney General Homer Cummings, who on December 27, 1933, responded. He, too, gave the president a brief account of the fire and the litigation, and he then discussed the circumstances of the settlement. Cummings's opinion was that:

> While there does not appear to be any legal liability in the matter on the part of the United States, both because the United States is not suable in tort and because the claimants executed binding releases at the time of settlement, nevertheless the contention that there is a moral and equitable obligation on the part of the Federal Government in the matter is not devoid of merit. It seems to me to be entitled to further study and consideration.[20]

This constituted a departure from the arguments of the reimbursement association lawyers and from the opinion of Judge Dancer, who asserted that the government's obligation in the matter was a legal, and not a moral, one. But more important, this was a moderately favorable opinion by the chief legal officer of the government. Roosevelt, in response, took the unusual step of sending letters to the chairmen of the House and Senate claims committees on January 24, 1934, quoting the attorney general's view that the subject should be looked at further. Cummings also wrote to Josiah W. Bailey, chairman of the Senate Committee on Claims, in which he again summarized the situation and concluded, "Accordingly, in my opinion, the bill is meritorious."[21]

All of this Roosevelt administration support seemed promising, but it still did not bring immediate success. The House Committee on Claims considered the bill again, and on February 9, Loring M. Black, the chairman, reported the bill favorably. The Senate bill was passed unanimously on March 20 without debate. On April 4 Chairman Black attempted to have the House rules suspended in order to pass the bill immediately. Thomas Blanton of Texas objected. Blanton had been instrumental in defeating the measure in 1932, and he had not changed his opinion on the issue in two years. He argued that the bill should stay on the private calendar, where, failing to receive unanimous consent, it would be doomed to defeat. Blanton also said that there had been no misrepresentation or duress in the government settlement, that no "responsible representative of this Government" had ever promised to pay the original "claims in full" (ignoring completely the signed stipulations in the Cloquet and Moose Lake cases). Relying on James Davis's statements at the 1930 hearings, Blanton heatedly claimed, "All this cry of duress raised years after these claimants and their lawyers accepted $13,000,000 in full settlement from the Government is an afterthought, is a subterfuge, is a sham, is a camouflaged scheme to get some more millions out of the United States." Blanton even stated that the bill did not have the Roosevelt administration's support, quoting part of Attorney General Cummings's letters, "there does not appear to be any legal liability in the matter," but ignoring the rest of the sentence, which asserted that there was "a moral and equitable obligation on the part of the Federal Government." Congressmen Robert Ramspeck, John Taber, Cassius

Clay Dowell, and David D. Glover joined Blanton in attacking the measure, and Louis T. McFadden lashed out at what he saw as the insidious influence of a paid lobbyist, Arthur Mullen.[22]

The Minnesota congressmen, of course, attempted to refute these charges. Einar Hoidale and Paul J. Kvale gave a brief account of the fire, the legal battle, and the legislative struggle. They were joined by three Wisconsin congressmen, George W. Blanchard (who raised the point of the Railroad Administration's agreement in the stipulations of the Cloquet and Moose Lake cases), Gerald J. Boileau (who noted that the dollar amounts claimed were figures set by the Minnesota courts, not by the lawyers or the claimants), and Hubert H. Peavey (who pointed out the quick and full congressional settlement of claims arising out of fires and explosions of munitions at Morgan, New Jersey, in 1918, for which the administration was held responsible). The reasoning of the Minnesota congressmen and their supporters did not prevail, however. When Chairman Black's motion came to a vote, it was defeated 65 to 44. The following day a second attempt to pass the bill under a suspension of the House rules failed by a vote of 123 to 99. Congressman Hoidale spoke again to the House on June 16 and 18, complaining of the near impossibility of getting a private bill through Congress and protesting specifically against the allegations of Edward E. Cox of Georgia that Hoidale's bill was the work of a "crooked lobby." Time had run out for Einar Hoidale, however. His bill (H.R. 4774) died in committee with the expiration of the Seventy-third Congress. Minnesota editors' and individuals' last-minute appeals to the White House for support for the Hoidale bill met with polite sympathy, but it was too late.[23]

In the congressional elections of 1934 William Pittenger was returned to his old seat in the House of Representatives, Hoidale having resigned to run unsuccessfully for the Senate. Shortly after the new Seventy-fourth Congress met, three bills were introduced to obtain compensation for the Minnesota fire claimants. Pittenger, a Republican; Paul Kvale, a Farmer-Laborite; and Elmer J. Ryan, the lone Democrat among the Minnesota representatives, introduced separate similar bills on January 10, 1935. In the Senate, Henrik Shipstead introduced a parallel bill, which moved quickly through the legislative stages and was passed unanimously on June 11. The House bills went to the Committee on Claims, and periodically in March and April

Ryan and Pittenger spoke in support of the fire sufferers from the floor of the House and submitted documents and editorials on the subject.[24]

Eventually the Ryan Bill (H.R. 3662) was designated as the measure to receive the support of the Minnesota caucus. (With Democrats in control of the House, the Senate, and the White House, it was expedient that the Democrat's bill be put forward.) Ryan's bill was included in an omnibus claims bill in the House (H.R. 8108), and President Roosevelt instructed his staff to monitor the situation and to ask Congressman Kvale "if he needs any help" in the matter. Governor Olson kept in touch with the White House by telegraph. Even then, there was some resistance from the floor during a reading of the bill on August 20, as Edward Cox attempted to get the Ryan Bill deleted from the package. Cox ridiculed the measure as the "notorious Minnesota fire-claim case, in behalf of which a lobby has been maintained here during the whole of the present administration." Congressmen Ryan, Kvale, Theodore Christianson (the former governor of Minnesota), and several others were quickly on their feet, vigorously defending the fire sufferers' provision. Cox's motion was defeated by a vote of 100 to 64, and when he called for yeas and nays he was again defeated, by 168 to 130. Congressman Pittenger then gave a short history of the plight of the fire sufferers and the succession of bills that had been attempted. The result was that the fire sufferers' bill remained in the omnibus claims bill and was passed later that day. After so long a fight, such an anticlimax was almost droll. President Roosevelt signed the bill on August 27, 1935. The survivors of the great fire had won their long struggle for justice.[25]

With the signing of the bill into law the matter was transferred to the Treasury Department to manage the payment of the actual claims. By September 13 the comptroller general announced the procedure by which claims could be made. The Treasury Department used the Railroad Administration's account records, in which were written the agreed-upon amounts of each eligible claim accepted in the early 1920s. From these claims the administration had calculated the 40 or 50 percent originally paid. In 1935 the task remained simply to verify the claim, calculate the remainder to be paid, and locate the claimant or survivor. The Minnesota Forest Fire Reimbursement Association

The Pine Knot *of December 6, 1935, celebrated the resolution of the claims cases (with panorama of rebuilt Cloquet by Olson).*

assisted the government by sending Ralph E. Burdick, its legal advisor, to Washington to help provide information. There he was joined by Congressman Pittenger; by Hanford Cox, one of the lawyers who had worked with the cases since 1919; and by Frank Yetka, now the Minnesota state insurance commissioner. A large staff of Treasury Department auditors and clerks processed the claims, and the first checks were sent out by mid-November. Thereafter, at a rate of about one thousand claims a month, $10,837,326.12 was paid to the fire sufferers. Thus, with both payments, a total of $23,538,990.29 was paid to the fire claimants between 1921 and 1935.[26]

In northern Minnesota there was a celebration and a sense of vindication. Years later Herbert Hubert, the chairman of the reimbursement association, remembered, "That was the day when people in Cloquet danced on Cloquet Avenue." On December 6, 1935, the *Pine Knot* published a special Fire Reimbursement Jubilee Edition, in which the story of the great fire was retold and generous praise was given to those who had struggled so hard during the legal and legislative battles. The paper declared the gratitude of the community "to the scores of people who worked so untiringly and gave of their time, services and money to bring about justice to the fire sufferers of 1918 in Northern Minnesota." Minnesotans would agree with the paper's bold proclamation, "The DEBT is PAID." It was a great triumph for the victims of the fire of 1918. For the first time in a forest fire disaster, a substantial proportion of the fire sufferers had been able to successfully sue in the courts for damages traceable to railroad origins. Openly defied by the Railroad Administration in the 1920s, the fire sufferers, their lawyers, and the elected officials of the state had, after more than ten years of struggle, pressed their claims victoriously in the halls of Congress.[27]

PART FOUR

Epilogue

Houses constructed during the rebuilding of Cloquet, about 1919

CHAPTER TEN

The Recovery of the Region

They are going to rebuild — we are going to rebuild, help is coming in from all over the country.
Orlo B. Elfes

The fires left the region devastated. What was to become of it? How could life be restored to normal for the fifty thousand people uprooted by the holocaust? How would people live in an area where their homes and livelihoods had been destroyed? Even after the immediate relief operations, the court cases, the railroad settlement, and the legislative struggle, questions remained: Could the region come back? What of the forests and the forest industries? Was it all over for them? And the farms — would people go back to the ruins of their lonely farmsteads, haunted by the memories of the sudden inferno and of the loss of family and neighbors? The economic and social recovery of the region is perhaps the most remarkable aspect of this whole narrative.

The revival of the region had several dimensions, because the impact of the fires was felt in several ways. Duluth, for example, was left relatively unthreatened by the economic consequences of the disaster. The fires had burned into farms, dairies, and houses on the outskirts of the city and had destroyed several suburbs, as well as bridges, dredges, and commercial property on St. Louis Bay; but the economic base of Duluth, serving the mining, shipping, and railroad industries, was largely untouched. Though individual Duluthians, whose farms, homes, or summer cottages were burned by fire, might have suffered, the economic survival of the city was never at issue.

For the farming community, however, economic survival was more precarious. Crops that had been harvested but not sold were burned. Seed and winter supplies were destroyed. Livestock was killed or maimed. Barns, outbuildings, and implements were lost. In many places the heat of the fires was so intense that the organic material in the soil was itself burned up, leaving the land bereft of its nutrients and fertility. Nevertheless, the people came back. In early November the *Carlton County Vidette* ran the headline "Moose Lake Will Rise from Ashes," and Charles Mahnke, the Moose Lake member of the relief commission, said to the farmers of that region, "We are going to put you back as well off as you were before." Indeed, the relief commission was instrumental in rescuing the rural community and the small farm-service towns. The commission adopted a deliberate policy of rebuilding the farming community, and to a large degree it worked. Relief assistance provided not only shelters for the farm families but also the means of reconstructing barns and replacing farm implements. Surviving livestock was fed and lost livestock was replaced (with the assistance of other agricultural organizations). The local newspapers announced when seeds and implements were being distributed. A year after the fire, the Moose Lake *Star Gazette* reported, "Over 90 per cent of the people are back on their farms or in new homes in the towns that were destroyed." In the words of the newspaper, these people "have truly shown that they have faith in the country."[1]

The leadership of H. C. Hanson of Barnum, and others in the area, in improving breeds of dairy cattle had an important result in many of the devastated parts of Carlton and St. Louis counties. Hanson had started his efforts in the years before the fires, but the need to replace dairy herds after the fires served as an opportunity to accelerate this process. The Minnesota Guernsey and Holstein-Friesian breeders' associations, the University of Minnesota, and the U.S. Department of Agriculture assisted. By the mid-1930s some 80 percent of the dairy herds in Carlton County were purebred Guernseys or Holsteins, and southern St. Louis County dairy farms kept pace. Hanson's initiative was also instrumental in improving area egg and poultry production; what was in most places typically a peripheral element of farming became a serious source of agricultural income in the fire area. The shortage of cash in the hands of farmers and of local capital in the farm-service towns, together with the old-world experience of the Finnish community in the region, stimulated the growth and development of cooperative societies after the fires. Both cooperative retail stores and cooperative produce marketing facilities (particularly dairies) multiplied and prospered in the 1920s in Kettle River, Moose Lake, Wright, Cromwell, and Cloquet. In fact, by the end of the 1930s, Cloquet had the largest cooperative society in the United States. The claims of the *Star Gazette* were not exaggerated: not only did people come back to the farms, but farming actually increased in the region in the 1920s. During that decade, Carlton County enjoyed a 50 percent increase in the number of people engaged in farming, from 1,938 in 1920 to 2,899 in 1930.[2]

Efforts were made to get the rural centers on their feet as soon as possible. Rail service in Brookston, where most of the Great Northern facilities had been saved, was held up for only twenty-four hours, and Moose Lake and Kettle River had trains in from Sunday morning on. Electrical power for both Brookston and Moose Lake came from Cloquet and depended on resetting the poles and wires. The Northwestern Telephone company restored connections with Moose Lake by 7:00 P.M. on Sunday. Thanks to the relief commission, rebuilding in towns could begin almost at once. Even school was reopened in Moose Lake on January 6, 1919, as soon as the troops and the Red Cross moved out of the unburned high school building. The economic life of the small towns (farm-service centers) recovered on the strength of the revived farming community. The relief commission supported small-town merchants by purchasing from them the relief supplies it intended to distribute rather than bringing in vast amounts of goods acquired in bulk in Duluth or Minneapolis. But not every settlement made it. Bain, Lawler, Automba, and Harney, to name but four, never regained their old positions.[3]

If there were questions about the possible revival of the farming community, the prospects of the forest industries, and with them the city of Cloquet, were even more seriously in doubt. The pattern of the lumber industry in the United States had been to cut the white pine and move west. Across Maine, New York, Michigan, and Wisconsin, this was how the industry had operated. Michigan and Wisconsin were by the 1920s filled with ghost towns that had once buzzed with the sound of sawmills. Indeed, the Weyerhaeuser interests had already opened substantial operations in Idaho, Washington, and Arkansas. By 1918 the white pine forests of northern Minnesota, and certainly of the St. Louis River valley, had only a few years left to sustain full-scale logging operations. The Brooks-Scanlon Lumber Company, founded in 1901, packed up in 1912 and pulled out of the town that bears its name, Scanlon. Would the Weyerhaeuser lumber interests simply dismantle the remaining sawmills and planers in Cloquet, load them on trains, and take them to the new timber regions? Would Cloquet and the forest industries survive? The newspapers attempted to be optimistic. The *Carlton County Vidette* on October 18, 1918, urged its readers, "Don't Lose Courage!" and promised, "Cloquet will arise from its ashes and ruins a better and more beautiful city than it has been in the past." The relief commission was instrumental in assisting the dispersed fire sufferers to return as soon as possible to begin the rebuilding, with shelters in which they could survive the winter. But the matter of Cloquet's long-term survival hinged on the decision to be made by the owners of the lumber mills.[4]

The fire had burned through the city in a curious way. The peculiar topography of the curving river and the steep banks on the north side of the river, together with the prevailing wind out of the northwest on the night of the fire and, no doubt, the efforts of the men who stayed by the mills and fought fire, resulted in only a partial destruction of the industries. Most of the secondary industries survived: the Northwest Paper Company, the Cloquet Tie and Post Company, the Berst-Forster-Dixfield Company toothpick factory, and the Rathborne, Hair and Ridgeway Company box factory. The big lumber companies took the brunt of the destruction, and then unevenly. The biggest of all, the Northern Lumber Company, lost almost everything of its Cloquet operations (two sawmills, planer, power plants, shops, barns, offices, and sixty-five million board feet of cut lumber). The Cloquet Lumber Company lost one planing mill and forty million board feet of lumber, but its two sawmills and some of its cut lumber were saved. The Johnson-Wentworth Lumber Company, owned jointly by the other two firms, was largely undamaged by the fire.

How then would the lumber interests respond? Would they rebuild or move out?[5]

On Sunday, October 20, a week after the fire, anxious Cloquet citizens met in Carlton to discuss the city's future. Henry Oldenburg, a Carlton lawyer who had represented the Weyerhaeuser interests in the past, presided at the meeting, and he attempted to assure his listeners that the manufacturers would give the reconstruction of the city the "fullest and most hearty co-operation."[6]

But when asked whether the Northern Lumber Company would rebuild, Oldenburg replied that he had no authority to actually speak for the company. He did say that the directors of the company had left the decision in the hands of Rudolph Weyerhaeuser, the manager. The directors — including Rudolph's brothers, Frederick E. and Charles A. Weyerhaeuser; Frederic Somers Bell; and others — met on Saturday, but even Sherman Coy had to admit, "There are no plans for the future yet."[7]

Within another two weeks Rudolph Weyerhaeuser had worked out a plan to reorganize the lumber industry along the St. Louis River. The Northern Lumber Company, which had substantial stands of timber in northern Minnesota, would take over the Johnson-Wentworth Lumber Company, with its sawmill and planer, in early 1919. Neither the Cloquet Lumber Company nor Johnson-Wentworth had large standing timber reserves (about 150 million board feet of logs combined), and Weyerhaeuser estimated that in another three years the Cloquet Lumber Company would be out of business. At that time, he thought, the Northern could also take over the Cloquet and thus run both mills to cut its timber; this was a sufficiently workable plan to justify continued sawmill operations in Cloquet. The Northern and the Cloquet Lumber Company had owned the Johnson-Wentworth jointly since 1902, but the takeover arrangement depended on the cooperation of the non-Weyerhaeuser shareholders of the Cloquet Lumber Company. This was eventually worked out, and it had the benefit of bringing Northern Lumber Company timber into the market without any serious interruption for its customers.

The position of the lumber companies was complicated. Only the fire claim payment of $169,349.72 from the Railroad Administration in 1921 enabled the Northern Lumber Company to show a profit that year. In 1924 the Northern discovered that its timber reserves were smaller than had been calculated. The account books for all three companies during the second half of the 1920s reveal a steady decline in assets and in the volume of lumber cut. Nevertheless, both the Cloquet and the Johnson-Wentworth remained in operation until 1929 and the Northern until 1937.[8]

As for the rebuilding of the Northern sawmills on the old site, eventually one sawmill was rebuilt, but Rudolph Weyerhaeuser also began to develop other plans. Considering the forest reserves in northern Minnesota and the existing mills in Cloquet, he did not feel initially that the construction of new sawmills would be justified. In 1919, however, Dr. Howard F. Weiss and Dr. A. W. Schorger, scientists working for the C. F. Burgess Laboratories of Madison, Wisconsin, received instructions from the Weyerhaeuser Timber Company to develop a commercial use for aspen, birch, balsam, and jack pine. What was needed was a product that would enable the Northern Lumber Company to utilize the secondary timber that was already on its own lands and that could be expected to regenerate on the burned-over lands in the future. By October 1919 Rudolph Weyerhaeuser was able to write to one of his brothers that sufficient progress had been made for him and a group of other owners to recommend that they go ahead with production plans for the Burgess proposition. Weiss and Schorger had developed a process that separated wood fibers in a method similar to the manufacture of paper pulp, but that recombined the fibers not in a flat sheet but in a loose and fluffy form that resembled sheep's wool and had important insulating properties. This became "Balsam Wool," a wood-fiber insulation manufactured for industrial (and later household) purposes. The Wood Conversion Company was formed in early 1921, and a plant was built on the site of the old Northern Lumber Company on the banks of the St. Louis River. The Wood Conversion Company, managed by Edwin Weyerhaeuser Davis, a grandson of Frederick Weyerhaeuser and a recent graduate of Yale University's forestry school, went into production in August 1922, and over the next several decades developed a whole range of wood-fiber products. By 1926 a slightly different process of recombining the fibers resulted in the manufacture of a fiber board that would be used in building industry for either insulation or panelling, and eventually for acoustical noise control. This was initially marketed as "Nu-Wood."[9]

The survival of the secondary industries was more important in the long run than was immediately apparent. The machinery and plant facilities of a pulp and paper mill or a match factory were such that it was not convenient to dismantle them like a sawmill and move them off to a new site. Once built, they were there to stay. Furthermore, particularly in the case of a pulp and paper mill, they were more labor intensive than the sawmills. As a result of substantial expansion during the 1920s and 1930s, the Northwest Paper Company emerged within twenty years as the major industry in Cloquet and by far the largest employer. The Diamond Match Company's acquisition of the Berst-Forster-Dixfield Company, and subsequent plant expansion, also increased its production and workforce.

The city would remain a forest industry center, although not the sawmill town of the days before the great fire. The Northwest Paper Company (which became a division of the Potlatch Corporation in 1964), the Wood Conversion Company (which became part of the United States Gypsum Company in 1985), and the Berst-Forster-Dixfield Company (which eventually became Diamond Brands Incorporated in 1986) were the fitting heirs to the big lumber companies.[10]

§

With the decisions made regarding Cloquet's heavy industry, discussion of the city's reconstruction was not an empty charade. "They are going to rebuild — we are going to rebuild, help is coming in from all over the country," cried an anxious and relieved Orlo Elfes to his family when he returned from a meeting with Mayor John Long. "CLOQUET IS COMING BACK!" The community's fears as to whether the city could be fully restored were gradually eased. People did begin coming back.

The Northwest Paper Company resumed production the week after the fire, providing immediate employment for a large number of people. Workmen slept in warehouses and quiet parts of the surviving mills while relief shelters were being put up. Ten or so of the mill managers "bunked" at the Weyerhaeuser summer cottage at Chub Lake, while others stayed with Henry Oldenburg in Carlton, but they

"Shacks" for temporary shelter, Cloquet, probably winter 1918–19

all drove into Cloquet or Duluth (where temporary offices were acquired) to work long hours getting things started. Typically, the men returned first, while their wives and children stayed in Duluth, Superior, or somewhere else with family or friends.[11]

Gradually, as the "Red Cross" shacks were built, families were reunited. For many, the occasion was an emotional Thanksgiving or Christmas dinner, cooked on the relief commission "kitchen kit." Eighteen years later Elise Wenzel, then living in Klamath Falls, Oregon, still had her "Red Cross butcher knife," and "wouldn't part with it for anything."[12]

School Superintendent Peter Olesen, his wife Anna, and their daughter Mary lived in a cloakroom in the Garfield School once the National Guard had moved out. Food was cooked for them and others in the school cafeteria by Mr. and Mrs. A. F. Peterson. Tena Smith remembered the sound of the "rat ta tat of the hammer" from early in the morning until late into the night. By November 15 there were at least 250 shelters built, and new ones were constructed every day. Pearl Drew later compared the Red Cross shacks to "mushrooms springing up over night, one shack after another dotted the snow-covered city." Although "primitive," they were not distasteful, she said. "With smoke curling from the chimneys, they looked quaint and inviting, snuggled in the snow."[13]

Kathryn Gray noted that there was determined effort to put up a good front. "A brave 'oh-this-is-fun-and don't you dare make us cry by saying otherwise,' " attitude. But the reality must have been grim. "You could see from one end of the town to another — gaping basements, ruined walls, smoke-blackened chimneys; and here and there bright new shacks that were offices, homes and stores. Only the water tank and the Garfield school looked familiar." Frederick E. Weyerhaeuser visited the city one week after the fire and concluded "it was one of the saddest looking sights I ever saw — nothing but black ruin and desolation almost as far as one could see." He went to the Johnson-Wentworth office, which was "crowded with soldiers, women, cots, and everything more or less in confusion." In fact, the Reverend Dr. William E. Williams of the First Presbyterian church, who had been on a tour of duty with the YMCA in Europe, said that Cloquet looked "worse than anything I saw in Belgium."[14]

Cloquet businesses attempted to resume operations almost immediately. Railroad facilities had been almost completely destroyed: the Union Depot and one bridge burned, and both the Great Northern and the Northern Pacific tracks bent and twisted by the heat. Using spare track at the ore docks in Superior, the Great Northern was able to open a single track by 4:00 P.M. Sunday and double track by late Monday or early Tuesday. Two boxcars on a siding served as the depot. Telephone connections with Duluth were established via Carlton by 10:00 A.M. Monday, and a direct line was put in two days later. By the end of the week 150 Northwestern telephones were in service. The Cloquet newspaper, the *Pine Knot*, was given the use of the presses and facilities of the *Carlton County Vidette* in Carlton, so that an edition of the *Pine Knot* came out the Friday after the fire, October 18, as usual. By October 25 the *Vidette* reported an incredible amount of activity in Cloquet. The St. Louis River Mercantile Company (which, among other things, outfitted the lumber camps in the woods) had set up temporary quarters on Avenue C and Market Street; the First National Bank opened on Arch Street and the Northwestern Bank built a wood-frame structure; the Northern Lumber Company (whose property was also used for the relief commission headquarters) started work on a warehouse; and the Cloquet Lumber Company rebuilt its barns. The Northern went back into operation in February using the Johnson-Wentworth mill, and the Cloquet opened in late April. The General Light and Power Company, whose electric plant had been spared by the fire, had to reset the transmission lines throughout Cloquet, as well as to Brookston, Moose Lake, and the several other communities that the company served.

Smaller businesses also sprang back to life. C. P. Cleveland started a hardware store on Avenue C and Arch Street, J. A. Fesenbeck resumed his law practice on Avenue C, and Joe Kleckner reopened his barber shop in a shanty. Throughout the rest of 1918 and 1919 the local newspapers frequently reported in triumph the return to business of some former establishment or the reconstruction of some enterprise.[15]

The Cloquet City Council held the first of a series of meetings in the Garfield School on October 21 to discuss the future of the city. Although the minutes are not precise, they reveal the uncertainty that prevailed. By December, however, the mood had changed sufficiently that concrete plans for the reconstruction of public buildings were discussed and approved. Symbolically, the first contract let was for the building of a new fire hall; and when Rudolph Weyerhaeuser made an offer of the property on Arch Street between Avenues A and B for a new city hall, it was gratefully accepted. The Duluth architectural firm of Holstead & Sullivan was commissioned to design what was to be one of the most handsome buildings in Cloquet. Special appropriations by the Minnesota legislature for the reconstruction of schools in the fire district enabled work to begin in March 1919 on the new high school. When school began in September 1919, students went in shifts to both the old Garfield School, which had survived the fire, and the new Leach School, which had just been put up. In July 1919 Hattie Marie Shaw DeLescaille and Cordelia Elizabeth Shaw Lynds, the two daughters of the early Cloquet lumberman George Shaw, each contributed $15,000 for the building of a new library. These contributions, together with the insurance money for the old library, financed the construction of the new Shaw Memorial Library; designed by Kelly & Shefchik of Duluth, it was the most elegant of the new buildings built after the fire.[16]

As the industrial, commercial, and public life of Cloquet began to take shape, people talked of a city plan. The city council discussed ways to redesign the streets, creating a more rational geometrical pattern, and to bring together in one concentrated location the businesses of the "West End" and the "East End." Redesigning the city proved impossible. Nevertheless, the results of the rebuilding were dramatic and not unpleasing. Lucile Watkins observed that Cloquet was not rebuilt as a grim industrial town with rows of identical workers' houses, but in her words, "It now became in very truth, the City of Cloquet." Property owners built homes to suit their own specifications, with help from the relief commission, the lumber companies, the Railroad Administration, perhaps some insurance, and, finally, Congress. People worked fast. Photographs taken even a year after the fire show what looks like a completely rebuilt city. It was an impressive achievement that was not lost on outside observers.[17]

The incredible rebirth of Cloquet as a forest industries center should not mask the crippling effects of the city's destruction. There was a cost for all of this. Sherman Coy said, "The town cannot be what it was in our lifetime," and he was right. Cloquet not only looked different, it was different. For one thing, it was smaller. Although the town "came back" to a remarkable degree, and people took enormous pride in that fact, the truth was that not all of the people came back. The census figures told an interesting story. The 1910 census showed the population of Cloquet to have been 7,031, although it was widely believed that at the time of the 1918 fire the population was between 8,000 and 9,000 (estimates of more than 10,000 were probably too high). The 1920 census revealed only 5,127 inhabitants in Cloquet. This census was taken almost two years after the fire and at a time when the industries were back in operation and the community, if not fully rebuilt, was at least resettled. Officially, Cloquet's population between 1910 and 1920 had fallen by 1,904. If the estimated population for 1918 is to be believed, the actual decline in the city's size may have been somewhere between 3,000 and 4,000. Even the more conservative figure of 1,904 would represent a major decline in population over a decade, and the larger figure is probably more correct. By 1930 the census showed that Cloquet's population had risen to 6,782 and by 1940 to 7,304. It took more than twenty years for Cloquet's population to reach the prefire figure.[18]

By contrast, the population of Carlton County rose steadily throughout the whole period from 1910 to 1920, despite the devastation and much larger loss of life in the rural areas of the northern part of the county and particularly the southwestern regions near Moose

Cloquet with ruins of Rudolph Weyerhaeuser's house on Park Place in foreground and city water tower in distance, October 1918 (Olson)

Lake and Kettle River. In 1910 the population of the county was 17,559 and in 1920 (even with the official decline in Cloquet and the deaths in the Moose Lake–Kettle River areas) it had grown to 19 391. Cloquet may have been "The Miracle City," but its recovery, even on the basis of the strong wood-fiber industry, should not be exaggerated.[19]

One year after the great fires, on Sunday, October 12, 1919, the region paused to remember the tragedy. A fair was held in Brookston for the Culver, Brevator, and Paupores settlements. In Moose Lake, the site of the mass grave of two hundred fire victims was covered with

Cloquet rebuilt, with new houses on Park Place for Weyerhaeuser (foreground) and Sherman Coy (second from right), 1923 (Olson)

flowers for a memorial service. More than two thousand people came to pay their respects and to remember. Governor Burnquist, who had witnessed the burial itself twelve months before, returned to speak at the service.[20]

In Cloquet there was an interdenominational religious service at noon in the new Leb Theatre and an outdoor public meeting later in the afternoon at Pinehurst Park. The official party toured the reconstructed city, and had dinner in the newly built Solem Hotel while being entertained by the city band. Mayor Long presided at the ceremony, and Governor Burnquist and other dignitaries spoke — Mayor Clarence Magney of Duluth, William McGonagle of the relief commission, and Henry Oldenburg of Carlton. Burnquist talked of

Burial in mass grave, Moose Lake, October 15, 1918, with photographer and motion-picture camera operator recording event (Olson)

the need to prevent a recurrence of such a disaster and of the "spirit of determination" to rebuild the community. In a warm tribute he said, "The generous aid which came from all parts of the state, as well as from many places in other states, did much to awaken courage and hope when the people of the city were in despair. But to the people of Cloquet themselves belongs the great share of the credit for the magnificent work that has been done."[21]

As part of the ceremony, the Cloquet City Council presented a resolution, which while admitting "the impossibility of expressing . . . the sentiment in the heart of each of us," offered thanks on behalf of the city and the people of Cloquet. The council declared,

> That we do hereby extend to the people of Carlton, Superior and Duluth; to the Governor and other officials of the State of Minnesota; to the American Red Cross Society and especially the branches at Duluth and Superior; to all the people of the State of Minnesota and other states contributing to our assistance; and to the legislature of the State of Minnesota, and each member thereof, our sincere appreciation and gratitude for all that they have done for us at the time of our misfortune.[22]

So the fires of autumn 1918 burned themselves out, the relief agencies brought assistance, the people came back, the farms and towns were

An obelisk in Riverside Cemetery, Moose Lake, was "Erected to the Memory of the Men, Women and Children Who Perished in the Forest Fire of October 12, 1918" and was dedicated on October 12, 1929.

built up, and the Railroad Administration and Congress paid their debts. But the great fires were never over, never forgotten. Not for sixteen-year-old Earl Miettunen, whose automobile crashed and whose mother was killed as he and his father escaped to the St. Louis River east of Brookston. Not for Rudolph Weyerhaeuser and Sherman Coy, standing amid their burning lumber company; nor for Evelyn Elshoss, squeezed into a crowded, smelly boxcar at Johnson's Crossing; nor for young Lester Blomberg, watching a burning board land in the street while he filled the gas tank of the delivery truck loaded with the family belongings that he was to drive to Carlton. Not for Daniel Welleck, south of Grand Lake, who thought he was witnessing the end of the world; nor young Katharine Luomala, who saw her sister as a mythical goddess with her hair streaming out, driving their team of horses through the night; nor Captain Wallace West, who during twenty years as a fireman in Duluth had never seen anything like it. Not for Nick and Hulda Koivisto, who braved the flames all night to keep the fire away from a root cellar, only to find that seven of their children had suffocated; nor for William Maki, whose last view of Automba was that of his store engulfed in flames; nor for Mayor Richard Hart, who spent the night beneath the bridge at Kettle River and who then made his way through Dead Man's Curve to burned-out Moose Lake and on to Sturgeon Lake to cable the governor for help. For all those who survived that night, and for their children and grandchildren, the great fires have never been over. The tragedy, the horror, and the adventure of that night have been a permanent legacy to each generation that has followed.

Photographers and the Fires

By Alan R. Woolworth

The effects of the catastrophic Cloquet–Moose Lake fires were vividly captured by photographers who traveled through the area recording the tragic event and its aftermath. Using a variety of photographic equipment, they were soon on the scene taking powerful pictures of destruction and despair that were quickly reproduced in newspapers. After the immediate crisis passed and the enormous task of relief work and reconstruction got under way, photographers continued to make and distribute images that showed the devastation of the fires and the determination of the survivors to rebuild. The disaster had so strong an impact on the region that some photographers labeled their work with the single date of "October 12, 1918" even though no pictures of the fires are yet known to have actually been taken on that day.

Among the most prominent fire photographers were Hugh McKenzie of Duluth, Olaf Olson of Duluth and Cloquet, Earl L. Irish of Rochester, and Fred Levie of Sandstone. McKenzie (1879–1957) had owned a studio in Duluth since 1905. Long accustomed to photographing city scenes, he also knew the rural areas of the region. Many of his better fire photographs were made with a sturdy five-by-seven-inch camera, more suited for field work than the larger, more fragile view cameras of the period; he also made some eight-by-ten-inch views. After the fires of October 12 broke out, McKenzie appears to have secured an automobile with a driver and to have gone to northwestern Duluth, where he photographed the remains of burned buildings and automobiles. He also visited the Duluth Armory to make a series of indoor views showing Red Cross members and other relief workers assisting refugees.

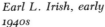
Earl L. Irish, early   *Hugh McKenzie, 1954*   *Olaf Olson, about*
1940s   *1906*

Next McKenzie made the first of at least two trips to Moose Lake and took views of the burned-out main street, refugees, and relief activities. Finally he drove to Cloquet, where he shot many photographs of the almost total devastation of that city. Then he rushed back to his Duluth studio to make prints for the *Duluth Herald* and other newspapers such as the *Minneapolis Journal*. The earliest published McKenzie photographs of the disaster are in the last edition of the *Herald* for the evening of Monday, October 14. Others appeared with photographs by Olson in *The Fury of the Flames: A Pictorial Record of the Great Forest Fires Which Raged in Northern Minnesota, Oct. 12–15, 1918*, a booklet published in Duluth the next year.[1]

Since about 1910 Olaf Olson (1883–1949) had worked at various times as a photographer for the *Duluth News Tribune* and the Duluth Photo Engraving Company in Duluth, where he used the first name of Oliver, mostly likely to differentiate himself from the many other Olsons in the city. When news came of the October 12 fires, Olson was probably provided by the newspaper with an automobile and driver. He appears to have used an eight-by-ten-inch view camera with a strong tripod and quantities of cut-sheet film. At Moose Lake, Olson took a few views of the burned-out business district and the Minnesota Home Guard units that had arrived shortly before his visit. Other photographs by Olson show scenes of relief work, refugees, and rescue workers in automobiles searching for survivors. About Monday, October 14, Olson visited his home town of Cloquet and prepared a detailed series of panoramic and other views of this devastated community that were published in the local *Pine Knot* on October 10, 1919. On October 15 he photographed the mass burial at Moose Lake, where Governor Burnquist was also present. Olson prepared prints in his studio at the newspaper, and the prints were immediately made into half-tone engravings for newspaper printing. Several Olson photos appeared in the *News Tribune* soon after they were taken.[2]

Earl Irish (1878–1953) was a medical photographer in Rochester, where he had been in charge of the photographic department of the Mayo Clinic since 1913. A member of a Home Guard medical unit, he was called into service on Friday, October 18, 1918. Irish's unit joined a Winona unit en route to Moose Lake, where they relieved other guards. The Rochester unit aided fire survivors, buried dead animals, and hauled food and hay until returning home by October 26. Irish apparently brought along photographic equipment, perhaps a small view camera on a tripod, and took a large number of striking photographs of refugees and fire-damaged buildings, mostly in the Moose Lake area. He appears to have had light guard duties or may even have been assigned to create a photographic record of the disaster and its effects. The photographs were later made into lantern slides and apparently used in an illustrated presentation about the fires and relief work, perhaps given by Irish himself. This presentation also incorporated photographs taken by Levie.[3]

Comparatively little is known about Fred Levie. By 1916, after running his own studio in Minneapolis, he had purchased another photographer's operation in Sandstone, a small town in northern Pine County about twenty-five miles south of Moose Lake. He also had a second studio in Hinckley, about ten miles south of Sandstone, where he spent part of each week. When the fires of 1918 struck, Levie climbed into his Model T Ford with one or two folding Kodak cameras of the popular "postcard" size and plenty of roll film. He made several dozen photographs around Moose Lake, depicting Home Guards and refugees, ruins and relief work. Then he returned to his Sandstone studio to process the film and by the next day or two was selling postcard views of the disaster. Levie also appears to have made later trips to Moose Lake. The Sandstone *Pine County Courier* noted on October 31 that "Photographer Levie was one of the first on the ground to take pictures of the big fire at Moose Lake. He secured some fine ones and has been doing a rushing business with them for the past two weeks." Although not technically comparable to the larger, more finished documentary photographs by McKenzie and Olson, Levie's postcard views furnish interesting everyday glimpses of life in the Moose Lake area during the relief operations.[4]

Other photographers also made invaluable documents, but were not as prolific or well-known or do not usually have their names associated with their pictures. William Bull (1877–1942) of St. Paul, for example, may have been one of the unidentified photographers for the *St. Paul Pioneer Press* and *St. Paul Dispatch* who traveled on the relief trains to the devastated area soon after the fires. Bull, a commercial photographer working for the Buckbee Mears printing company in St. Paul, took the poignant picture of Aina Jokimaki Johnson, the young refugee with bandaged hands and legs (see p. 85). Thomas J. Horton (about 1883–1965), a photographer who managed a photo lab at the University of Minnesota, recorded forest scenes in the burned-over area around Moose Lake. After news of the disaster spread through the country, journalistic teams representing the International Film Service and Underwood and Underwood arrived on the scene and took still pictures and probably newsreel footage of the devastation at Moose Lake, Duluth, and Cloquet.[5]

The work of all these photographers, known and unknown, created for posterity a dramatic and priceless graphic account of suffering and rebirth.

Notes

PREFACE

1. Ray E. Hemingson, *Death by Fire: The Story of the Great Northeastern Minnesota Forest Fire* (Waupaca, Wis., 1983); Edwin E. Manni, comp., *Kettle River, Automba, Kalevala, and Surrounding Area: History, Stories: Also 1918 Forest Fire* (n.p., 1978); Arnold R. Alanen, ed., *The 1918 Fire in Eastern Aitkin County: Personal Accounts of Survivors* (n.p., 1970). For more information on the essay contest sponsored by the Women's Friday Club, see Chapter Three.

2. Stewart H. Holbrook, *Burning an Empire: The Story of American Forest Fires* (New York: Macmillan Company, 1943), 31–45; Ralph W. Hidy, Frank Ernest Hill, and Allan Nevins, *Timber and Men: The Weyerhaeuser Story* (New York: Macmillan Company, 1963), 196–204.

3. Narrative of Steve Tomczak, p. 114 (quotation), in Manni, comp., *Kettle River*.

CHAPTER ONE. Fires in the Woods

1. R. DeC. Ward, "Smoke from the Minnesota Forest Fires of October, 1918," *Geographical Review* 7 (April 1919): 264; *Pine Knot* (Cloquet), October 25, 1918, p. 4; Hansen Evesmith to U.S. Weather Bureau, Duluth, January 29, 1932, News Clippings File, Northeast Minnesota Historical Center, University of Minnesota-Duluth (hereafter NEMHC).

2. Stephen J. Pyne, *Fire in America: A Cultural History of Wildland and Rural Fire* (Princeton, N.J.: Princeton University Press, 1982), 204; Minnesota Forest Fires Relief Commission, *Final Report* (Duluth, 1921), 6.

3. Minnesota Forest Fires Relief Commission, *Final Report*, 6; Western Adjustment & Inspection Company, *Forest Fires in Northern Minnesota, 1918: The Greatest Conflagration Since San Francisco* (Chicago: The Company, 1919). The *Carlton County Vidette* (Carlton) estimated the property loss to be more than $80 million and the loss in Cloquet alone to be about $20 million. *Carlton County Vidette*, October 18, 1918, p. 1.

4. Transcript of interview of Tena MacMillan Smith with John Esse, Cloquet, October 9, 1975 (quotation), Forest History and Lumbering Project, Oral History Collections, Minnesota Historical Society, St. Paul (hereafter MHS).

5. Pyne, *Fire in America*, 52–53; Holbrook, *Burning an Empire*, 46–48. Statistics on the causes of forest fires were collected in 1921 by the National Board of Fire Underwriters, who ranked the causes. Brush burning was responsible for 13.7 percent of all

forest fires in the United States, campers 12.7 percent, arson 12.5 percent, lightning 9.8 percent, and lumbering 6.2 percent. The fire underwriters also noted that 24.2 percent of forest fires had unknown causes and 6.0 percent were listed as miscellaneous. "A Record of Five Years' Forest Fires," *Safeguarding America against Fire* (National Board of Fire Underwriters, New York) 4 (April 1921): 6–7.

6. Ralph C. Hawley, *Forest Protection* (New York: John Wiley & Sons, 1937), 168–70; Franklin Moon and Nelson Courtlandt Brown, *Elements of Forestry*, 3d ed. (New York: John Wiley & Sons, 1937), 204–5.

7. Henry Solon Graves, *The Principles of Handling Woodlands* (New York: John Wiley & Sons, 1911), 294–96 (quotation, 294). Graves also commented that even with spark arresters it was probably impossible to completely eliminate railroad fires in dry weather. *Forest Fire Protection in Minnesota* (St. Paul: Department of Conservation, n.d.), 19–20; Smith Riley to R. H. Aishton, June 1, 1918, file no. 61, Records of the Forest Service, Record Group 95, National Archives, Washington, D.C. (hereafter NA, Washington, D.C.); William T. Cox, *Forest Protection and Conservation in Minnesota* (n.p., n.d.), 27. The National Board of Fire Underwriters regarded railroads as the largest single cause of forest fires, at 14.9 percent of the total fires of identifiable origins; "A Record of Five Years' Forest Fires," 6. During the 1920s and 1930s the proportion of fires caused by railroads fell sharply, while those started by smokers and campers rose dramatically. For statistics see Hawley, *Forest Protection*, 158–6L.

8. Miron L. Heinselman, "Fire in the Virgin Forests of the Boundary Waters Canoe Area, Minnesota," *Quaternary Research* 3 (October 1973): 329–82. Heinselman himself did research on living trees in northern Minnesota and was able to date forest fires back to the seventeenth century; he referred to other scientists whose work with charcoal fragments and fossil remains extracted from sediment in lake bottoms and from peat bogs revealed a steady pattern of fires since the last ice age.

9. The Hinckley fire of 1894 killed 418 people, destroyed Hinckley and several small towns, and burned 160,000 acres. The story of that dramatic event and the associated heroism and courage has been well preserved in several excellent accounts. See Holbrook, *Burning an Empire*, 13–30; Pyne, *Fire in America*, 207–10. Although there are several full-length studies of the Hinckley fire, the best is Grace Stageberg Swenson's *From the Ashes: The Story of the Hinckley Fire of 1894* (1979; rev. ed., Stillwater, Minn.: Croixside Press, 1988). The Baudette–Spooner fire of 1910 killed 42 people and burned 300,000 acres.

10. Pyne, *Fire in America*, 199–218; Holbrook, *Burning an Empire*, 13–53; *Forest Fire Protection in Minnesota*, 19–20.

11. For descriptions of fire-fighting techniques before 1918, see Graves, *Principles of Handling Woodlands*, 297–308; John Gifford, *Practical Forestry for Beginners in Forestry, Agricultural Students, Woodland Owners, and Others Desiring a General Knowledge of the Nature of the Art* (New York: D. Appleton & Company, 1909), 154–59; Samuel B. Green, *Principles of American Forestry* (New York: John Wiley & Sons, 1913), 153–55; *Pine Knot*, December 6, 1935, Fire Reimbursement Jubilee Edition, special section, [pt. 1], p. 5 (quotation).

12. Donald A. Haines and Rodney W. Sando, *Climatic Conditions Preceding Historically Great Fires in the North Central Region*, USDA Forest Service Research Paper NC 34 (St. Paul: North Central Forest Experiment Station, Forest Service, U.S. Department of Agriculture, 1969), 1–18, especially 15 (quotation).

13. H. W. Richardson, "The Northeastern Minnesota Forest Fires of October 12, 1918," *Geographical Review* 7 (April 1919): 221, 223, 231 (quotation, 231); testimony

of H. W. Richardson, Record 3:1755, *Jacob Anderson v. Minneapolis, St. Paul & Sault Ste. Marie Railway Company and Others* (hereafter *Soo Line*), 146 Minnesota Reports 430 (decisions of the Minnesota Supreme Court, hereafter Minn.) and 179 North Western Reporter 45 (reports of regional appeals courts, hereafter N.W.) and Minnesota Supreme Court case file 21,855.

14. Pyne, *Fire in America*, 200–211 (quotations, 200, 205). For descriptions of the Yellowstone park fires of 1988 see Ted Williams, "Incineration of Yellowstone," and Jim Dale Vickery, "Run!" *Audubon* 89 (January 1989): 38–85, 86–89; David Jeffery, "Yellowstone: The Fires of 1988," *National Geographic* 175 (February 1989): 254–73.

15. Pyne, *Fire in America*, 361–498.

16. Although the language used to describe forest fires is fairly precise and technical, many of the words used are relatively common. Thus, "small" fires and "large" fires refer to two specifically different kinds of fires. Within the category of "large" fires are several other generally used terms, which Stephen Pyne has put in a specific context. "Fires with a very large rates [*sic*] of spread are called *runaway fires*, or *conflagrations*, and fires with very large reaction intensities are known as *mass fires*, or *firestorms.*" Pyne, *Introduction to Wildland Fire: Fire Management in the United States* (New York: John Wiley & Sons, 1984), 52.

17. For good discussions of the dynamics of forest fires see the chapters on "Fire Behavior" in Craig Chandler et al., *Forest Fire Behavior and Effects*, vol. 1 of *Fire in Forestry* (New York: John Wiley & Sons, 1983), 91–108; Pyne, *Introduction to Wildland Fire*, 43–80 (quotation, 48). In regard to spot fires, Arthur A. Brown and Kenneth P. Davis in *Forest Fire: Control and Use*, 2d ed. (New York: McGraw-Hill Book Company, 1973), 186, said that several fires burning in conjunction with each other increase significantly the amount of heat generated — "A number of small fires burning together build up a much higher level of heat energy than will develop from a single fire front moving through the same area" — and they felt that this may be "the triggering action in the fire storm."

18. Here and below, see Pyne, *Introduction to Wildland Fire*, 80–86. The Sundance fire of 1967 in Idaho burned 50,000 acres in ten hours, during which time it generated winds of 80 and 120 miles per hour and a convection column 35,000 feet high. The fire-line intensity released energy at a rate of 22,500 Btu per second/per foot, or the equivalent of a Hiroshima-type (20-kiloton) bomb.

19. Here and below, see Richardson, "Northeastern Minnesota Forest Fires," 220–23.

20. For a good description of the topography of the region and particularly the watersheds, see Thomas F. Waters, *The Streams and Rivers of Minnesota* (Minneapolis: University of Minnesota Press, 1977), 25–43.

21. For more detailed descriptions of rural life in the region, see Francis M. Carroll, *Crossroads in Time: A History of Carlton County, Minnesota* (Cloquet, Minn.: Carlton County Historical Society, 1987), 129–78.

22. The history of the growth and function of the rural towns in Carlton County can be found in Carroll, *Crossroads in Time*, 186–98. An excellent book on Duluth that looks at several aspects of that city's economic life is Ryck Lydecker and Lawrence J. Sommer, eds., *Duluth Sketches of the Past: A Bicentennial Collection* (Duluth: American Revolution Bicentennial Commission, 1976).

23. Carroll, *Crossroads in Time*, 170; Walter O'Meara, *We Made It through the Winter: A Memoir of Northern Minnesota Boyhood* (St. Paul: Minnesota Historical Society Press, 1974), 2–7.

24. For a more detailed history of the origins of the lumber industry in Cloquet, see Carroll, *Crossroads in Time*, 139–51. There is a good account of the Weyerhaeuser interests in Hidy, Hill, and Nevins, *Timber and Men*, 115–20, 188–90.

25. Hidy, Hill, and Nevins, *Timber and Men*, 192–95; Carroll, *Crossroads in Time*, 151–54, 206–16. See also *Cloquet: Home of White Pine: Queen City of the St. Louis* (1907; reprint, Cloquet, Minn.: Cloquet Diamond Jubilee Committee, 1979.).

26. Carroll, *Crossroads in Time*, 206–16.

CHAPTER TWO. Milepost 62 and the Fires in Brookston and Fond du Lac

1. For a more detailed description of the origins of the Fond du Lac reservation and some of its history, see Carroll, *Crossroads in Time*, 61–64, 68–70.

2. The Office of Indian Affairs reckoned the Indian population on the Fond du Lac reservation to be 1,074 in 1920, although it has also been estimated as being as high as 1,227. See Carroll, *Crossroads in Time*, 70. Robert E. L. Newhouse to Commissioner of Indian Affairs, February 24, 1920, Central Classified Files, 1907–39, Fond du Lac, file 700, Records of the Bureau of Indian Affairs, Record Group 75 (hereafter RG 75), NA, Washington, D.C.

3. Fires had been burning for about two weeks before October 12 in the township of Fine Lakes, near Prairie Lake, south of Floodwood. Between Paupores and Gowan there was a fire, started by a Great Northern locomotive on October 10, at Milepost 67. This fire burned southeast into the farmsteads in the Rogers road and Nygaard road area. This fire also burned into the region between Brookston and Cloquet and was a contender for the fire that destroyed the reservation and Cloquet. There were also several bog fires of undetermined origins burning in the area. See Record, *Hans J. Borsheim v. Great Northern Railway Company*, 149 Minn. 210 and 183 N.W. 519 and Minnesota Supreme Court case files 22,267 and 22,268 (files in Minnesota State Archives, MHS).

4. Testimony of Steve Koskela, Record 1:25–53 (quotation, 35), *Philip Hall v. James C. Davis, As Agent of the President under the Transportation Act*, 150 Minn. 35 and 184 N.W. 25 and Minnesota Supreme Court case file 22,425 (file in Minnesota State Archives, MHS). O'Brien's Spur was named for William O'Brien, the lumberman who had been instrumental in getting the Brooks-Scanlon Lumber Company to locate at Scanlon and who had cut logs in this northern part of the Fond du Lac reservation several years before. Carroll, *Crossroads in Time*, 151–52.

5. Testimonies of Koskela, Record 1:44, Anton LaFave, Record 2:1668–74 — both in *Hall v. Davis*.

6. Haines and Sando, *Climatic Conditions*, 15.

7. Testimonies of Koskela, Record 1:54–70 (quotation, 56), Theodore Kunelius, Record 1:239, 258–59 — both in *Hall v. Davis*.

8. Here and following paragraph, see testimony of John Iwasko, Record 1:333–58 (quotations, 346, 339), *Hall v. Davis*. Mrs. Iwasko later died of her burns.

9. Kunelius testimony, Record 1:240, 252–60, *Hall v. Davis*. Kunelius had started working for the railroad at age twelve.

10. Testimony of Charles DeWitt, Record 1:179–81, 203–8 (quotation, 208), *Hall v. Davis*.

11. DeWitt testimony, Record 1:179–81, *Hall v. Davis;* Superior Fire Relief Committee, Superior, Wisconsin, *Northeastern Minnesota Forest Fires of October 12, 1918: Report to Donors* (Superior, Wis., 1919), 4–5; W. P. Kenney to R. H. Aishton, October 13, 14, 1918 (telegrams), President's subject file, no. 6907, Great Northern Railway Company, St. Paul, Records (hereafter GN Records), Manuscripts Collections, MHS.

12. DeWitt testimony, Record 1:208–12, *Hall v. Davis.*

13. Testimony of Fred Mader, Record 1:658–75 (quotation, 672), *Hall v. Davis;* interview of Lester J. Blomberg with Francis M. Carroll, Cloquet, December 1978, transcript in the possession of the authors.

14. Testimony of "Earl H. Miettunen," Record 1:840–61, *Harry E. McCool and Another v. James C. Davis,* 158 Minn. 146 and 197 N.W. 93 and Minnesota Supreme Court case file 23,650 (file in Minnesota State Archives, MHS).

15. Testimony of J. M. Miettunen ("K. M. Mietteunen" and "J. T. Mittunen"), Record 1:472–87 (quotations, 477, 479), *McCool v. Davis.* See also testimony of J. M. Miettunen ("Matt J. Miettunen"), Record 1:439–66, *Hall v. Davis; Duluth Herald,* October 15, 1918, p. 15; *Brookston Herald,* October 16, 1915, p. 1, January 29, 1916, p. 1.

16. Testimony of Mrs. Grace Sheehy, Record 1:627–38 (quotations, 637, 638), *Hall v. Davis.* A mosquito bar is a protective framework, draped with netting, that usually fits over a bed.

17. Here and below, see testimony of Dr. M. K. Whittemore, Record 2:2461–72 (quotations, 2462, 2464, 2465, 2466), *Hall v. Davis.*

18. Testimony of Joseph Petite, Record 1:902–10 (quotations, 906, 910), *Hall v. Davis.*

19. Testimony of Frank Houle, Record 1:923–31 (quotation, 928), *Hall v. Davis.*

20. Testimony of William Wiselan, Record 1:998–1021 (quotations, 1018), *Hall v. Davis.*

21. [George W.] Cross to Indian Office, Washington, D.C., October 13, 1918 (quotation), Indexes and Schedules of Fire Claims, Fond du Lac, Records of the Bureau of Indian Affairs, Record Group 75 (hereafter RG 75), National Archives, Kansas City, Kansas (hereafter NA, Kansas City).

22. Geo[rge] W. Cross to Commissioner of Indian Affairs, October 18, 1918, Index to Fond du Lac Fire Claims — both in Indexes and Schedules of Fire Claims, Fond du Lac, RG 75, NA, Kansas City; *Pine Knot,* October 25, 1916, p. 3. The figure of fifty-seven houses destroyed was later reduced to forty-seven. See also Lists of Indian Claimants, Central Classified Files, 1907–39, Fond du Lac, file 260, RG 75, NA, Washington, D.C.

23. G. W. Cross, "Fond du Lac Annual Report," quoted in *Pine Knot,* October 23, 1986, p. 8; *Pine Knot,* October 25, 1918, p. 3 (quotation); William T. Cox, *Annual Report of the State Forestry Board of the State of Minnesota for the Year Ending July 31, 1918* ([St. Paul, 1918?]), 16. See also testimony of Anna D[ickie] Olesen in United States Congress, House, Committee on Claims, *Relief of Certain Claimants Who Suffered Loss by Fire in the State of Minnesota during October, 1918. Hearings before a Subcommittee of the Committee on Claims . . . on H.R. 5660,* 71st Cong., 2d sess., March 26, 27, 28, 29, 1930 (Washington, D.C.: Government Printing Office, 1930; hereafter *Hearings on H.R. 5660*), 221.

24. Testimony of Peter M. Nelson, Record 1:874–95 (quotation, 876), *Hall v. Davis.*

25. Testimony of Archie Campbell, Record 1:1255–65, *Hall v. Davis.*

26. Sr. Alicia Panger, "I Remember the Great Fire," *Catholic Digest*, January 1964, p. 24–28.

27. Campbell testimony, Record 1:1255 (quotation), *Hall v. Davis*. The Mack Lake fire traveled at an average speed of 2.1 miles per hour, although both it and the Cloquet-Moose Lake fires experienced surges of much greater speeds. See Pyne, *Introduction to Wildland Fire*, 86.

CHAPTER THREE. The Miracle of Cloquet

1. Pearl E. (Mrs. Herbert J.) Drew, "The Forest Fire of 1918," Women's Friday Club, Cloquet, comp., "A Group of Essays Written by Cloquet Fire Sufferers," 31–32, copies in Carlton County Historical Society, Cloquet (hereafter CCHS), and Manuscripts Collections, MHS; published in *Pine Knot*, June 12, 1936, p. 6. In 1936 the Women's Friday Club sponsored a contest for essays about the Cloquet-Moose Lake fires. For announcements of the contest and publication of essays, see *Pine Knot*, January 3, February 7, May 15, 22, 29, June 5, 12, 19, July 3, 10, 17, 24, 1936. "A Group of Essays" contains essays by Katharine (Katherine) Luomala, Mayme C. Bey, Betty B. Erickson, Drew, Elise Cook Wenzel, Evelyn Swanson Elshoss, Mrs. W. H. Slavel, Mrs. A. F. Peterson, Margaret Wiirst, Eulalie Turcotte, and Evelyn E. Erickson; the *Pine Knot* contains essays by Luomala, Bey, B. Erickson, Drew, Wenzel, Elshoss, Slavel, Peterson, E. Erickson, and Charles Cormier. See also "Drew, Herbert J.," in C. N. Cornwall, comp., and Esther Stutheit, ed., *Who's Who in Minnesota* (Minneapolis: Minnesota Editorial Association, 1941), 205; testimony of Percy P. Vibert, Record 2:1880–1907, *Hall v. Davis*. Although Kenety left the experimental forest and took a relief train at Cloquet, Mark J. Thompson, his family, and several others stayed and fought the fire until they were driven to seek shelter in Otter Creek under a bridge. Thompson, the superintendent of the University of Minnesota's Northeast Demonstration Farm and Experiment Station near Duluth, said years later, "We thought of the Belgian refugees of World War I." Four hundred acres burned, but several buildings, the tree nursery, and the celebrated stand of red pine were saved. Mark J. Thompson, "Four Decades of Reminiscence," "Remarks–50th Anniversary Luncheon; Spalding Hotel, Duluth; Aug. 8, 1962" (quotation), Mark J. Thompson Reminiscences, Manuscripts Collections, MHS; testimony of W. H. Kenety ("Konety"), Record 3: 1789–93, *Anderson v. Soo Line*.

2. Elise Cook Wenzel, "My Experience in the Cloquet Fire of 1918," Mrs. A. F. Peterson, "My Personal Experience," Drew, "The Forest Fire of 1918," Evelyn Swanson Elshoss, "My Experiences in the Cloquet Fire of 1918," in Women's Friday Club, Cloquet, comp., "Group of Essays," 38, 57, 32, 45 (quotation), CCHS, MHS, and *Pine Knot*, July 3, p. 3, June 19, p. 6, June 12, p. 6, July 10, p. 3 – all 1936; Panger, "I Remember the Great Fire," 24; Smith interview, Oral History Collections, MHS.

3. Sher[man Coy] to Mayde [Mary D. Coy], October 17, 1918 (transcript; quotation), original letter in the possession of Elizabeth Coy Walter, Cloquet; "Sherman L. Coy," in J. A. A. Burnquist, ed., *Minnesota and Its People* (Chicago: S. J. Clarke Publishing Company, 1924) 4:496; [Rudolph M. Weyerhaeuser] to J[ohn] P. Weyerhaeuser, November 2, 1918, Frederick E. Weyerhaeuser Correspondence, Weyerhaeuser Family Papers, Manuscripts Collections, MHS.

4. Coy to Mayde, October 17, 1918 (quotation), in the possession of Elizabeth

Walter; [R. Weyerhaeuser] to J. Weyerhaeuser, November 2, 1918 (quotation), Weyerhaeuser Family Papers, MHS.

5. Testimonies of LaFave, Record 2:1674–77 (quotation, 1677), Wiselan, Record 1:1009–15 (quotation, 1015), Petite, Record 1:906–10 — all in *Hall v. Davis.*

6. [R. Weyerhaeuser] to J. Weyerhaeuser, November 2, 1918, Weyerhaeuser Family Papers, MHS; Campbell testimony, Record 1:1275, *Hall v. Davis.*

7. Holbrook, *Burning an Empire,* 33–35; Hemingson, *Death by Fire,* 131–37; W. H. Strachan to P. H. McCauley, October 29, 1918, list of special Northern Pacific train services related to the fire, October 12-November 1, 1918 — both in President's subject file, no. 494, A-3, Northern Pacific Railway Company, St. Paul, Records (hereafter NP Records), Manuscripts Collections, MHS; Superior Fire Relief Committee, *Report to Donors,* 4–5; [R. Weyerhaeuser] to J. Weyerhaeuser, November 2, 1918, Weyerhaeuser Family Papers, MHS; Kathryn Elfes Gray, "The Old Train Myth Exploded," *Cloquet Pine Knot,* June 28, 1979 (special edition for seventy-fifth anniversary of establishment of Cloquet), section C, p. 1C. There is also a strong tradition that Ranger Percy Vibert and Mayor John Long were instrumental in arranging for the trains. The available documents shed no light on their role in this matter.

8. The clearest descriptions of the four relief trains are to be found in Gray, "The Old Train Myth Exploded," *Cloquet Pine Knot,* June 28, 1979, section C, p. 1C; and Superior Fire Relief Committee, *Report to Donors,* 4–5. See also *Pine Knot,* January 27, 1912, p. 1; O'Meara, *We Made It through the Winter,* 71, 106.

9. Kathryn Elfes Gray, "Are You a 49'er? The 1918 Forest Fires in Minnesota," pt. 1, *Cloquet Vidette,* October 11, 1967, p. 3; *Pine Knot,* October 10, 1919 (Fire Anniversary Number), p. 17. No clear picture exists about any plans to fight the forest fire before it entered the city. Several survivors talk of brigades of volunteers who were to go north or out on the reservation. It may be that this was just rumor, or it may be that the fire came too quickly. One rather logical account suggests that the plan to fight the fire was based on the presumption that in the evening the wind would die down, which would give the fire fighters a better chance. Of course, that never happened.

10. Kathryn Elfes Gray, "My Story of the Cloquet Fire," carbon typescript (quotations), "The Fire," typescript — both in Kathryn Elfes Gray Papers (hereafter Gray Papers), Manuscripts Collections, MHS; Olesen testimony, *Hearings on H.R. 5660,* p. 220–21; *Pine Knot,* October 11, 1918, p. 1; Emmett Kavanaugh, reminiscence in "Holocaust of 1918 Holds Vivid Memories for Veteran Conwed Employees," *Conwed Contact* (Conwed Corporation, Cloquet, Minn.) 26 (July 1968): 8; Blomberg interview (quotation), transcript in the possession of the authors.

11. Wiselan testimony, Record 1:1019–21, *Hall v. Davis;* Gray, "The Fire" (quotations), Gray Papers, MHS; "Elfes, Orlo B.," in Cornwall, comp., *Who's Who in Minnesota,* 206; here and below, see Olesen testimony, *Hearings on H.R. 5660,* p. 220–21.

12. Gray, "My Story of the Cloquet Fire," Gray Papers, MHS; Olesen testimony, *Hearings on H.R. 5660,* p. 221.

13. Gray, "My Story of the Cloquet Fire," Gray Papers, MHS. The train stopped at Johnson's Crossing, at several other mill crossings, in Scanlon three miles down the line, and then finally in Carlton, where a larger engine was put on before the train continued to Duluth.

14. Gray, "Are You a 49'er?" pt. 2, *Cloquet Vidette,* October 18, 1967, p. 12; "Spoor, Eldon W.," in Cornwall, comp., *Who's Who in Minnesota,* 210; Elshoss, "My Experiences in the Cloquet Fire of 1918," in Women's Friday Club, Cloquet, comp., "Group of Essays," 47 (quotation), CCHS, MHS.

15. Drew, "The Forest Fire of 1918," in Women's Friday Club, Cloquet, comp., "Group of Essays," 34 (quotation), CCHS, MHS.

16. Gray, "Are You a 49'er?" pt. 1, p. 3, pt. 2, p. 12, *Cloquet Vidette*, October 11, 18, 1967; *Pine Knot*, December 29, 1959, p. 4; Gray, "My Story of the Cloquet Fire," Gray Papers, MHS; Vibert testimony, Record 2:1887–89, *Hall v. Davis;* Coy to Mayde, October 17, 1918, Coy to Ted, October 19, 1918 — both in the possession of Elizabeth Walter; Smith interview, Oral History Collections, MHS; Blomberg interview, transcript in the possession of the authors; Ruby Spurbeck, "The 1918 Cloquet Fire" (recollection, September 1975), NEMHC; "Spurbeck, Roy George," in Cornwall, comp., *Who's Who in Minnesota*, 210.

17. Western Adjustment & Inspection Company, *Forest Fires in Northern Minnesota*, 1918. A Northern Pacific pump engine kept water pressure in the Carlton system when the village plant failed. *Carlton County Vidette*, October 18, 1918, p. 2; *Cloquet Pine Knot*, October 19, 1978, p. 5.

18. *Carlton County Vidette*, October 18, 1918, p. 2; Gray, "The Fire," Gray Papers, MHS; Mrs. Henry C. Oldenburg to Margaret Oldenburg, October 14, 1918, Henry (Heinrich) Carl Albert Oldenburg Papers, Manuscripts Collections, MHS; Coy to Mayde, October 17, 1918, in the possession of Elizabeth Walter; Dr. Maurice H. Haubner in *Village Times* (Carlton) July 1, 1987, p. 17; "Hornby, Henry C.," Cornwall, comp., *Who's Who in Minnesota*, 207. The fears of Carlton residents are vividly described in Annie B. Cook Woodworth to Avis Woodworth, October 13, 1918, letter in the possession of Nancy Hursh Bagley, Seattle, Washington.

19. Campbell testimony, Record 1:1245–76 (quotations, 1246, 1275–76), *Hall v. Davis.*

20. Coy to Mayde, October 17, 1918, in the possession of Elizabeth Walter.

21. Testimonies of Petite, Record 1:908–20 (quotation, 920), LaFave, Record 2:1677–1711, Houle, Record 1:945–53 — all in *Hall v. Davis;* Gray, "Are You a 49'er?" pt. 2, *Cloquet Vidette*, October 18, 1967, p. 12. Joe Madwayosh's nickname was recalled by Ramona Thompson of the Fond du Lac reservation, whose husband, Joe Thompson, was also a log roller. Madwayosh was nearly one hundred years old when he died, probably in the late 1960s or the 1970s. Conversation of Ramona Thompson with Daniel W. Anderson (curriculum developer), Fond du Lac Indian Reservation, February 6, 1990; Patricia Maus (NEMHC) to Deborah Swanson (MHS), February 6, 22, 1990, in the files of the Minnesota Historical Society Press. See also *Fond du Lac Tri-Parish Pictorial Directory*, 1977 ([Louisville, Ky.: Bel-Air Studios, 1978]), 5.

22. Wenzel, "My Experience in the Cloquet Fire of 1918," in Women's Friday Club, Cloquet, comp., "Group of Essays," 38–41 (quotation, 41), CCHS, MHS.

23. For an interesting account of Cloquet while it was burning, written by someone who stayed through the night, see [R. Weyerhaeuser] to J. Weyerhaeuser, November 2, 1918, Weyerhaeuser Family Papers, MHS.

24. For the assertion that one hundred men could have saved the city, see F. E. Weyerhaeuser to Mrs. F. E. W[eyerhaeuser], October 15, 1918, Frederick E. Weyerhaeuser Correspondence, Weyerhaeuser Family Papers, MHS. The names of many of those who worked to save the lumber companies were published in the *Carlton County Vidette* of November 25, 1918, p. 1, as follows: Northern Lumber Company: Rudolph M. Weyerhaeuser and John Atkins; Cloquet Lumber Company: Henry ["Harry"] Hornby, H. G. Stevens, William F. Heasley, R. R. Macartney, John N. Anderson, Martin Bodin, Reuben Holmes, Arthur LeBrun, Dennis Dunn, Ira Gilbert, and two mill firemen; Johnson-Wentworth Lumber Company: Joseph Wilson

and Anthony McKale; and Cloquet Tie and Post Company: James A. Wilson and crew.

25. Pyne, *Fire in America*, 206–7; Richardson, "Northeastern Minnesota Forest Fires," 227. At the time, people certainly felt that the railroads had performed heroically. One Northern Pacific official wrote, "I think everything has been done that could be done by the railroads, and everyone that I have come in contact with here and along the line has nothing but praise for what has been done." J. M. Rapelje to J. M. Hannaford, October 14, 1918, President's subject file, no. 494 A-3, NP Records, MHS. C. I. McNair of Cloquet, writing to Louis W. Hill, president of the Great Northern, sent high praise for that line's handling of the situation in Cloquet. McNair to Hill, November 9, 1918, President's subject file, no. 6907, GN Records, MHS. The governor of Minnesota told the regional director of the U.S. Railroad Administration: "All of the railways in this section have given us very valuable assistance, and you may be sure that it is greatly appreciated." [J. A. A. Burnquist] to R. H. Aishton, October 17, 1918 (copy), file 648c, Gov. J. A. A. Burnquist in Governor's Records (hereafter Burnquist in Governor's Records), Minnesota State Archives, MHS. What is perhaps so difficult to understand now, in a world that hangs on roving reporters' news updates, mobile camera units, aerial photo coverage, and radio-television communications networks, is people's failure to appreciate the growing seriousness of the fire situation during the afternoon of October 12. In towns like Moose Lake, not to mention numerous smaller communities, no communications structure existed to channel information either to the public or to responsible officials.

CHAPTER FOUR. The Fires above Duluth

1. J. Miettunen testimony, Record 1:472–79 (quotation, 479), *McCool v. Davis*.

2. Jacqueline Moran, comp., *Recollections: An Informal History of the Alborn Area, St. Louis County, Minnesota* (Duluth: St. Louis County Historical Society, 1980), 26–28 (quotations, 26, 28); *Hearings on H.R. 5660*, p. 109–14.

3. Moran, comp., *Recollections*, 27–29.

4. Testimony of Mrs. Ida W. Thorwall, Record 1:1000–1007 (quotation, 1003), *McCool v. Davis*.

5. Testimony of Edward F. Gill, Record 1:639–45, 661–66 (quotations, 640, 665–66), *McCool v. Davis*.

6. Richardson, "Northeastern Minnesota Forest Fires," 227–31. At the hearings a compilation of testimony about wind direction in the Duluth fire showed a strong indication of wind from the west, but there was a substantial variety of opinions. The results of the compilation of testimony were as follows: for the wind out of the west 33, northwest 18, southwest 15, east 2, north 1, and southeast 1. *Hearings on H.R. 5660*, p. 300–302.

7. Testimony of Daniel Willeck, Record 1:732–39 (quotations, 739), *McCool v. Davis*.

8. Testimonies of Miss Viena Hill, Record 1:792–97 (quotations, 795, 796, 798), Willeck, Record 1:735 – both in *McCool v. Davis*.

9. Here and below, see Katharine Luomala, "The Cloquet Fire, October 12, 1918," in Women's Friday Club, Cloquet, comp., "Group of Essays," 1–9 (quotations 3, 4, 6), CCHS, MHS, and *Pine Knot*, May 15, 1936, p. 1, 8; *Pine Knot*, February 20, 1920, p. 1. Katharine Luomala (whose first name is spelled Katherine in the "Group

of Essays" typescript) was a student at the University of California at Berkeley when she wrote her prize-winning essay. She later became a well-known scholar at the University of Hawaii, specializing in the traditional literature of the Pacific. See Adrienne L. Kaeppler and H. Arlo Nimmo, eds., *Directions in Pacific Traditional Literature: Essays in Honor of Katharine Luomala*, Bernice P. Bishop Museum, Special Publication 62 (Honolulu, Hawaii: Bishop Museum Press, 1976), 1–58, especially 3–9.

10. Testimony of C. H. Barnes, Record 1:916–28, *McCool v. Davis.*

11. Testimony of Anna Hanson, Record 2:1090–98 (quotations, 1093, 1097), *McCool v. Davis.*

12. Testimony of Victor Leslie, Record 2:1242–69 (quotations, 1247, 1248), *McCool v. Davis.*

13. Olga Marie Gustafson Fremling reminiscence, quoted in "Postscripts," *Minnesota History* 49 (Spring 1985): 202–3; Frank [Murphy] to Mother, October 15, 1918, Frank Murphy Letter (hereafter Murphy Letter), NEMHC; Sher[man Coy] to Ted, October 19, 1918 (transcript), original letter in the possession of Elizabeth Walter; *Duluth Herald*, October 14, 1918, p. 9.

14. *Pine Knot*, December 6, 1935, p. 10 (from October 25, 1918, issue).

15. Report of Captain Henry L. Tourtelotte, Commanding Officer, Duluth District, Fourth Regiment, Minnesota Infantry, National Guard, to Adjutant General, October 27, 1918 (hereafter Tourtelotte report), report of Major Roger M. Weaver, Commanding Officer, Third Battalion, Minnesota Home Guard, to Commanding Officer, November 3, 1918 (hereafter Weaver report) — both in Roger M. Weaver Scrapbook (hereafter Weaver Scrapbook), NEMHC; Richardson, "Northeastern Minnesota Forest Fires," 225.

16. *Hearings on H.R. 5660*, p. 245–47 (quotations, 247); testimony of Edward L. Kimball, Record 2:1383–88, *McCool v. Davis;* Duluth city directories, 1917–30, for entries regarding Captain West.

17. Testimony of Harry E. McCool, Record 1:22–42 (quotation, 30), *McCool v. Davis.*

18. [Mildred Washburn] to Caroline [Marshall], November 3, 1918, transcript, NEMHC. In 1919 Washburn married Charles Russell McLean, the "Russell" mentioned in her letter.

19. Fremling reminiscence in "Postscripts," 203.

20. *Hearings on H.R. 5660*, p. 228, 272; Richardson, "Northeastern Minnesota Forest Fires," 221–25; photograph of Northland Country Club ruins in *The Fury of the Flames: A Pictorial Record of the Great Forest Fires Which Raged in Northern Minnesota, Oct. 12–15, 1918* (Duluth: Martin A. Olmem, 1919); Strachan to McCauley, October 29, 1918, NP Records, MHS; Kenney to Aishton, October 13, 14, 1918, GN Records, MHS.

CHAPTER FIVE. The Tragedy at Automba, Kettle River, and Moose Lake

1. For a full discussion of the building of the railroads through this region see Carroll, *Crossroads in Time*, 101–24.

2. Testimony of George Brand, Record 2:940–62, *Dennis Carr v. James C. Davis,*

159 Minn. 485 and 199 N.W. 237 and Minnesota Supreme Court case file 23,837 (file in Minnesota State Archives, MHS).

3. Testimonies of Ed. R. Jacobson, Record 1:27–35, J. P. Brenner, Record 1:70–81 — both in *Carr v. Davis*.

4. *Aitkin Independent Age*, October 15, 1975, p. 1B (quotation).

5. Strachan to McCauley, October 29, 1918, NP Records, MHS.

6. Testimony of Dennis Carr, Record 1:663–79, *Carr v. Davis*.

7. Narrative of Uno Lake, p. 4–5, in Alanen, ed., *1918 Fire*.

8. Narratives of Carl Maijala, p. 2–3, Oscar Rinta, p. 3, Aili Rosbacka Field, p. 5–7 (quotation, 6), Ina Pursi Alanen, p. 7–8, Miriam Sanda Shilstron, p. 8, in Alanen, ed., *1918 Fire*. The Rintas, the Lundeens, the Bakka girls, John Ulback, and Matt Luuki, Sr., found refuge in the Maijala house; the Pursis, the Rosbackas, the Haapanens, the Salos, and others went to the Illberg house.

9. Forest Fire Investigation Commission, "Report of Forest Fire Investigation Commission," in appendix to Minnesota, Governor (1915–21: Burnquist), *Inaugural Message of Gov. J. A. A. Burnquist to the Legislature of Minnesota, 1919* [St. Paul?, 1919], 34; C. A. Hanna, "Remember the Moose Lake Fire," *Conservation Volunteer* (Minnesota Department of Conservation) 24 (September-October 1961): 56–59 (quotation, 57). For a description of the fire at Palisade, a town in Aitkin County on the banks of the Mississippi where the Soo Line tracks crossed the river, see Eric K. Johnson, "Anna Hedin: Reluctant Immigrant," *Heritage* (Chisago County Historical Society, Minn.) 8 (December 1989-January 1990): 4–7.

10. Testimonies of Gilbert Buxter, Record 1:87–141, Jacob Anderson, Record 1:303–23 — both in *Anderson v. Soo Line*.

11. Brief for Respondent, 24, 32, 49, *Anderson v. Soo Line*; Forest Fire Investigation Commission, "Report," 34; Perry W. Swedberg, Summary of year's work, ca. late 1918, Records, Reports and Related Correspondence, Districts, 1914–1924, Minnesota Forestry Board Records, Minnesota State Archives, MHS.

12. Testimony of Gust Sahlstrom, Record 3:1457–78, *Anderson v. Soo Line*; Swedberg, Summary of year's work, ca. late 1918 (quotation), Minnesota Forestry Board Records, MHS. Swedberg here referred to the fact that the roads out of Automba were just dirt tracks in the woods, and in the circumstances very dangerous.

13. Narratives of Tomczak, p. 113–14, William Maki, p. 117 (quotation), Matt Reed, p. 121–23, in Manni, comp., *Kettle River*. There were at least three sawmills in Automba, as well as several stores, a post office, and the Soo Line depot. The yards held an estimated 60,000 cords of pulpwood, 80,000 railroad ties, and 5,000,000 board feet of lumber. Split Rock had no town site; Carroll, *Crossroads in Time*, 190–92.

14. Narrative of Aina Jokimaki Johnson, p. 99–100 (quotations, 99), in Manni, comp., *Kettle River*. Aina later married Carl J. Johnson.

15. Narrative of Fred Maki, p. 102–3 (quotation, 102), in Manni, comp., *Kettle River*. Many others in this area survived by going into recently plowed fields. Hulda Baakari Bisila told how her family and many neighbors saved themselves in this fashion. They suffered some burns, but survived. H. Bisila narrative, p. 106–7, *Kettle River*.

16. *Carlton County Vidette*, February 24, 1964, 75th Anniversary (Futurama) Edition, section 7, p. 4.

17. Narratives of Reiner Hattenberger, p. 116, W. Maki, p. 117, Mrs. Bernard Walzak, p. 118, Stella Homicz Dudek, p. 93–94, in Manni, comp., *Kettle River*.

18. Narrative of Clara Suchoski Caskey, p. 113 (quotation), in Manni, comp., *Kettle River*; testimony of Peter Suchoski, Record 1:555–65, *Anderson v. Soo Line*.

19. Narrative of Reed, p. 121–23 (quotation, 122), in Manni, comp., *Kettle River.*

20. Testimony of Lillian Peterson, Record 2:851–55 (quotation, 855), *Anderson v. Soo Line.*

21. Here and following paragraph, see testimony of Walfred Westholm, Record 4:2513–28 (quotation, 2521), *Anderson v. Soo Line.*

22. Narratives of Olga Silverberg, p. 125, George Maijala, p. 83, Gust Granrose, p. 116 (quotations), in Manni, comp., *Kettle River; Forest Fire Investigation Commission, "Report," 34.* For details about the problems of fighting this fire, see testimony of Frank Ronkainen, Record 4:2164–66, 2396–2428, *Anderson v. Soo Line.*

23. Narratives of Walfred Carlson, p. 95–96, Charles Eckman, p. 127, in Manni, comp., *Kettle River.*

24. Westholm testimony, Record 4:2513–28, *Anderson v. Soo Line.*

25. Testimony of Arthur C. Russell, Record 3:934–44, *Anderson v. Soo Line;* narratives of Ailie Leppa Nikkila, p. 84 (quotation), Mrs. Jack Kohtala, p. 120, Tillie N. Odberg Westman, p. 104, Joseph G. and Celia Kowalski, p. 111, in Manni, comp., *Kettle River.*

26. Testimonies of Ernest Vandervort, Record 3:2051–60 (quotation, 2053), I. B. Phelps, Record 3:2018–34 (quotation, 2021), *Anderson v. Soo Line.*

27. Russell testimony, Record 3:934–44 (quotations, 934, 944), *Anderson v. Soo Line.*

28. See also Holbrook, *Burning an Empire,* 35; Hemingson, *Death by Fire,* 38–39.

29. Westholm testimony, Record 4:2529–47, *Anderson v. Soo Line;* narrative of Nikkila, p. 84, in Manni, comp., *Kettle River; Duluth News Tribune,* November 1, 1918, p. 4; *Carlton County Vidette,* January 9, 1920, p. 1.

30. Narrative of J. and C. Kowalski, p. 111 (quotation), in Manni, comp., *Kettle River.* Everett Bisila and two friends walked through Dead Man's Curve, attempting to help others, and Matt O. Wilson and his brother Walter drove through. Narratives of Everett Bisila, p. 128, Matt O. Wilson, p. 128, in Manni, comp., *Kettle River.*

31. Narratives of Nikkila, p. 85, E. Bisila, p. 128, in Manni, comp., *Kettle River;* Westholm testimony, Record 4:2529–47, *Anderson v. Soo Line.*

32. Narratives of Arnold Lund, p. 94, Carlson, p. 95–97 (quotations, 95, 97), Eckman, p. 127–28, in Manni, comp., *Kettle River.*

33. Narratives of Hulda Portinen Koivisto, p. 100–101 (quotation, 101), Granrose, p. 116, Lund, p. 95, in Manni, comp., *Kettle River.* The Jalonens and Williamses died together in the root cellar on the Williams farm while Saima's husband, Frank, was directing fire fighters elsewhere. Apparently, Frank returned home, attempted unsuccessfully to keep the cellar from burning, and then died on the road to another farm.

34. Strachan to McCauley, October 29, 1918, NP Records, MHS; Superior Fire Relief Committee, *Report to Donors,* 5; *Carlton County Vidette,* October 18, 1918, p. 2; *Star Gazette* (Moose Lake), December 19, 1918, p. 1; Holbrook, *Burning an Empire,* 35; Memorandum, n.d., General Correspondence, Minnesota Forestry Board Records, MHS; E. G. Cheyney, "The Holocaust in Minnesota: A Greater Hinckley," *American Forestry* 24 (November 1918): 646. A Northern Pacific relief train was also sent into Moose Lake on October 13 after the town had burned. It took between fifteen and twenty people back to Carlton. The Soo Line also ran four relief trains on Sunday and Monday.

35. Narratives of Wilson, p. 129–30, Westman, p. 104, Kohtala, p. 119, in Manni, comp., *Kettle River.*

36. Narratives of Wilson, p. 130, Westman, p. 104 (quotation), Kohtala, p. 119

(quotations), in Manni, comp., *Kettle River;* "Williams; Elmer J.," in Cornwall, ed., *Who's Who in Minnesota,* 210; *Pine Knot,* October 8, 1987, p. 15.

37. R[ichard] T. Hart to [J. A. A.] Burnquist, October 13, 1918, Burnquist in Governor's Records, MHS. Farther south, the Millward-Arthyde fires had their origins in both Soo Line railroad fires and bog fires. The villages of Arthyde, Selana, and White Pine were saved by the crews of men working under District Ranger Swedberg. Forest Fire Investigation Commission, "Report," 34.

38. Minnesota Forest Fires Relief Commission, *Final Report,* 12; Forest Fire Investigation Commission, "Report," 33; Swedberg, Summary of year's work, ca. late 1918 (quotation), Minnesota Forestry Board Records, MHS.

CHAPTER SIX. Relief Operations

1. Tourtelotte report, October 27, 1918, in Weaver Scrapbook, NEMHC.

2. Weaver report, November 3, 1918, in Weaver Scrapbook, NEMHC.

3. Weaver report, November 3, 1918, in Weaver Scrapbook, [Murphy] to Mother, October 15, 1918, Murphy Letter — both in NEMHC. On the Motor Corps, see Arnold L. Luukkonen, "Brave Men in their Motor Machines — and the 1918 Forest Fire," *Ramsey County History* (Minn.) 9 (Fall 1972): 3–8. Between 15,000 and 18,000 gallons of gasoline were used in Duluth from October 12 to 14, and "practically every automobile in the city was drafted" for emergency use of some kind, according to C. H. Tanner of the Northwestern Oil Company. All of the gasoline in Carlton was used up, and new supplies had to be rushed in from Duluth. *Pine Knot,* December 6, 1935, special section, [pt. 2], p. 4 (from October 25, 1918, issue).

4. Weaver report, November 3, 1918 (quotation), in Weaver Scrapbook, NEMHC; American Red Cross, *The Work of the American Red Cross: Report by the War Council of Appropriations and Activities from Outbreak of War to November 1, 1917* (Washington, D.C.: American Red Cross, 1917), 32, 35, 37.

5. Weaver report, November 3, Tourtelotte report, October 27 — both 1918 and in Weaver Scrapbook, NEMHC; Blomberg interview, transcript in the possession of the authors; Gray, "Are You a 49'er?" pt. 1, p. 3, pt. 2, p. 12, *Cloquet Vidette,* October 11, 18, 1967.

6. Weaver report, November 3, 1918, in Weaver Scrapbook, NEMHC; narratives of Koivisto, p. 101 (quotation), Wilson, p. 130 (quotation), in Manni, comp., *Kettle River.*

7. Weaver report, November 3, 1918, in Weaver Scrapbook, NEMHC.

8. [Hubert V. Eva] to W. F. Rhinow, December 13, 1918, Eva to J. A. A. Burnquist, January 2, 1919 — both in Burnquist in Governor's Records, MHS; *Pine Knot,* November 1, 1918, p. 1, December 6, 1918, p. 1; *Star Gazette,* December 19, 1918, p. 1.

9. Weaver report, November 3, 1918, in Weaver Scrapbook, NEMHC; report of Frank J. Bruno (director of Bureau of Civilian Relief, Northern Division), October 1918 (hereafter Bruno report), in American Red Cross Report of Division Directors of Civilian Relief for the Month of October, 1918, p. 34–36, in American Red Cross, Northern Division, Minneapolis, Papers (hereafter American Red Cross Papers), Manuscripts Collections, MHS; Women's Friday Club, Cloquet, comp., "Group of Essays," p. 3, CCHS, MHS; letter about Kathleen Covey from Marjorie Adams and W. Gordon Adams to Alan Woolworth (MHS), April 24, 1990, in the files of the Minnesota Historical Society Press.

10. Bruno report, October 1918, p. 34–36, American Red Cross Papers, MHS; [Murphy] to Mother, October 15, 1918 (quotations), Murphy Letter, NEMHC; Mrs. W. H. Slavel, "My Experiences the Night of the Cloquet Fire," in Women's Friday Club, Cloquet, comp., "Group of Essays," p. 54–55, CCHS, MHS, and *Pine Knot*, June 5, 1936, p. 9; Smith interview, Oral History Collections, MHS. For another interesting account of the experiences of someone who stayed at the Spalding Hotel, see [Washburn] to [Marshall], November 3, [1918], NEMHC.

11. Arthur N. Collins, Report of Medical Activities October 26, 1918, in Weaver Scrapbook, NEMHC; reports of Frank J. Bruno, December 1918, p. 97, January 1919, p. 76–77 (hereafter Bruno reports), in reports of division directors for the months of December 1918 and January 1919, American Red Cross Papers, MHS.

12. Bruno reports, December 1918, p. 97, January 1919, p. 76–77, American Red Cross Papers, MHS; Hanna, "Remember the Moose Lake Fire," 56–59; *Pine Knot*, November 1, 1918, p. 1. For a full account of the influenza problem, see Alfred W. Crosby, Jr., *Epidemic and Peace, 1918* (Westport, Conn.: Greenwood Press, 1976; reprinted as *America's Forgotten Pandemic: The Influenza of 1918* [New York: Cambridge University Press, 1990]), 3–90.

13. *Pine Knot*, November 1, 1918, p. 1, November 22, 1918, p. 1; Gray, "Are You a 49'er?" pt. 2, *Cloquet Vidette*, October 18, 1967, p. 12; *Pine Knot-Billboard* (Cloquet), October 11, 1984, p. 3, 10.

14. *Duluth News Tribune*, October 15, 1918, p. 2, October 16, 1918, p. 2, 4, October 17, 1918, p. 2, November 1, 1918, p. 7; *Pine Knot*, November 22, 1918, p. 1.

15. Report of J. L. Gillin (director of Bureau of Civilian Relief, Central Division), October 1918, in report of division directors for the month of October 1918, p. 71, American Red Cross Papers, MHS; Superior Fire Relief Committee, *Report to Donors*, [2]-10.

16. Superior Fire Relief Committee, *Report to Donors*, 56; Minnesota Forest Fires Relief Commission, *Final Report*, 14–23; Drew, "The Forest Fire of 1918," in Women's Friday Club, Cloquet, comp., "Group of Essays," 35–36 (quotation, 35), CCHS, MHS; *Hearings on H.R. 5660*, p. 221–22 (quotations); Iva Andrus Dingwall, "Memories of the Cloquet Forest Fire" (quotation), Iva Andrus Dingwall Reminiscences, Manuscripts Collections, MHS. Drew observed about the volunteer effort in Superior: "The churches, theaters, schools, and lodges opened their doors wide. Women cooked and donated food — washed countless dishes — made over clothes for children — took care of the sick and there were so many sick with the flu at this time, everyone giving themselves at this crucial time. Such sympathy, kindness, and unselfishness can never be forgotten" (p. 36).

17. Superior Fire Relief Committee, *Report to Donors*, [3–23]. The final number of refugees registered in Superior was 9,039. Although part of a different Red Cross geographical division, the Superior Chapter nevertheless worked carefully and cooperatively with its counterpart in Duluth.

18. *Duluth News Tribune*, October 14, 1918, p. 4; *Pine Knot*, December 6, 1935, special section, [pt. 2], p. 7.

19. J. A. A. Burnquist, public announcement, ca. October 15, 1918, Joseph Alfred Arner Burnquist Papers (hereafter Burnquist Papers), Manuscripts Collections, MHS; Minutes, October 16, 22, 29, 1918, Minnesota Commission of Public Safety Records, Minnesota State Archives, MHS; *Duluth News Tribune*, October 17, 1918, p. 1, 3. For issues arising out of the question of appropriating public money for relief, see *Pine Knot*, January 10, 1919, p. 2, January 24, 31, 1919, both p. 1, February 7, 14, 21, 1919,

all p. 1; *Laws of Minnesota*, 1919, p. 53–55. On other activities of the MCPS, see Carol Jenson, "Loyalty as a Political Weapon: The 1918 Campaign in Minnesota," *Minnesota History* 43 (Summer 1972): 42–57.

20. Minnesota Forest Fires Relief Commission, *Final Report*, 14–21; "Colonel Hubert V. Eva," in Burnquist, ed., *Minnesota and Its People* 4:606.

21. Minnesota Forest Fires Relief Commission, *Final Report*, 19–21.

22. Minnesota Forest Fires Relief Commission, *Final Report*, 19–23 (quotation, 22). The expression "long-term" had to be used with some caution. In response to an inquiry from the house appropriations committee of the state legislature, Attorney General Clifford L. Hilton said that public money could not be give for "long term relief" or permanent rehabilitation, but only for emergency circumstances; *Pine Knot*, February 21, 1919, p. 1. The commission, which of course also had private money at its disposal, took a broad interpretation of the attorney general's opinion.

23. C. I. McNair to J. A. A. Burnquist, October 23, 1918 (quotation), W. A. McGonagle to Burnquist, October 26, 1918 (typescript copy of telegram) — both in Burnquist in Governor's Records, MHS.

24. Minnesota Forest Fires Relief Commission, *Final Report*, 22–24, 38, 40; *Carlton County Vidette*, November 15, 1918, p. 1.

25. Minnesota Forest Fires Relief Commission, *Final Report*, 8, 22.

26. Minnesota Forest Fires Relief Commission, *Final Report*, 8, 21–30. By mid-April farmers were encouraged to apply for seed and farm implements. *Pine Knot*, April 25, 1919, p. 1.

27. Minnesota Forest Fires Relief Commission, *Final Report*, p. 23–30.

28. Minnesota Forest Fires Relief Commission, *Final Report*, 23–30; Bruno report, January 1919, p. 76–77, American Red Cross Papers, MHS.

29. Charles Koster to Henry W. Libby, December 16, 1918, Perry W. Swedberg to William T. Cox, January 11, 1919, main file 262, Minnesota Commission of Public Safety Records, MHS; Minnesota Forest Fires Relief Commission, *Final Report*, 26 (quotation). For a public discussion of the equity of the relief distribution policy, see *Pine Knot*, March 7, 14, 1919, p. 1. Praise for the relief efforts can be found in many passages of fire sufferers' accounts. See Manni, comp., *Kettle River*, 88, 95, 135.

30. Minnesota Forest Fires Relief Commission, *Final Report*, 23–30 (quotation, 28); Crosby, *Epidemic and Peace*, 203–94.

31. Minnesota Forest Fires Relief Commission, *Final Report*, 4, 26, 30; Burnquist, Public announcement, ca. October 15, 1918 (quotation), Burnquist Papers, MHS. The work for fire refugees in Minneapolis is shown in Civilian Relief, Records of Miscellaneous Departments, Adjutant General's Office, Minnesota Home Guard, Records, Minnesota State Archives, MHS. For examples of letters of sympathy and offers of help sent to Governor Burnquist in 1918, see Thomas Van Lear (mayor of Minneapolis), October 14 (telegram), R. E. Leonard (secretary of Rotary Club of St. Paul), October 15, A. F. Wright (city clerk of Rochester), October 15 (telegram), E. L. Philipp (spelled "Phillips"; governor of Wisconsin), October 15 (telegram), Samuel W. McCall and Calvin Coolidge (spelled "Colledge"; governor and lieutenant governor of Massachusetts), October 17 (telegram), Frank O. Lowden (governor of Illinois), October 19 (letter and telegram), Axel, Prince of Denmark, October 19 — all in Burnquist in Governor's Records, MHS. On the closing of the relief offices in Cloquet, see *Pine Knot*, August 1, 1919, p. 1.

32. Memorandum, October 15, 1918, President's subject file, no. 494 A-3, NP

Records, MHS; R. H. Aishton to W. P. Kenney, ca. October 16, 1918 (telegram), Burnquist in Governor's Records, MHS.

33. Carl G. Schulz to Superintendents and Principals, October 19, Clarence W. Wigington to J. A. A. Burnquist, October 14 (quotation) — both 1918 and in Burnquist in Governor's Records, MHS. The Junior Red Cross was an organization for schoolchildren that carried on its activities through schools; American Red Cross, *Work*, 27–28. See also Minnesota Forest Fires Relief Commission, *Final Report*, 32; *Star Gazette*, December 19, 1918, p. 1; *Pine Knot*, October 25, 1918, p. 1, December 6, 1935, special section, [pt. 1], p. 8 (from October 25, 1918, issue); *Duluth News Tribune*, October 18, 19, 1918, both p. 1.

34. Cross to Commissioner, October 18, 1918 (quotation), Indexes and Schedules of Fire Claims, Fond du Lac, RG 75, NA, Kansas City; Cross to Commissioner of Indian Affairs, October 28, 1918, E. B. Merritt to Cross, November 6, 1918 — both in Central Classified Files, 1907–39, Fond du Lac, file 330, RG 75, NA, Washington, D.C. See also N. Connor (superintendent of Nett Lake Indian Reservation, Minnesota) to Commissioner, December 16, 1919, Merritt to Cross, December 27, 1919 — both in Central Classified Files, 1907–39, Fond du Lac, file 330, RG 75, NA, Washington, D.C. Of course, the Indian agency office in Cloquet had been destroyed by the fire. Cross not only had the task of trying to look after the Ojibway fire victims, but he also had to get his office functioning again. Facilities were eventually established in Superior.

35. George W. Cross to Commissioner of Indian Affairs, January 10, 1919, E. B. Merritt to Cross, January 27, 1919 (telegram), Merritt to Leo S. Bonnin, August 20, 1919, S. G. Hopkins to Bonnin, October 17, 1919 — all in Indexes and Schedules of Fire Claims, Fond du Lac, RG 75, NA, Kansas City.

36. Leo S. Bonnin to Commissioner of Indian Affairs, August 1, 1919, Bonnin to Commissioner of Indian Affairs, September 24, 1919, Bonnin to Indian Office, October 17, 1919 (telegram) — all in Central Classified Files, 1907–39, Fond du Lac, file 410, RG 75, NA, Washington, D.C.; E. B. Merritt to Bonnin, August 20, 1919, Indexes and Schedules of Fire Claims, Fond du Lac, RG 75, NA, Kansas City.

CHAPTER SEVEN. Fire in the Courts

1. Swedberg, Summary of year's work, ca. late 1918, Minnesota Forestry Board Records, MHS; *Pine Knot*, October 25, 1918, p. 2.

2. Cox, *Annual Report*, 15–17 (quotations, 15); *Pine Knot*, November 22, 1918, p. 1. See also " 'Unusual Freaky Conditions Caused Fire' — Forester Cox," *Duluth News Tribune*, October 14, 1918, p. 9; Cox, *Comments on Report of Duluth Fire Committee* ([St. Paul?]: Printed by the Minnesota Forestry Association, [1923?]), copy in Reference Library, MHS. Cox's first impression was that weather and bog fires were responsible, but the *Pine Knot* later reported that he blamed the state legislature for reducing appropriations to the forest service, "making efficient forest patrol work impossible," and thus allowing "the flames to cause such historic devestation." *Pine Knot*, December 6, 1935, special section, [pt. 2], p. 2 (from October 25, 1918, issue).

3. Statement of Governor J. A. A. Burnquist, n.d., ca. October 1918 (quotations), Burnquist to J. L. Washburn, November 7, 1918 (quotation) — both in Burnquist Papers, MHS. See also Washburn to Burnquist, November 19, 1918, Burnquist in Governor's Records, MHS.

4. Forest Fire Investigation Commission, "Report," 32–40 (quotation, 33). When

submitting his report, Washburn wrote, "We could keep on all winter investigating the origin of a multitude of individual fires. The general facts would remain the same, and the recommendations be unchanged." Washburn to Burnquist, November 27, 1918, Burnquist Papers, MHS. For the opinion of the forestry journals, see Cheyney, "The Holocaust in Minnesota," 643–47; J. F. Hayden, "The Great Minnesota Fire," and an editorial, "Minnesota's Forest Fire Disaster," *American Forestry* 24 (November 1918): 648–52, 654–55. See also B. E. F., review of *Annual Report of the State Forestry Board of the State of Minnesota for the Year Ending July 31, 1918*, by William T. Cox, and L. M., review of "The Northeastern Minnesota Forest Fires of October 12, 1918," by H. W. Richardson, *Journal of Forestry* 17 (May; November 1919): 567–69; 867–70.

    5. Testimony of N. B. Arnold, *Hearings on H.R. 5660*, p. 111–12.

    6. R. H. Aishton to Walker D. Hines, February 5, 1919, Aishton to John Barton Payne, February 5, 1919 (quotation), Memorandum for the Director General from Oscar Price, February 8, 1919 — all in file no. I 19–1, Records of the United States Railroad Administration, Record Group 14 (hereafter RG 14), NA, Washington, D.C.

    7. The cases were tried in the Minnesota courts as a result of both state and federal legislation. The relevant section (4426) of the *General Statutes of Minnesota*, 1913, made railroad companies operating in Minnesota liable for damage caused by fires set by their locomotives:

> Each railroad corporation owning or operating a railroad in this state shall be responsible in damages to every person and corporation whose property may be injured or destroyed by fire communicated directly or indirectly by the locomotive engines in use upon the railroad owned or operated by such railroad corporation, and each such railroad shall have an insurable interest in the property upon the route of the railroad owned or operated by it and may procure insurance thereon in its own behalf for its protection against such damages.

The Federal Control Act of 1918 provided specifically that railroads could be sued in the state courts:

> That carriers while under Federal control shall be subject to all laws and liabilities as common carriers, whether arising under State or Federal laws or at common law, except in so far as may be inconsistent with the provisions of this Act or any other Act applicable to such Federal control or with any order of the President. . . . Nor shall any such carrier be entitled to have transferred to a Federal court any action heretofore or hereafter instituted by or against it, which action was not so transferable prior to the Federal control of such carrier. (*United States Statutes at Large*, 65th Cong., 2d sess., 1918, 40, pt. 1:456 [section 10].)

The Transportation Act of 1920 (Esch-Cummings Act) transferring the railroads back to private ownership provided that:

> Actions at law, . . . based on causes of action arising out of the possession, use, or operation by the President of the railroad or system of transportation of any carrier (under the provisions of the Federal Control Act, or of the act of August 29, 1916) of such character as prior to Federal control could have been brought against such carrier, may, after the termination of Federal control, be brought against an agent designated by the President for such

purpose. *(United States Statutes at Large,* 66th Cong., 2d sess., 1920, 41, pt. 1:461 [section 206a].)

8. Arnold testimony, *Hearings on H.R. 5660,* p. 109, 113–14 (quotation, 109); *Sivert Holten v. Duluth, Missabe & Northern Railway Company* (in Minnesota Supreme Court case file 21,617; file in Minnesota State Archives, MHS).

9. Testimonies of James C. Davis, p. 14–22, D. S. Holmes, p. 52–54, *Hearings on H.R. 5660;* Aishton to Hines, February 5, 1919, Aishton to Payne, February 5, 1919, Memorandum for the Director General from Price, February 8, 1919 — all in file no. I 19–1, RG 14, NA, Washington, D.C.

10. Arnold testimony, *Hearings on H.R. 5660,* p. 113–14; J. E. Diesen to G. W. Cross, March 11, 1922, Central Classified Files, 1907–39, Red Lake file 260, RG 75, NA, Washington, D.C. The Northern Minnesota Fire Sufferers Association's official publication invited "items of news from members of the Association and others, especially if same has a bearing on the forest fires of October 12, 1918, on matters pertaining to forestry, forest fire relief work and many other subjects closely related to the affairs of the fire sufferers." *Fire Sufferers Bulletin* (Duluth) 1 (March 10, 1921): 4.

11. Appellants' Brief, 1–13, Brief for Respondent, 1–61 — both in *Anderson v. Soo Line; Cook v. Minneapolis, St. Paul & Sault Ste. Marie Railway Company,* 89 Wis. (decisions of the Wisconsin Supreme Court) 622 and 74 N.W. 561.

12. Testimony of Judge Herbert A. Dancer, *Hearings on H.R. 5660,* p. 91–92. For Dancer quotation, see Record 4: 2965–66, *Anderson v. Soo Line;* the entire charge to the jury can be found in Record 4:2957–83.

13. Davis testimony, *Hearings on H.R. 5660,* p. 20 (quotation); *Anderson v. Soo Line,* 146 Minn. 430 (quotation, 431).

14. *Hans J. Borsheim v. Great Northern Railway Company,* 149 Minn. 210 and 183 N.W. 519.

15. Memorandum for Mr. [Walker D.] Hines from Max Thelen, January 3, 1920 (see especially George Schlecht to Hines, October 13, 1919 [quotations], enclosed copy), January 7, 1920, Memorandum for Hines from M. B. C., December 5, 1919 — both in file no. I 19–1, RG 14, NA, Washington, D.C.

16. Memorandum for Hines from Thelen, January 3, 1920 (quotation), file no. I 19–1, RG 14, NA, Washington, D.C.

17. Walker D. H[ines] to [E. Marvin] Underwood, January 16, 1920 (quotation), file no. I 19–1, RG 14, NA, Washington, D.C.

18. Memorandum for the Director General, January 13, 1920 (quotation), file no. I 19–1, RG 14, NA, Washington, D.C.

19. Memorandum for the Director General from LaRue Brown, February 5, 1920, file no. I 19–1, RG 14, NA, Washington, D.C. In a statement to the House Committee on Claims in 1928, Sidney F. Andrews, the then general solicitor of the Railroad Administration, recorded that only $22,193.87 had been paid to settle claims on a 100-percent basis; that is, those claims were the railroads' admitted liability. This actually amounted to .17 percent of the total of $12,693,973.00 paid by the Railroad Administration in settlement by May 1928. *Hearings on H.R. 5660,* p. 2–4.

20. Arnold testimony, *Hearings on H. R. 5660,* p. 108–27.

21. Arnold testimony, *Hearings on H.R. 5660,* p. 108–27. See also Stipulation to Submit Cases to Judges, etc., *A. R. Peterson v. Walker D. Hines as Agent of the President under the Transportation Act,* April 8, 1920 (quotation), file no. I 19–1, RG 14, NA, Washington, D.C.

22. Findings, *A. R. Peterson v. Walker D. Hines as Agent of the President under*

the Transportation Act, September 11, 1920 (copy), file 649c, Gov. Jacob A. O. Preus in Governor's Records (hereafter Preus in Governor's Records), Minnesota State Archives, MHS.

23. *Philip Hall v. James C. Davis as Agent of the President under the Transportation Act*, 150 Minn. 35 and 184 N.W. 25; Arnold testimony, p. 109-27, James C. Davis to Albert Baldwin, December 7, 1920, p. 303-4 (quotation, 303) — both in *Hearings on H.R. 5660*. Davis was a lawyer who specialized in railroad litigation. He was appointed general counsel for the Railroad Administration in June 1920 and served as director general from March 1921 to December 1925. "Davis, James Cox," in Clarence L. Barnhart, ed., *The Cyclopedia of Names* (New York: Appleton-Century-Crofts, 1954) 1:1206. See also Caleb Forbes Davis and James Cox Davis, "The Autobiographies of an Iowa Father and Son," *Annals of Iowa*, 3d ser., 19 (January 1935): 483-538 (pt. 2 by J. Davis, p. 501-38), especially 517.

24. James C. Davis to E. B. Merritt, December 9, 1920, Central Classified Files, 1907-39, Red Lake, file 260, RG 75, Washington, D.C.

25. *Hall v. Davis*, 150 Minn. 35 (quotations, 37, 38, 39) and 184 N.W. 25.

CHAPTER EIGHT. The Railroad Administration Settlement

1. W. A. Cant, Martin Hughes, Herbert A. Dancer, Bert Fesler, and Edward Freeman (judges of Eleventh Judicial District, Minnesota) to Wm. D. Mitchell, January 7, 1921 (quotation; copy), Governor's Records, MHS. Mitchell became solicitor general of the United States in 1925 and attorney general in Herbert Hoover's cabinet in 1929. His father was a Minnesota Supreme Court justice after whom the William Mitchell College of Law in St. Paul was named. *Dictionary of American Biography*, s.v. "Mitchell, William DeWitt"; James F. Heinlen, "The Honorable William Mitchell," *Chronicles* (Winona County Historical Society, Minn.) 5 (Fall 1986): 1-5. James Davis, as general counsel for the Railroad Administration, had concluded that a commission would not be suitable but that the administration should make a settlement offer following a supreme court decision on the Cloquet cases. Davis to Albert Baldwin, December 7, 1920, *Hearings on H.R. 5660*, p. 303-4.

2. W. A. Cant to J. A. O. Preus, February 16, 25, 26 (quotation), 1921, Preus to Cant, February 14, 1921 (copy) — all in Preus in Governor's Records, MHS.

3. John B. Payne to E. C. Lindley, January 19, 1921, file no. I 19-1, RG 14, NA, Washington, D.C.

4. Charles W. Bunn to Charles Donnelly, January 29, 1921, President's subject file, no. 494 A-3, NP Records, MHS; A Concurrent Resolution Memorializing the Congress of the United States to Reimburse Claimants Who Suffered Loss and Damage on Account of the Forest Fires that Devastated Northern Minnesota in October, 1918, March 15, 1921 (quotation), file no. I 19-1, RG 14, NA, Washington, D.C. See also Governor [J. A. O. Preus] to Warren G. Harding, March 17, 1921 (copy), Geo. B. Christian, Jr., to Preus, March 21, 1921 — both in Preus in Governor's Records, MHS.

5. [J. A. O. Preus] to James C. Davis, March 31, 1921 (copy), Preus in Governor's Records, MHS.

6. Davis to Baldwin, December 7, 1920, *Hearings on H.R. 5660*, p. 303-4; Davis to J. A. O. Preus, April 5, 1921 (quotation), file no. I 19-1, RG 14, NA, Washington

D.C. See also N. B. Arnold to Preus, March 28, 1921, Preus in Governor's Records, MHS.

7. [J. A. O. Preus] to James C. Davis, July 23, 1921 (quotation; copy). See also Preus to W. R. Ryan, May 24, 1921 (copy) — both in Preus in Governor's Records, MHS.

8. James C. Davis to J. A. O. Preus, July 30, 1921 (quotation), Davis, Memorandum, July 29, 1921 (quotation) — both in file no. I 19–1, RG 14, NA, Washington, D.C.

9. James C. Davis to J. A. O. Preus, August 11, 1921 (quotation); for reinforcement of the view that the Railroad Administration should not have been held liable, see E. C. Lindley to John Barton Payne, February 3, 1921 — both in file no. I 19–1, RG 14, NA, Washington, D.C. Davis's view was also based on the *Cook* case of 1898, which said, "If plaintiff's property was damaged by a number of fires combining, one . . . being the fire pleaded . . . the others being of no responsible origin, but of such sufficient or such superior force that they would have produced the damage to plaintiff's property regardless of the fire pleaded, then defendant was not liable." *Cook v. Minneapolis, St. Paul & Sault Ste. Marie Railway Company*, 98 Wis. 622 and 74 N.W. 561. The Minnesota Supreme Court considered the *Cook* case, pointed out challenges to it from other sources, and said that it was not relevant to the circumstances in the *Anderson* case; 146 Minn. 430 and 179 N.W. 45.

10. Director General to Albert Baldwin, August 29, 1921, J. C. D., Memorandum for Mr. McLaughlin, August 29, 1921 — both in file no. I 19–1, RG 14, NA, Washington, D.C.

11. Abbott MacPherran Gilbert & Doan to Baldwin Baldwin Holmes & Mayall, August 6, 1921, Memorandum on Minnesota Fire Cases against the Government, from Senator Frank B. Kellogg to A. A. McLaughlin, ca. August 1921 — both in *Hearings on H.R. 5660*, p. 57–59.

12. Davis to Baldwin, December 7, 1920 (quotation), *Hearings on H.R. 5660*, p. 303–4.

13. A. A. McLaughlin to Albert Baldwin, September 22, 1921, Davis testimony (quotation, 46), *Hearings on H.R. 5660*, p. 46, 60.

14. *Hearings on H.R. 5660*, p. 145–48, 153–63.

15. Stipulation, *Peterson v. Hines*, April 8, 1920, file no. I 19–1, RG 14, NA, Washington, D.C.

16. James C. Davis, Final Proposition of Settlement by the Railroad Administration as a Result of Hearing Representatives of Fire Claimants in Carlton and St. Louis Counties, Minnesota, January 25, 1922, file no. I 19–1, RG 14, NA, Washington, D.C.; testimonies of Holmes and Dancer, *Hearings on H.R. 5660*, p. 64–68, 86–102.

17. James C. Davis to Frank B. Kellogg, January 25, 1922, *Hearings on H.R. 5660*, p. 36–37; Davis to J. A. O. Preus, January 26, 1922, file no. I 19–1, RG 14, NA, Washington, D.C. A set of correspondence that reveals the process of submitting questionnaires to the Railroad Administration officials and then reaching agreement about the figures is that of the General Light and Power Company of Cloquet, which provided electrical service to Cloquet, Scanlon, Brookston, and Moose Lake. Much of its equipment had been destroyed by the fires in the several fire districts, so it made claims under several of the cases. (The company was later acquired by the Minnesota Power & Light Company, which became Minnesota Power in 1980.) See Correspondence, 1920–22, Records Division, Minnesota Power, Duluth, Minnesota; Bill Beck, *Northern Lights: An Illustrated History of Minnesota Power* (Duluth: Minnesota Power, [1981]), 151–57, 447.

18. *Harry E. McCool and Another v. James C. Davis*, 158 Minn. 146 and 197 N.W. 93; see also 162 Minn. 281 and 202 N.W. 900; and Offer by United States Railroad Administration of Settlement as to Eastern Area, March 28, 1925, *Hearings on H.R. 5660*, p. 68–70. Still another case decided by the Minnesota Supreme Court was *Carr v. Davis*, 159 Minn. 485 and 199 N.W. 237, which confirmed the Railroad Administration's responsibility for fires in the Tamarack area along the Northern Pacific tracks in Aitkin County. Two cases in which the appeals of the plaintiffs were turned down are *Smith v. Davis*, 162 Minn. 256 and 202 N.W. 483; and *Johnson v. Davis*, 207 N.W. 23.

19. Here and below, see J. A. Fesenbeck to G. W. Cross, October 12, 1920, Cross to Commissioner of Indian Affairs, December 30, 1921, January 24, September 3, 1922, F. M. Goodwin to Cross, January 18, 1922, J. E. Diesen to Cross, March 11, 1922 — all in Central Classified Files, 1907–39, Red Lake, file 260, RG 75, NA, Washington, D.C.

20. G. W. Cross to Commissioner of Indian Affairs, May 17, 1922, T. Scott to Joseph LaVeirge, August 1, 1923, Webster Ballinger to F. M. Goodwin, August 13, 1923 — all in Central Classified Files, 1907–39, Red Lake, file 260, RG 75, NA, Washington, D.C.; *LaVeirge v. Davis*, 166 Minn. 14 and 206 N.W. 939. The Office of Indian Affairs seemed generally suspicious of the Minnesota lawyers and their contingent fees — a view that was not discouraged by the Railroad Administration — and stated categorically that "the best interest of the Indians will be served" if the OIA represented them. Charles S. Burke, Commissioner, to Congressman O. J. Larson, December 23, 1922, Central Classified Files, 1907–39, Red Lake, file 260, RG 75, NA, Washington, D.C. The Consolidated Chippewa Agency is mentioned in Edmund Jefferson Danziger, Jr., *The Chippewas of Lake Superior*, The Civilization of the American Indian Series, vol. 148 (Norman: University of Oklahoma Press, 1978), 110–11, 135.

21. Sidney F. Andrews to Charles L. Underhill, May 23, 1928, *Hearings on H.R. 5660*, p. 2–4. For an interesting contemporary article that casts the fire claimants in the role of shrewd and slightly sharp-practicing country rustics, see Oliver P. Newman, "A Forest Fire That Cost Uncle Sam Fifteen Million Dollars," *American Forests* 31 (June 1925): 323–26. This settlement in 1925 virtually ended the fire sufferers' struggle to recover damages from the Railroad Administration through the courts. The records of the director general show that there was some, but not much, resistance. Two suits were taken out in the United States Court of Claims to recover the unpaid balance of what had been set by the state district court as the value of property destroyed by the fire, but both suits were dismissed in October 1926. *Hearings on H.R. 5660*, p. 3.

22. Testimonies of Davis and Holmes, *Hearings on H.R. 5660*, p. 14–47, 50–76.

23. Here and below, see Dancer testimony, *Hearings on H.R. 5660*, p. 87–108.

CHAPTER NINE. Congress and the Final Claims

1. *Hearings on H.R. 5660*, p. 3; *Congressional Record*, 70th Cong., 1st sess., 1928, 69, pt. 6:6675 (H.R. 13107), 6737 (S. 4147).

2. *Congressional Record*, 71st Cong., 2d sess., 1930, 72, pt. 1:739 (H.R. 5660); Davis testimony, *Hearings on H.R. 5660*, p. 14–47, especially 32 (quotation, 32). On January 27, 1930, Senator Shipstead introduced S. 3329; *Congressional Record*, 71st Cong., 2d sess., 1930, 72, pt. 3:2416. After leaving government service in 1925, Davis

went back to Iowa where he formed a law partnership with, among others, Angus A. McLaughlin, who had been general solicitor for the Railroad Administration and who had been put in charge of making payments under the terms of the settlement. J. Davis, "Autobiographies," 531–32.

3. Davis testimony, *Hearings on H.R. 5660*, p. 26, 33, 41–42 (quotations, 26, 33).

4. James C. Davis to Walter H. Newton, March 20, 1930, Newton to Davis, March 25, 1930, Subject file: Fire Prevention, 1930, Herbert Hoover Papers, Herbert Hoover Presidential Library, West Branch, Iowa (hereafter Hoover Papers, Hoover Library).

5. Holmes testimony, *Hearings on H.R. 5660*, p. 50–72, 81–86.

6. Dancer testimony, *Hearings on H.R. 5660*, p. 86–108, especially 94–95 (quotations, 93–94, 95).

7. Arnold testimony, *Hearings on H.R. 5660*, p. 108–27 (quotation, 116).

8. Testimonies of Victor J. Michaelson, p. 127–66, 168–73, especially 152 (quotation), Theo[dore] Hollister, p. 228–82, *Hearings on H.R. 5660*.

9. Testimonies of Frank Yetka, p. 175–210, 212–13, Carl D. Ohman, p. 213–18 (quotation, 216), Olesen, p. 218–28, especially 224–25 (quotation, 224), *Hearings on H.R. 5660*.

10. Congressmen who spoke or presented appeals from constituents were Hubert H. Peavey, John W. Palmer, Wilbur Cartwright, Thomas J. Halsey, Paul J. Kvale, Godfrey G. Goodwin, Frank Clague, Melvin J. Maas, August H. Andresen, Samuel B. Hill, William I. Nolan, Harold Knutson, and Conrad G. Selvig. *Hearings on H.R. 5660*, p. iii–iv.

11. United States, Congress, House, Committee on Claims, *Relief of Certain Claimants Who Suffered Loss by Fire in the State of Minnesota during October, 1918. Hearing before the Committee on Claims . . . on H.R. 5660*, 71st Cong., 3d sess., January 16, 1931 (Washington, D.C.: Government Printing Office, 1931), 1–46. Several problems also arose out of the Transportation Act of 1920 (Esch-Cummings Act) that transferred the railroads back to the private companies.

12. United States, Congress, House, Committee on Claims, *For the Relief of Certain Claimants Who Suffered Loss by Fire in the State of Minnesota during October, 1918*, 71st Cong., 3d sess., 1931, H. Rept. 2703, pt. 1, p. 10 (quotations) (Serial 9377). In regard to the lawyers' fees, problems emerged over the fee arrangements that led to two court cases: *Diesen v. Cox, et al.*, 238 N.W. 785 (settled on November 6, 1931), a complicated case involving disputes about how fees should have been shared in the multiparty actions, and *Hollister, et al. v. Ulvi, et al.*, 271 N.W. 493 (settled on February 19, 1937), which hinged on the litigants' freedom to change counsel after proceedings had begun.

13. F. J. Morse to Walter H. Newton and George Akerson, February 11, Lawrence Richey to Morse, February 20, Newton to Morse, February 21, Godfrey G. Goodwin to the President, April 21, Harold Knutson, et al., to the President, February 20, Richey to Andrew W. Mellon, April 14, Sidney F. Andrews to Newton and Mellon, May 26 (quotation), Theodore Christianson to Newton, May 22, Newton to Christianson, May 31, Newton to Mellon, May 31, Ogden L. Mills to Newton, June 5 – all 1930 and in Subject file: Fire Prevention, 1930, Hoover Papers, Hoover Library.

14. *Congressional Record*, 72d Cong., 1st sess., 1931, 75, pt. 1:100 (H.R. 491); 1932, 75, pt. 2:1287 (S. 2667); United States, Congress, House, Committee on Claims, *For the Relief of Certain Claimants Who Suffered Loss by Fire in the State of Minnesota during October, 1918*, 72d Cong., 1st sess., 1932, H. Rept. 493, p. 1–23 (Serial

9491). See also Concurrent Resolution from the Minnesota Legislature to the President, January 20, 1931, Subject file: Fire Prevention, 1931–33, Hoover Papers, Hoover Library.

15. Memorandum — in re Fire Sufferers' Bill, April 9 (unsigned, but clearly from William A. Pittenger; quotation), Frank Yetka to Pittenger, April 15, Yetka to Anna Dickie Olesen, April 27 (quotations) — all 1932 and in Frank Yetka Papers (hereafter Yetka Papers), Manuscripts Collections, MHS. Both Yetka and Governor Olson were in Washington lobbying in early 1932. See also Petition to the Honorable Herbert Hoover, President of the United States, and to Congress, ca. November 1931, Yetka Papers, MHS; Yetka to Floyd B. Olson, January 3, 1932, file: U. S. Appropriation for Forest Fire Sufferers in Minnesota, Gov. Floyd B. Olson in Governor, Executive Letters (hereafter Olson in Governor, Executive Letters), Minnesota State Archives, MHS. For Republican-party considerations, see Arthur E. Nelson to Walter H. Newton, March 7, J. R. McCarl to Ralph E. Burdick, April 5 — both 1932 and in Subject file: Fire Prevention, 1931–33, Hoover Papers, Hoover Library. In fact, early in 1931 Newton told a friend in Minnesota in regard to Congress passing a claims bill that it had always been "my judgment [that] there was no chance whatever of doing any thing of the kind." Newton to Arthur J. Schunk, February 16, 1931, Hoover Papers.

16. Anna Dickie Olesen to Frank Yetka, November 19, 1932 (quotation), Yetka Papers, MHS.

17. Frank Yetka to Henrik Shipstead, March 8 (identical copies were sent to the entire Minnesota delegation in Congress), Anna Dickie Olesen to Yetka, March 18 (quotations) — both 1933 and in Yetka Papers, MHS; *Congressional Record*, 72d Cong., 1st sess., 1932, 75, pt. 11:11710.

18. Frank Yetka to Henrik Shipstead, April 6, Yetka to Einar Hoidale, April 6 (quotation), Hoidale to Yetka, May 12 — all 1933 and in Yetka Papers, MHS; *Congressional Record*, 73d Cong., 1st sess., 1933, 77, pt. 1:785 (S. 770), pt. 2:1374 (H.R. 4774).

19. Anna Dickie Olesen to Frank Yetka, March 21, 1933, Yetka Papers, MHS. Olesen eventually had a thirty-minute meeting with Eleanor Roosevelt about the claims bills, although the details of their conversation have not been preserved. Letter from Olesen's daughter, Mary Olesen Gerin, to authors, January 27, 1984; letter in the possession of the authors.

20. Frank Yetka to Howard T. Abbott, April 29, Yetka to John Manni, May 22, Abbott to Yetka, December 5, 11 — all 1933 and in Yetka Papers, MHS; Floyd B. Olson to Franklin D. Roosevelt, December 8, Memorandum for the Attorney General by M. H. McIntyre, December 19, Homer Cummings to The President, December 27 (quotation) — all 1933 and in Official File, folder OF 409, Franklin D. Roosevelt Papers, Franklin D. Roosevelt Presidential Library, Hyde Park, New York (hereafter Roosevelt Papers, Roosevelt Library).

21. Franklin D. Roosevelt to Loring M. Black, January 24, Roosevelt to Josiah W. Bailey, January 24, Homer S. Cummings to Bailey, January 23 (quotation), Bailey to Roosevelt, January 29 — all 1934 and in Official File, folder OF 409, Roosevelt Papers, Roosevelt Library. Roosevelt had written a more noncommittal reply to Governor Olson on January 4, 1934, in which he merely said that he would be happy to have the governor discuss the matter with the attorney general. Roosevelt to Olson, Roosevelt Papers. Instructions were given to keep Senator Henrik Shipstead informed, and both Shipstead and Olson sent their thanks for presidential support. Shipstead to Roosevelt, February 5, Olson to Roosevelt, March 19 — both 1934 and in Roosevelt Papers.

22. *Congressional Record*, 73d Cong., 2d sess., 1934, 78, pt. 2:2292, pt. 5:4891, pt. 6:6057–66 (quotations, 6064, 6059).

23. *Congressional Record*, 73d Cong., 2d sess., 1934, 78, pt. 2:6057–66, pt. 11:12301–2, 12489–90 (quotation, 12489). For correspondence with journalists see, M. F. Hanson (copublisher of the *Duluth Herald* and the *Duluth News-Tribune*) to Franklin D. Roosevelt, May 29, Louis McH. Howe to Hanson, June 1, Fred Schilplin (owner and publisher of the *St. Cloud Daily Times and the Daily Journal-Press*) to Roosevelt, May 21 (telegram), Howe to Schilplin, May 22 — all 1934 and in Official File, folder OF 409, Roosevelt Papers, Roosevelt Library. As the bill moved closer to a vote, anxiety rose, and when the bill appeared to be in trouble, desperate efforts were made to get stronger presidential intervention. See Frank Yetka to Floyd B. Olson, March 17, Yetka to Olson ("Aboard Capitol Limited B & O Enroute Chicago"), April 4 (telegram) — both 1934 and in Olson in Governor, Executive Letters, MHS; Olson to M. H. McIntyre, April 5, 1934, McIntyre to The President, n.d., McIntyre to Steve Early, April 5, 1934, Early to McIntyre, April 5, 1934 — all in Roosevelt Papers.

24. Kvale (H.R. 3661), Ryan (H.R. 3662), Pittenger (H.R. 3663), in *Congressional Record*, 74th Cong., 1st sess., 1935, 79, pt. 5:4708–10, 4969, 5177, pt. 6:6383, pt. 8:8985; United States, Congress, House, Committee on Claims, *Certain Claimants Who Suffered Loss by Fire in the State of Minnesota during October 1918*, 74th Cong., 1st sess., 1935, H. Rept. 255, p. 1–8 (Serial 9890).

25. Floyd B. Olson to The President, June 13, 1935, unsigned Roosevelt memo, n.d. (quotation), Olson to President, August 19, 1935 — all in Official File, folder OF 409, Roosevelt Papers, Roosevelt Library; *Congressional Record*, 74th Cong., 1st sess., 1935, 79, pt. 13:13846–49 (quotation, 13846); *United States Statutes at Large*, 74th Cong., 1st sess., 1935, 49, pt. 2:2194–95. See also *Duluth News Tribune*, August 14, 21, 1935.

26. *Pine Knot*, November 22, December 6 — both 1935, p. 1. The Railroad Administration had an opportunity to at least delay the payments. Ten months after the passage of the bill, lawyers in Moose Lake were complaining to President Roosevelt that the claims filed in October had not yet been paid. The comptroller general reported to the White House that there was enough staff to handle the claims, but that the Railroad Administration was not processing and returning the papers fast enough. L. H. Blacklock to the Office of the President, May 23, J. R. McCarl to M. H. McIntyre, June 12, McIntyre to Blacklock, May 26, June 15 — all 1936 and in Official File, folder OF 409, Roosevelt Papers, Roosevelt Library. For correspondence and papers for one Ojibway family, see Mother (Charlotte La Prairie) to Son (Louis La Prairie), September 29, 1935, J. R. McCarl to Joseph LaPrairie [*sic*], March 3, 1936, McCarl to Louis LaPrairie [*sic*,], Jr., August 7, 1936 — all in Louis La Prairie and Family Papers, Manuscripts Collections, MHS. The statistical information is taken from U.S. Treasury Department, *Combined Statement of Receipts and Balances, Etc., of the United States for Fiscal Year Ended June 30, 1936* (Washington, D.C.: Government Printing Office, 1937), 146, and *Combined Statement of Receipts and Expenditure Balances, Etc., of the United States for Fiscal Year Ended June 30, 1937* (Washington, D.C.: Government Printing Office, 1938), 151.

27. *Cloquet Pine Knot*, November 21, 1974, p. 1 (quotation); *Pine Knot*, December 6, 1935, special section, [pt. 1], p. 1 (quotations). Even at this point there were individual problems with the government payments. For matters concerning Fond du Lac reservation Ojibway, see W. J. Clark (chief clerk in charge of the Consolidated Chippewa Agency, Duluth) to C. H. McArthur (United States Indian Service, Clo-

quet), July 8, 1938, Fire Claims: Checks Received and Deposited, n.d., ca. 1940 — both in Indexes and Schedules of Fire Claims, Fond du Lac, RG 75, NA, Kansas City. Several law suits sorted out claims: *United States v. City National Bank of Duluth*, 31 F. Supp. 530 (settled January 24, 1939) affirmed the right of the estate of a deceased fire victim to receive government payments; *Bang v. United States*, 31 F. Supp. 535 (February 10, 1940), and *United States v. Bang*, 117 F. 2d 515 (February 10, 1941), which affirmed the right of a fire sufferer to claim personal injury damages as well as property loss.

CHAPTER TEN. The Recovery of the Region

1. *Carlton County Vidette*, November 8, 1918, p. 1 (quotation); Minnesota Forest Fires Relief Commission, *Final Report*, 23–30; *Star Gazette*, October 16, 1919, p. 1 (quotations).

2. Carroll, *Crossroads in Time*, 262–67; United States, Bureau of the Census, *Census, 1920, Population*, vol. 1, p. 91, 1930, *Population*, vol. 3, pt. 1, p. 1223.

3. Kenney to Aishton, October 13, 14, 1918, GN Records, MHS; *Star Gazette*, December 19, 1918, p. 1; *Carlton County Vidette*, December 13, 1918, p. 1; *Cloquet Pine Knot*, October 8, 1987, p. 15; Minnesota Forest Fires Relief Commission, *Final Report*, 20. For a useful description of the region some twenty years after the fire, see Federal Writers' Program, Minnesota, *The WPA Guide to the Minnesota Arrowhead Country*, with an introduction by Francis M. Carroll (St. Paul: Minnesota Historical Society Press, Borealis Books, 1988; first published as *The Minnesota Arrowhead Country* [Chicago: Albert Whitman & Co., 1941]).

4. For a description of the westward migration of the lumber industry across the United States, see Stewart H. Holbrook, *Holy Old Mackinaw: A Natural History of the American Lumberjack* (New York: Macmillan Company, 1957), 152–60.

5. In addition to the sawmills and lumber, the big companies also lost the roundhouse and some rolling stock for the Duluth and Northeastern Railroad, the warehouse of the St. Louis River Mercantile Company, some of the property of the Cloquet Tie and Post Company, the Northern Lumber company store and company houses, and an office building in town shared by several enterprises. Almost all of the property was at least partially covered by insurance, so that some compensation was immediate. See F. E. Weyerhaeuser to J. P. W[eyerhaeuser], October 21, 1918, [R. Weyerhaeuser] to J. Weyerhaeuser, November 2, 1918, Frederick E. Weyerhaeuser Correspondence, Weyerhaeuser Family Papers, MHS.

6. *Carlton County Vidette*, October 25, 1918, p. 1.

7. Sher[man Coy] to Ted, October 19, 1918, in the possession of Elizabeth Walter.

8. [R. Weyerhaeuser] to J. Weyerhaeuser, November 2, 1918, Weyerhaeuser Family Papers, MHS; Hugo Schlenk to R. M. Weyerhaeuser, January 7, 1922, April 4, 1924; annual reports of the Johnson-Wentworth Lumber Company, the Cloquet Lumber Company, and the Northern Lumber Company, in F. Weyerhaeuser and Company, St. Paul, Records (hereafter Weyerhaeuser and Company Records), Manuscripts Collections, MHS.

9. Rudolph M. Weyerhaeuser to J. P. Weyerhaeuser, October 20, 1919, Weyerhaeuser and Company Records, MHS; Hidy, et al., *Timber and Men*, 199–200, 358–61; Holbrook, *Burning an Empire*, 41–43.

10. Hidy, et al., *Timber and Men*, 201–4; Carroll, *Crossroads in Time*, 254–59,

300–301; *St. Paul Pioneer Press and Dispatch*, October 29, 1986, p. 9B. The Rathborne, Hair and Ridgeway Company box factory remained in operation until 1935, when it moved to Deer River.

11. Gray, "Are You a 49'er?" pt. 1, *Cloquet Vidette*, October 11, 1967, p. 3 (quotation); Sher[man Coy] to Ted, October 19, 1918, in the possession of Elizabeth Walter.

12. Wenzel, "My Experience in the Cloquet Fire of 1918," in Women's Friday Club, Cloquet, comp., "Group of Essays," 42, CCHS, MHS.

13. Gray, "Are You a 49'er?" pt. 1, *Cloquet Vidette*, October 11, 1967, p. 3 (quotations); Smith interview (quotation), Oral History Collections, MHS; Drew, "The Forest Fire of 1918," in Women's Friday Club, Cloquet, comp., "Group of Essays," 37 (quotations), CCHS, MHS.

14. Gray, "Are You a 49'er?" pt. 1, *Cloquet Vidette*, October 11, 1967, p. 3; *Pine Knot*, December 6, 1935, special section, [pt. 2], p. 5 (quotation; from October 25, 1918, issue); F. Weyerhaeuser to J. W[eyerhaeuser], October 21, 1918 (quotations), Weyerhaeuser Family Papers, MHS; *Carlton County Vidette*, November 15, 1918, p. 1.

15. The first iron ore train passed through Cloquet at 7:00 A.M. Monday, traffic having been held up by the fire for about forty-eight hours. Kenney to Aishton, October 13, 14, 1918, GN Records, MHS; Rapelje to Hannaford, October 14, 1918, NP Records, MHS; *Carlton County Vidette*, October 25, 1918, p. 1, November 15, 1918, p. 1. The *Pine Knot* acquired new presses and equipment and was operating on its own by mid-December 1918; *Pine Knot*, December 13, 20, 1918, p. 1, October 8, 1987, p. 15; *Star Gazette*, April 24, 1919, p. 1. See also Beck, *Northern Lights*, 151–57. Beck indicated that the financial burden of this extensive rebuilding for the General Light and Power Company, together with the obligations arising from the purchase of the Little Falls Water Power Company earlier in 1918, was too much. The company was acquired by the more financially secure Minnesota Power and Light Company in 1924.

16. Cloquet City Council proceedings from October 21, 1918, to July 7, 1919, in Cloquet City Council Minute Book, Cloquet City Hall, Cloquet, Minnesota; *Pine Knot*, March 7, 1919, p. 1, June 27, 1919, p. 1, September 5, 1919, p. 1; Carroll, *Crossroads in Time*, 259–60. In 1987 this building was acquired by the Carlton County Historical Society for its museum; *Pine Knot*, November 12, 1987, p. 1, 2. Both the city hall and the library have been placed on the National Register of Historic Places; Minnesota Historical Society, State Historic Preservation Office, *The National Register of Historic Places: Minnesota Checklist* (St. Paul: The Office, 1986), 6.

17. Cloquet City Council Minute Book, October 21, 23, 1918, Cloquet City Hall; Holbrook, *Burning an Empire*, 41; Lucile Booker Watkins, "Introduction," in Women's Friday Club, Cloquet, comp., "Group of Essays," 12 (quotation), CCHS, MHS.

18. Sher[man Coy] to Ted, October 19, 1918, in the possession of Elizabeth Walter; United States, Bureau of the Census, *Census*, 1910, *Population*, vol. 1, p. 92, 1940, *Population*, vol. 1, p. 39.

19. United States, Bureau of the Census, *Census*, 1940, p. 39, 1910, p. 92, 1920, p. 111.

20. *Duluth Sunday News Tribune*, October 12, 1919, p. 6; *Star Gazette*, October 16, 1919, p. 1. A granite obelisk was dedicated on October 12, 1929, at Riverside Cemetery in Moose Lake as a monument to those who died in the Moose Lake-Kettle River area. June Drenning Holmquist and Jean A. Brookins, *Minnesota's Major Historic Sites: A Guide*, rev. 2d ed. (St. Paul: Minnesota Historical Society, 1972), 179.

21. Summary of speech by Governor Burnquist at Cloquet, October 12, 1919,

Burnquist to Orlo B. Elfes, October 16, 1919 (quotations) – both in Burnquist Papers, MHS.

22. For the Cloquet resolution, see Cloquet City Council Minute Book, October 6, 1919, Cloquet City Hall. See also *Pine Knot*, October 17, 24, 1919 – both p. 1. The authors recall that for many years the only notice taken of the fire in Cloquet was a sign outside the district forest service headquarters, which provided a brief sketch of the fire. In Cloquet on October 17, 1968, a stone marker was dedicated to the people who returned to rebuild the city after the fire. It was placed in Fauley Park, renamed from Railroad Park in honor of Lawrence Fauley, the station agent who was instrumental in evacuating the city by train. *Cloquet Pine Knot*, October 17, 1968, p. 1, 7; Ellen Quinn (Carlton County Historical Society) to David Nystuen (MHS), February 12, 1990, in the files of the Minnesota Historical Society Press.

APPENDIX. Photographers and the Fires

1. Some McKenzie photographs appear in Cheyney, "The Holocaust in Minnesota." Cornwall, comp., *Who's Who in Minnesota*, 1121; *Cloquet: Home of White Pine*, [50]; *Duluth News-Tribune*, February 7, 1954, Cosmopolitan section, 8–9, April 9, 1967, second news section, 17; *Duluth Herald*, July 15, 1957, p. 12.

2. When Olson (who was born in Norway) returned to Cloquet in 1923 to live as a photographer, he resumed the first name Olaf and the nickname Ole. *Pine Knot*, May 6, 1949, p. 7; telephone conversation of LaVerne L. Olson (son of Olaf) with Alan R. Woolworth (MHS), April 18, 1990.

3. In May 1929 Irish established the Irish Studio in Rochester, which he operated until it was destroyed by fire in May 1953, at which time he retired. Lantern slides, popular from the 1890s into the 1930s, have positive images placed on photo emulsion fixed to a small glass sheet with a second sheet to protect the emulsion. After the death of Earl Irish, about eighty of his slides came into the possession of Dr. Frederick Smith, who had also served in the Rochester unit. In 1955 Smith donated them to the Moose Lake community; they are now in the possession of the Moose Lake Historical Society. Cornwall, comp., *Who's Who in Minnesota*, 659; *Rochester Daily Post and Record*, October 18, 1918, p. 4, October 26, 1918, p. 5; *Rochester Post-Bulletin*, April 23, 1936, p. 7, July 28, 1953, p. 7; *Duluth News-Tribune*, Cosmopolitan section, September 4, 1955, p. 4.

4. Levie closed his Sandstone and Hinckley studios in 1919 and returned to Minneapolis, where he is known to have worked as a photographer into the 1930s. *Pine County Courier* (Sandstone), August 3, 1916, p. 7, 8, June 21, 1917, p. 7, September 5, 1917, p. 7, October 31, 1918, p. 5, February 6, 1919, p. 5; Minneapolis city directories, 1912–16, 1920–21, 1931.

5. *St. Paul Pioneer Press*, October 14, 1918, p. 3; *St. Paul Dispatch*, October 14, 1918, p. 1. On Bull, see *St. Paul Pioneer Press*, October 19, 1942, p. 2. On Horton, see John McLaren, "The Great Minnesota Fire," folder O, Fires, October 12, 1918 Fires, Central Correspondence 1918, Forestry Division, Conservation Department, Minnesota State Archives, MHS; *Minneapolis Journal*, February 14, 1965, p. 17B. For published photographs by Horton, the International Film Service, and Underwood and Underwood, see Hayden, "The Great Minnesota Fire."

Bibliography

MANUSCRIPTS

Carlton County Historical Society, Cloquet, Minnesota
    Newspaper collection
    Thorvald Schantz-Hansen. "Cloquet and the Forest Industries"
    Women's Friday Club, Cloquet, comp. "A Group of Essays Written by
        Cloquet Fire Sufferers" (copy also in Minnesota Historical Society,
        Manuscripts Collections). For announcements of the essay contest
        sponsored by the club and publication of most essays, see *Pine Knot*
        (Cloquet), January 3, February 7, May 15, 22, 29, June 5, 12, 19, July
        3, 10, 17, 24, 1936.
Cloquet City Hall, Cloquet, Minnesota
    Cloquet City Council Minute Book
Cloquet Public Library, Cloquet, Minnesota
    1918 Forest Fire Collection
Herbert Hoover Presidential Library, West Branch, Iowa
    Herbert Hoover Papers
Minnesota Historical Society, St. Paul, *Manuscripts Collections*
    American Red Cross, Northern Division, Minneapolis, Papers
    Joseph Alfred Arner Burnquist Papers
    Iva Andrus Dingwall Reminiscences
    Kathryn Elfes Gray Papers
    Great Northern Railway Company, St. Paul, Records
    Louis La Prairie and Family Papers
    Northern Pacific Railway Company, St. Paul, Records
    Henry (Heinrich) Carl Albert Oldenburg Papers
    Mark J. Thompson Reminiscences
    (F.) Weyerhaeuser and Company, St. Paul, Records
    Weyerhaeuser Family Papers
    Women's Friday Club, Cloquet, comp. "A Group of Essays Written by
        Cloquet Fire Sufferers" (copy also in Carlton County Historical
        Society)
    Frank Yetka Papers
Minnesota Historical Society, *Minnesota State Archives*

Adjutant General's Office, Minnesota Home Guard, Records
Governor, Executive Letters
Governor's Records
Minnesota Commission of Public Safety Records
Minnesota Forestry Board Records
Minnesota Supreme Court, Case Files
Minnesota Power, Duluth
Records Division
National Archives, Washington, D.C.
Records of the Bureau of Indian Affairs (Record Group 75)
Records of the Forest Service (Record Group 95)
Records of the United States Railroad Administration (Record Group 14)
National Archives — Kansas City Branch, Kansas
Records of the Bureau of Indian Affairs (Record Group 75)
Northeast Minnesota Historical Center, University of Minnesota — Duluth
Frank Murphy Letter (October 15, 1918)
News Clippings File
Ruby Spurbeck. "The 1918 Cloquet Fire" (recollection; September 1975)
Mildred Washburn McLean Letter (November 3, 1918)
Roger M. Weaver Scrapbook
Franklin D. Roosevelt Presidential Library, Hyde Park, New York
Franklin D. Roosevelt Papers

INTERVIEWS

Blomberg, Lester J. Interview with Francis M. Carroll. Cloquet. December 1978. Transcript in the possession of the authors.
Gerin, Mary Olesen. Interview with authors. October 24, 25, 1982. Notes in the possession of the authors.
Smith, Tena MacMillan. Interview with John Esse. Cloquet. October 9, 1975. Forest History and Lumbering Project, Oral History Collections, Minnesota Historical Society.

OFFICIAL PUBLICATIONS

Cox, William T. *Annual Report of the State Forestry Board of the State of Minnesota for the Year Ending July 31, 1918.* [St. Paul, 1918?]
Forest Fire Investigation Commission. "Report of Forest Fire Investigation Commission." In appendix to Minnesota, Governor (1915–21: Burnquist), *Inaugural Message of Gov. J. A. A. Burnquist to the Legislature of Minnesota. 1919.* [St. Paul?, 1919.]
Minnesota. *General Statutes of Minnesota.*
———. *Laws of Minnesota.*

——. Supreme Court. Briefs.

Minnesota Forest Fires Relief Commission. *Final Report*. Duluth, 1921.

Superior Fire Relief Committee, Superior, Wisconsin. *Northeastern Minnesota Forest Fires of October 12, 1918: Report to Donors*. Superior, Wis., 1919.

United States. Bureau of the Census. *Census*. 1910. *Population*, vol. 1.

——. *Census*. 1920. *Agriculture*, vol. 6, pt. 1. *Population*, vol. 1.

——. *Census*. 1930. *Population*, vol. 3, pt. 1.

——. *Census*. 1940. *Population*, vol. 1.

United States. Congress. *Congressional Record*. Washington, D.C., 1928–35.

United States. Congress. House. Committee on Claims. *Relief of Certain Claimants Who Suffered Loss by Fire in the State of Minnesota during October, 1918. Hearings before a Subcommittee of the Committee on Claims . . . on H.R. 5660*. 71st Cong., 2d sess., March 26, 27, 28, 29, 1930. Washington, D.C.: Government Printing Office, 1930.

——. *Relief of Certain Claimants Who Suffered Loss by Fire in the State of Minnesota during October, 1918. Hearing before the Committee on Claims . . . on H.R. 5660*. 71st Cong., 3d sess., January 16, 1931. Washington, D.C.: Government Printing Office, 1931.

——. *For the Relief of Certain Claimants Who Suffered Loss by Fire in the State of Minnesota during October, 1918*. 71st Cong., 3d sess., 1931; H. Rept. 2703, pts. 1–2; Serial 9327. 72d Cong., 1st sess., 1932; H. Rept. 493; Serial 9491.

——. *Certain Claimants Who Suffered Loss by Fire in the State of Minnesota during October 1918*. 74th Cong., 1st sess., 1935. H. Rept. 255. Serial 9890.

United States. Treasury Department. *Combined Statement of Receipts and Balances, Etc., of the United States for Fiscal Year Ended June 30, 1936*. Washington, D.C.: Government Printing Office, 1937.

——. *Combined Statement . . . for Fiscal Year Ended June 30, 1937*. Washington, D.C.: Government Printing Office, 1938.

United States Statutes at Large. 1918–35.

LEGAL CASES

Jacob Anderson v. Minneapolis, St. Paul & Sault Ste. Marie Railway Company and Others, 146 Minn. 430 and 179 N.W. 45

Bang v. United States, 31 F. Supp. 535

Hans J. Borsheim v. Great Northern Railway Company, 149 Minn. 210 and 183 N.W. 519

Dennis Carr v. James C. Davis, 159 Minn. 485 and 199 N.W. 237

Cook v. Minneapolis, St. Paul & Sault Ste. Marie Railway Company, 89 Wis. 622 and 74 N.W. 561

Diesen v. Cox, et al., 238 N.W. 785

Philip Hall v. James C. Davis, As Agent of the President under the Transpor-
tation Act, 150 Minn. 35 and 184 N.W. 25

Hollister, et al. v. Ulvi, et al., 271 N.W. 493

Henry Johnson v. James C. Davis, 207 N.W. 23

Joseph LaVeirge v. James C. Davis, 166 Minn. 14 and 206 N.W. 939

Harry E. McCool and Another v. James C. Davis, 158 Minn. 146 and 197
N.W. 93; and also 162 Minn. 281 and 202 N.W. 900

G. A. Ringquist v. Duluth, Missabe & Northern Railway Company, 145
Minn. 147 and 176 N.W. 344

E. M. Smith v. James C. Davis, 162 Minn. 256 and 202 N.W. 483

United States v. Bang, 117 F. 2d. 515

United States v. City National Bank of Duluth, 31 F. Supp. 530

NEWSPAPERS

Aitkin Independent Age
Carlton County Vidette (Carlton)
Cloquet Pine Knot
Cloquet Vidette
Duluth News Tribune
Pine Knot (Cloquet)
Pine Knot-Billboard (Cloquet)
Star Gazette (Moose Lake)

BOOKS AND PAMPHLETS

Alanen, Arnold R., ed. *The 1918 Fire in Eastern Aitkin County: Personal Accounts of Survivors.* N.p., 1970.

Beck, Bill. *Northern Lights: An Illustrated History of Minnesota Power.*
Duluth: Minnesota Power, [1986].

Brown, Arthur A., and Kenneth P. Davis. *Forest Fire: Control and Use.* 2d
ed. New York: McGraw-Hill Book Company, 1973.

Carroll, Francis M. *Crossroads in Time: A History of Carlton County, Minnesota.* Cloquet, Minn.: Carlton County Historical Society, 1987.

Chandler, Craig, et al. *Fire in Forestry.* Vol. 1, *Forest Fire Behavior and
Effects.* Vol. 2, *Forest Fire Management and Organization.* New York:
John Wiley & Sons, 1983.

Cloquet: Home of White Pine: Queen City of the St. Louis. 1907. Reprint.
Cloquet, Minn.: Cloquet Diamond Jubilee Committee, 1979.

Cox, William T. *Forest Protection and Conservation in Minnesota.* N.p.,
n.d.

Crosby, Alfred W., Jr. *Epidemic and Peace, 1918.* Westport, Conn.: Greenwood Press, 1976. Reprinted as *America's Forgotten Pandemic: The Influenza of 1918* (New York: Cambridge University Press, 1990).

Federal Writers' Program, Minnesota. *The WPA Guide to the Minnesota Arrowhead Country*, with an introduction by Francis M. Carroll. St. Paul: Minnesota Historical Society Press, Borealis Books, 1988. First published as *The Minnesota Arrowhead Country* (Chicago: Albert Whitman & Company, 1941).

Forest Fire Protection in Minnesota. St. Paul: Department of Conservation, n.d.

The Fury of the Flames: A Pictorial Record of the Great Forest Fires Which Raged in Northern Minnesota, Oct. 12–15, 1918. Duluth: Martin A. Olmem, 1919.

Gifford, John. *Practical Forestry for Beginners in Forestry, Agricultural Students, Woodland Owners, and Others Desiring a General Knowledge of the Nature and Art.* New York: D. Appleton & Company, 1909.

Graves, Henry Solon. *The Principles of Handling Woodlands.* New York: John Wiley & Sons, 1911.

Green, Samuel B. *Principles of American Forestry.* New York: John Wiley & Sons, 1913.

Haines, Donald A., and Rodney W. Sando. *Climatic Conditions Preceding Historically Great Fires in the North Central Region.* USDA Forest Service Research Paper NC 34. St. Paul: North Central Forest Experiment Station, Forest Service, U.S. Department of Agriculture, 1969.

Hawley, Ralph C. *Forest Protection.* New York: John Wiley & Sons, 1937.

Hemingson, Ray E. *Death by Fire: The Story of the Great Northeastern Minnesota Forest Fire.* Waupaca, Wis., 1983.

Hidy, Ralph W., Frank Ernest Hill, and Allan Nevins. *Timber and Men: The Weyerhaeuser Story.* New York: Macmillan Company, 1963.

Holbrook, Stewart H. *Burning an Empire: The Story of American Forest Fires.* New York: Macmillan Company, 1943.

——. *Holy Old Mackinaw: A Natural History of the American Lumberjack.* New York: Macmillan Company, 1957.

Lydecker, Ryck, and Lawrence J. Sommer, eds. *Duluth Sketches of the Past: A Bicentennial Collection.* Duluth: American Revolution Bicentennial Commission, 1976.

Manni, Edwin E., comp. *Kettle River, Automba, Kalevala, and Surrounding Area: History, Stories: Also 1918 Forest Fire.* N.p., 1978.

Moon, Franklin, and Nelson Courtlandt Brown. *Elements of Forestry.* 3d ed. New York: John Wiley & Sons, 1937.

Moran, Jacqueline, comp. *Recollections: An Informal History of the Alborn Area, St. Louis County, Minnesota.* Duluth: St. Louis County Historical Society, 1980.

Niemi, Harriette. *Awfullest Fire Horror in State's History.* Cloquet, Minn.: Cloquet Public Library, n.d.

O'Meara, Walter. *We Made It through the Winter: A Memoir of Northern Minnesota Boyhood*. St. Paul: Minnesota Historical Society, 1974.

Pyne, Stephen J. *Fire in America: A Cultural History of Wildland and Rural Fire*. Princeton, N.J.: Princeton University Press, 1982.

———. *Introduction to Wildland Fire: Fire Management in the United States*. New York: John Wiley & Sons, 1984.

A Romance in Fire and Wood. Duluth: Stewart-Taylor Company, n.d.

Sommer, Barbara. *Cloquet and the Fire of 1918: The City That Really Came Back*. Cloquet, Minn.: Carlton County Historical Society, 1985.

Swenson, Grace Stageberg. *From the Ashes: The Story of the Hinckley Fire of 1894*. 1979. Rev. ed. Stillwater, Minn.: Croixside Press, 1988.

Waters, Thomas F. *The Streams and Rivers of Minnesota*. Minneapolis: University of Minnesota Press, 1977.

Western Adjustment and Inspection Company. *Forest Fires in Northern Minnesota, 1918: The Greatest Conflagration Since San Francisco*. Chicago: The Company, 1919.

ARTICLES

B. E. F. Review of *Annual Report of the State Forestry Board of the State of Minnesota for the Year Ending July 31, 1918*, by William T. Cox. *Journal of Forestry* 17 (May 1919): 567–69.

Bachmann, Elizabeth. "Early Days of the Forest Service." Pt. 3 of "The Golden Forestry Story." *Conservation Volunteer* (Minnesota Department of Conservation) 24 (November–December 1960): 13–18.

Carroll, Francis M., and Franklin R. Raiter. "'At the Time of Our Misfortune': Relief Efforts following the 1918 Cloquet Fire." *Minnesota History* 48 (Fall 1983): 270–82.

———. "The People Versus the Government: The 1918 Cloquet Fire and the Struggle for Compensation." *Journal of Forest History* 29 (January 1985): 4–21.

Cheyney, E. G. "The Holocaust in Minnesota: A Greater Hinckley." *American Forestry* 24 (November 1918): 643–47.

"Fire!!!" *Potlatch Story* (Potlatch Corporation, San Francisco) 23 (June 1983): 4–7.

Fremling, Olga Marie Gustafson. Reminiscence quoted in "Postscripts," *Minnesota History* 49 (Spring 1985): 202–3.

Hanna, C. A. "Remember the Moose Lake Fire." *Conservation Volunteer* 24 (September–October 1961): 56–59.

Hayden, J. F. "The Great Minnesota Fire." *American Forestry* 24 (November 1918): 648–52.

Heinselman, Miron L. "Fire in the Virgin Forests of the Boundary Waters

Canoe Area, Minnesota." *Quaternary Research* 3 (October 1973): 329–82.

Jeffery, David. "Yellowstone: The Fires of 1988." *National Geographic* 175 (February 1989): 254–73.

Jenson, Carol. "Loyalty as a Political Weapon: The 1918 Campaign in Minnesota." *Minnesota History* 43 (Summer 1972): 42–57.

Kavanaugh, Emmett, and Paul Wagtskjold. Reminiscences in "Holocaust of 1918 Holds Vivid Memories for Veteran Conwed Employees." *Conwed Contact* (Conwed Corporation, Cloquet, Minn.) 26 (July 1968): 8–9. Reprinted in *Cloquet Pine Knot*, June 28, 1979, p. 1C.

L. M. Review of "The Northeastern Minnesota Forest Fires of October 12, 1918," by H. W. Richardson. *Journal of Forestry* 17 (November 1919): 867–70.

Luukkonen, Arnold L. "Brave Men in Their Motor Machines–and the 1918 Forest Fire." *Ramsey County History* 9 (Fall 1972): 3–8.

"Minnesota's Forest Fire Disaster" (editorial). *American Forestry* 24 (November 1918): 654–55.

Newman, Oliver P. "A Forest Fire That Cost Uncle Sam Fifteen Million Dollars." *American Forests* 31 (June 1925): 323–26.

Panger, Sr. Alicia. "I Remember the Great Fire." *Catholic Digest*, January 1964, p. 24–28.

"A Record of Five Years' Forest Fires." *Safeguarding America against Fire* (National Board of Fire Underwriters, New York) 4 (April 1921): 6–7.

Richardson, H. W. "The Northeastern Minnesota Forest Fires of October 12, 1918." *Geographical Review* 7 (April 1919): 220–32.

Vickery, Jim Dale. "Run!" *Audubon*, January 1989, p. 86–89.

Ward, R. DeC. "Smoke from the Minnesota Forest Fires of October, 1918." *Geographical Review* 7 (April 1919): 264.

Wolff, Julius F., Jr. "Of Fire, Forests and People." *Minnesota Volunteer* (Minnesota Department of Natural Resources) 37 (March–April 1974): 12–20.

Williams, Ted. "Incineration of Yellowstone." *Audubon*, January 1989, p. 38–85.

Index

Picture Credits

Photographs and other images reproduced in this book are located on the following pages and appear through the courtesy of the persons and organizations noted below. Works by photographers discussed in the appendix are listed first. The names of other photographers or artists, when known, are given in parentheses in the remaining entries.

Photo by William Bull: p. 85 — Phyllis M. (Mrs. Harold C.) Johnson on behalf of the children of Aina Jokimaki Johnson and Carl J. Johnson

Photos by Earl L. Irish: p. 21, 80, 90, 99, 101, 109, 112, 152 — Moose Lake Historical Society

Photo by Fred Levie: p. 107 — Minnesota Historical Society (MHS)

Photos by Hugh McKenzie: *frontispiece*, p. 1, 9, 53, 63, 69, 128 — MHS; 72 (probably by McKenzie), 110 — Northeast Minnesota Historical Center, University of Minnesota-Duluth (NEMHS)

Photos by Olaf (Oliver) Olson: p. 24, 42, 50, 55, 143 — Carlton County Historical Society (CCHS); 173, 188, 189, 190 — MHS

P. 12 & 14 (both *St. Paul Dispatch*), 18, 36 (bottom), 45, 67 (photo by E. D. Berg, Cloquet), 73 *(St. Paul Dispatch)*, 94, 98 (Governor's Records, Minnesota State Archives), 106, 114 (cartoon by Coleman F. Naughton), 116 (*St. Paul Dispatch*), 120 (Minnesota Forest Fires Relief Commission, *Final Report*), 121 *(St. Paul Dispatch)*, 130 (Forestry Division, Department of Conservation Records, Minnesota State Archives), 140 (about 1920), 157, 161, 164 & 167 (both *St. Paul Daily News*), 175, 184, 191 (about 1930), 194 (center), 196 (published by R. L. Polk & Company) — MHS

P. 34, 194 (right) — CCHS

P. 36 (top) — Records of the Bureau of Indian Affairs, National Archives-Kansas City Branch, Kansas

P. 52 — Elizabeth Coy Walter

P. 118, 150 (Harris and Ewing Studio) — NEMHC

P. 146 — State Historical Society of Iowa-Special Collections

P. 194 (left) — Olmsted County Historical Society Archives

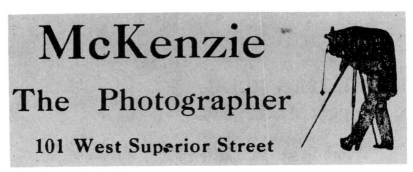

Advertisement, Duluth city directory, 1916